Subcellular
Psychobiology
Diagnosis Handbook

Books from the Institute for the Study of Peak States Press

Peak States of Consciousness: Theory and Applications, Volume 1: Breakthrough Techniques for Exceptional Quality of Life, by Dr. Grant McFetridge with Jacquelyn Aldana and Dr. James Hardt (2004)

Peak States of Consciousness: Theory and Applications, Volume 2: Acquiring Extraordinary Spiritual and Shamanic States by Grant McFetridge Ph.D. with Wes Gietz (2008)

Peak States of Consciousness: Theory and Applications, Volume 3: Subcellular Psychobiology, Disease, and Immunity by Grant McFetridge Ph.D., *et al.* (forthcoming)

The Basic Whole-Hearted Healing™ Manual (3rd Edition) by Grant McFetridge Ph.D. and Mary Pellicer M.D. (2004)

The Whole-Hearted Healing™ Workbook, Volume 1 by Paula Courteau (2013)

Subcellular Psychobiology Diagnosis Handbook: Subcellular Causes of Psychological Symptoms - Peak States® Therapy, Volume 1 by Grant McFetridge Ph.D. (2014)

Silence the Voices: The Fungal Cause of Schizophrenia - Peak States® Therapy, Volume 2 by Grant McFetridge Ph.D. (forthcoming)

Suicide Prevention - Peak States® Therapy, Volume 3 by and Grant McFetridge Ph.D. *et al.* (forthcoming)

Spiritual Emergencies - Peak States® Therapy, Volume 4 by Grant McFetridge Ph.D. *et al.* (forthcoming)

Addiction and Withdrawal - Peak States® Therapy, Volume 5 by Grant McFetridge Ph.D. *et al.* (forthcoming)

Breakthrough Research: Techniques, Insights, and Mindset by Grant McFetridge Ph.D., Frank Downey, Ken Solomon Ph.D., and Rene Jaeger (forthcoming)

To order, go to www.PeakStates.com

Subcellular Psychobiology Diagnosis Handbook

Subcellular Causes of Psychological Symptoms

Peak States® Therapy, Volume 1

By Grant McFetridge Ph.D.
Illustrations by Lorenza Meneghini and Piotr Kawecki

Institute
for the Study
of Peak States

"Methods for Fundamental Change in the Human Psyche"

First Edition
First Printing, 2014

Library and Archives Canada Cataloguing in Publication

McFetridge, Grant, 1955-, author
    Subcellular psychobiology diagnosis handbook : subcellular causes of psychological symptoms / by Dr. Grant McFetridge ; illustrations by Lorenza Meneghini.

Includes bibliographical references and index.
ISBN 978-0-9734680-5-2 (pbk.)

    1. Mental illness--Diagnosis--Handbooks, manuals, etc.
2. Mental healing--Handbooks, manuals, etc. 3. Psychobiology--Handbooks, manuals, etc. 4. Medicine and psychology--Handbooks, manuals, etc. I. Institute for the Study of Peak States, issuing body II. Title.

RC469.M34 2014   616.89'075   C2014-900626-8

Peak States®, Whole-Hearted Healing®, Silent Mind Technique™, Body Association Technique™, Tribal Block Technique™, Triune Brain Therapy™, Crosby Vortex Technique™, and the Courteau Projection Technique™ are trademarks of the Institute for the Study of Peak States.

Institute for the Study of Peak States Press
3310 Cowie Road
Hornby Island, British Columbia
V0R 1Z0 Canada
http://www.PeakStates.com

This book is dedicated to all of my large extended family, whose encouragement and emotional support over the years has been very precious to me. In particular, I want to acknowledge:

My brother, Scott McFetridge
My uncle, Frank Downey
My aunt, Brenda and her husband Hugh Blair
And my cousin, Ian and his wife Marina Harriman

Legal Liability Agreement
IMPORTANT!
READ THE FOLLOWING BEFORE CONTINUING WITH THE TEXT

The material in this book is provided for educational purposes only, and is *not* intended to be used by the general public as a self-help aid. The processes in this book are for the benefit of professionals in the field of trauma healing, and are not meant to be used by lay people without *competent and qualified supervision*. As this is a relatively new and specialized field of study, even most licensed professionals do not have adequate background and training in both prenatal and perinatal psychology and power therapies.

It is possible, and in some cases probable that you will feel extreme distress, both short and long term, if you use the processes in this book. As with any intense psychological process, life-threatening problems might occur due to the possibility of stressing a weak heart, from activating suicidal feelings, and other causes. Although we've explicitly indicated in the text the potential problems that you might encounter using these processes, you may encounter something we haven't seen before. You may experience serious or life-threatening problems with any of the processes in this book. The possibility that you may die from using these processes *does* exist. If you are not willing to be TOTALLY responsible for how you use this material, and any consequences to doing so, then we require that you not use the processes in this book. This should be obvious, but we wanted to make it totally explicit.

Given what we've just said, the following common sense statements constitute a legal agreement between us. This applies to everyone, including licensed professionals and lay people. Please read the following statements carefully:

1.   The author, any people associated with the Institute for the Study of Peak States, and other contributors to this text cannot and will not take responsibility for what you do with the material in this book and these techniques.
2.   You are required to take complete responsibility for your own emotional and physical well-being if you use these processes or any variations of them.
3.   You are required to instruct others on whom you use these processes, or variations of these processes, that they are completely responsible for their own emotional and physical well-being.
4.   Use these techniques under the supervision of a qualified therapist or physician as appropriate.
5.   You must agree to hold harmless the author and anyone associated with this text or with the Institute for the Study of Peak States from any claims made by anyone, yourself included, on whom you use these processes, or variations of them.
6.   Many of the process names in this book are trademarked, and so the usual legal restrictions apply to their public use.

Out of consideration for the safety of others:

•   You are required to instruct other people on whom you use these processes or variations of these processes of the dangers involved, and that they are completely responsible for their own emotional and physical wellbeing.
•   If you write (or communicate in other ways) to others about the new and experimental material in this book, you agree to inform them that there are possible dangers involved with working with this material, and to give specifics where applicable.

Continuing with this text constitutes a legal agreement to these conditions. Thank you for your understanding.

Contents

Diagnosis and Treatment

Subcellular Diseases and Disorders

Applications

Acknowledgements

I'd like to start by thanking my present and past colleagues at the Institute for the Study of Peak States. They freely volunteered their time and energy, in some cases over many years, to help in the research efforts needed to derive so much basic, previously unknown biology. In particular, I'd like to acknowledge our CEO Frank Downey who has acted as an elder statesman and who has a talent for helping very different people work together.

I'd also like to thank our training instructors Nemi Nath and Ingka Malten, and research staff members Samsara Salier, Paula Courteau, Lars Vestby and Steve Hsu who reviewed the text and the tedious details of the subcellular cases for content errors and omissions. In particular, my thanks to Lisbeth Ejiertsen who first assembled my original class notes into tabular form. I'd also like to thank the many, many therapists who took our trainings over the years, who participated in the slow and often frustrating process of deriving the material in this manual; or who acted as guinea pigs for the rough drafts as I tested for usefulness and clarity.

My illustrator, the certified PeakStates therapist Lorenza Meneghini has also been invaluable in making illustrations from the often poorly explained rough sketches made for her. (Incidentally, I asked her to make these very simple line drawings – otherwise each one would have been an intricate, detailed piece of art!) And my sincerest thanks to Piotr Kawecki, another certified therapist who came to my rescue by dreaming up and cheerfully making the amazing cover you hold in your hands.

I would also like to thank the friends who believed in me and helped me in those hard times when I needed encouragement to continue with the research, especially Chant and Bahar Thomas, Lita Stone, Sheelo Bolm, and Dr. Art MacCarley. And to Dr. Jim Harris, the Cal Poly EE department chair who took a chance, hired and mentored me at my first faculty position all those years ago. And my deepest gratitude to Tony Clarkson, founder of the Sanctuary of Healing in the UK for his financial donation that helped keep us going during the difficult financial downturn of 2008.

Each of the models and subcellular cases in this manual involved hundreds, and often thousands of hours of effort as we slowly made the breakthroughs necessary to understand the subcellular biology. This work was also unbelievably painful, tedious, and disheartening as trial after trial failed while we slowly derived techniques that would actually work. Again, I would like to acknowledge my past and current core research staff, who routinely faced great pain and suffering in the hope that their efforts would make a difference in the world, especially (in roughly chronological order): Dr. Marie Green, Dr. Deola Perry, Dr. Mary Pellicer, Maureen Chandler, Paula Courteau, Tal Laks,

Nemi Nath, Matt Fox, Samsara Salier, Lars Vestby, and Leif Pedersen. And special thanks to Kasia Presalek, whose exceptional integrity and commitment to the Institute led her to freely help many in Poland who desperately needed her during 2010-13.

I would also like to acknowledge those staff members who were injured in the research, and who, in some cases waited years in continuous pain and disability before we were able to help them. And finally, I send out into the universe my deepest thanks to my colleagues and dear friends whose deaths in our explorations pushed the boundaries of our understanding and made it safer for those who followed: Dorothy Gail, Edward Kendricks, Brian Beard, Dr. Adam Waisel, and Edward Rodziewicz – you are sorely missed.

Introduction

This manual was written as a desk reference for therapists who use Peak States®
Therapy with its Whole-Hearted Healing® regression trauma technique. It is also
written for our training program - appendices in the back are for teachers to give
their students in-class practice in identifying the various subcellular cases they
may encounter with clients.

In teaching our material, we've found that one of the biggest hurdles
therapists have is in doing diagnosis. This book is an attempt to address that
problem. It gives therapists an easy to use desk reference for the various
subcellular cases that clients can have; and reinforces, by using illustrations, the
fundamental principle that psychological issues are caused by various problems
found in the subcellular biology of the client.

This first edition manual is also an ongoing project. We continue to
improve it as we make new discoveries and, where possible, simplify our
techniques.

Why write another psychology book?

The material in this book is fundamentally different than anything you
have ever seen before, as it utilizes a biological breakthrough in understanding
and treating psychological and medical problems. One of the main problems in
current psychology and psychiatry is that there is no clear understanding of why
clients suffer from mental (or even many physical) disorders or issues. The
newer PTSD and trauma therapies have been a major boon to the field, but there
is still no understanding of why these therapies actually work (or don't as the
case may be); or how to apply them to many other problems.

Fortunately, it turns out that there *is* an underlying basis for these issues
and disorders, but in a place that no one had ever imagined – inside the cells
themselves. Thus, this manual covers specifics of a new field, that of
'subcellular' psychobiology. We list many subcellular problems, their mental
and physical symptoms, and new non-drug psychological-like techniques that
actually interact directly with these subcellular issues to eliminate them in a
reliable, efficient and fast way.

What assumptions do we make about your background?

This manual assumes you are already a trained therapist who uses
various modern, fast and effective trauma treatment techniques such as EFT
(meridian tapping), EMDR (bilateral stimulation), and TIR (regression); or are
currently studying them. It also helps if you have some background in prenatal

and transpersonal psychology. We've found that therapists who train with us are generally the ones who have reached the edge of what is possible with other approaches, but want to be even more effective; or are young students who want to learn a practical, cohesive biological framework for psychology, spirituality and medicine.

In the class setting, we spend a lot of time illustrating basic subcellular biology. Hence, reading a primer on eukaryotic subcellular biology (Wikipedia has good articles) and watching some of the excellent videos available on the web can be very useful.

This book does *not* explain treatments or techniques. We assume you already know the Whole-Hearted Healing or Peak States Therapy techniques that each subcellular case requires. These techniques are either taught in our therapist training classes, or found in:

- *The Basic Whole-Hearted Healing™ Manual* by Grant McFetridge and Mary Pellicer MD,
- *The Whole-Hearted Healing™ Workbook* by Paula Courteau,
- Other books in our *Peak States® Therapy* series,
- *Peak States of Consciousness, Volumes 1-3* by Dr. Grant McFetridge *et al.*

How this handbook evolved

This manual started as wall charts we had our therapist students fill in for practice during our therapist trainings. Each poster had a subcellular case, with listings of the phrases that typical clients used when describing their issue, along with other possible causes for the same symptoms (for differential diagnosis). When the students got to the stage where they were doing supervised work with clients, they could look at the posters at the back of the room to help them diagnose. This book formalizes that process for therapists who have finished the training but may have forgotten some of the material they learned.

The book is *not* organized starting from symptoms and going to causes. As handy as this would be, the problem is that most symptoms have a variety of causes. Thus, we took a different tack. Similar to how physicians or mechanics are taught, our students learn the subcellular problems first, and then learn to apply them to clients' symptoms. Fortunately, most client issues are only due to trauma or one of just a few particular subcellular cases. Hence, we first focus students on understanding and using these few common subcellular cases, and then add more specialized or rare cases later. To help this process, we found that drawings of the primary cell problem greatly enhanced student's ability to recall the subcellular cases; understanding the subcellular damages made symptoms and treatment much more obvious. This is similar to having a car manual or anatomy book with pictures that show the problem you need to repair.

Once that part of the book was done, we realized that the manual really needed to include systematic ways to diagnose issues, as some clients need a little detective work to figure out what the problem really is. Then we added two chapters on specific problems whose causes are not obvious by inspection. The last one is particularly interesting from a paradigm viewpoint, as it uses western subcellular biology to explain the basis of (and treatment for) spiritual, psychic, and related problems.

'Charging for Results'

The chapter on 'charging for results' is in many ways the most important chapter in this book, both from an ethical and functional viewpoint. We've found that therapists who get paid if they are successful get competent very fast; therapists who get paid for time actually have an unconscious disincentive to heal clients. Again drawing on the car analogy, this is similar to a car mechanic who charges by the hour versus one that charges by the job.

Safety issues: certifying therapists, and clinic backup

Although this may not be obvious since many people think of therapy as equivalent to chatting with a favorite aunt, one of the biggest problems technique developers face is that of safety. It has only been in the last 20 years or so that effective processes for trauma (or the more extreme version PTSD) have appeared, and it took quite a while for the field to realize that there were also risks with these very effective treatments (or in fact, with any therapy or spiritual practice). Because the Institute was developing techniques that had never existed before, we originally established several strategies to minimize unexpected problems or identify risk factors in our new product development process. One of these was to train therapists in our techniques and models; verify their relevant professional backgrounds in such areas as suicide intervention; and then license these therapists to use our new techniques. This allowed us to use our Institute clinics as 24/7 back-ups for these therapists in case any problems arose, and allowed us to update them with newer versions as our techniques and understanding improved. And since these therapists agreed to only 'charge for results' in all their work (clients pay only if an agreed upon treatment works), there was very good feedback to the research group if there were a problem with a new process or technique.

So, what happens when we publish a book on our techniques that anyone can read? Well, the techniques we describe are only ones that have had a good, long testing period to find any atypical responses. However, some techniques have intrinsic issues that a therapist has to know how to recognize and treat – like the mechanic or physician has to be able to spot and treat any unusual issues or side effects (such as the smell of gas while changing a water pump). Hence, this book is specifically written for therapists who have or are taking our training. Thus, for most readers, this book is for educational purposes only, and not a book on how to do therapy – but we make it available to the public to act as a catalyst for radical change in the fields of psychology, psychiatry and medicine, to a new, clear biological model that allows far more effective ways of helping clients.

Licensed Peak States processes

Again due to safety issues, there are a number of processes taught at our trainings that the participants agree to not use unless they have are licensed by the Institute to do so. This is for their protection as well as those of their clients (or their family and friends). These are usually also processes that continue to evolve over time, either to become more effective or to minimize some problem that may have arisen in some clients. They are called out in this manual as "licensed Peak States therapist processes". They generally involve healing key developmental event trauma that is the cause of a particular problem.

Trademark issues

Historically, as soon as a new therapy comes out that has some commercial success, two problems arise. First, some people read the book and became 'instant authorities' and teach the material, because teaching new therapies can sometimes be very lucrative, or make the teacher feel important; but this can have the unfortunate outcome that clients are not helped, or worse are injured, giving the new therapy a completely undeserved negative reputation. Secondly, people teach other material but call it by the same name to attract clients or students, making the original name meaningless.

To avoid these problems, we've trademarked our work, as is now customary in this and other technology fields for those exact reasons. Hence, only current staff from the Institute for the Study of Peak States are authorized to teach Whole-Hearted Healing® and Peak States® Therapy. This is not due to wanting to earn a living from it (although that would be a wonderful change!), but rather due to the nature of our material - it continues to change and evolve, so the teachers have to stay up to date. More importantly, for the safety of students we only allow very skilled and trained therapists to teach, who have far more understanding and skills than can be found from our published materials, and who work directly with the Institute's research group in case there are any unforeseen problems or new developments.

Techniques for acquiring peak states are not included

This manual does *not* cover our work on acquiring peak states of consciousness; rather, it only focuses on psychological problems and diseases.

In the last chapter we do briefly cover some of the psychological problems that apply specifically to peak states and spiritual experiences – for a complete coverage of this topic, see our *Spiritual Emergencies - Peak States*® *Therapy, Volume 4.*

The limitations of this handbook

First, this whole new field is a work-in-progress. Although the material in this book allows therapists and physicians to treat and understand many problems that they could not before, we do not yet have treatments for every client illness. This is not a problem with the theoretical basis of this approach – rather, it simply takes a tremendous amount of time to explore this huge new field of biology and apply its principles. Over time we expect that more and more treatments for specific diseases and disorders will be worked out, but it will be decades before all of the applications of this new approach are developed. Thus, we tell our students to use any and all techniques that they might know, not just the ones we teach – the only thing that matters is that the client gets well. However, this new way of understanding therapy and disease – subcellular psychobiology – gives our students a priceless framework to put these other techniques into, so they have a better understanding of limitations, advantages and areas of application.

Secondly, this book is just a snapshot in time of our theory and techniques. For the most part it is limited to material that was released to our therapists before 2010. This is because it just takes time and a significant number of clients to verify safety and reliability, so there is typically a built-in delay of four years to six years. Hence, more recent techniques and subcellular cases are generally not included.

Finally, this book is *not* designed to give a solid, detailed grounding in theory. Instead, it was designed to be a desk reference for practicing therapists who might need to quickly review possible causes and treatments for a client. For more in-depth theory, we refer you to our *Peak States of Consciousness* textbooks.

We also hope that in the future this handbook will become obsolete. Our current theoretical model and experiments suggest that there are far simpler and more comprehensive ways to heal psychological and medical issues.

About the cover art...

The cover illustration, created by Piotr Kawecki, is a stylized eukaryotic cell with what is intended to look like three close-up magnifications of areas of the cell. Shown as if they were actual photographs, these boxes illustrate three subcellular problems. The top box shows the case of 'copies', where a parasitic bacterial organism attaches to ribosomes along stuck mRNA copies of genes. The middle box shows the case of a body association, with a side view of two ribosomes stuck in the rough endoplasmic reticulum membrane. The lowest box shows the case of a vortex, with a mitochondrion continuously sucking in cytoplasm at its top (due to histone damage on an internal gene).

Dr. Grant McFetridge
Institute for the Study of Peak States,
Hornby Island, Canada

Section 1

Basic Principles

.

Chapter 1

Understanding the Subcellular Causes
of Emotional and Physical Symptoms

One of the biggest problems in psychology and medicine is that, despite a plethora of tools and techniques, there is still no clear theoretical understanding of why people have psychological symptoms. Yes, in some cases there are biological causes, such as brain damage or toxins – but these by far are the exception, not the rule. Since the 1950s, researchers assumed that symptoms have something to do with bad biochemistry – but attempts to follow up with that model have failed. And failed so thoroughly and for so long that the large drug companies have abandoned research into mental disorders. The latest hypothesis is that disorders are due to damaged neural networks, and again, some interesting work is coming from this, but no breakthroughs have materialized. Since these ideas seem reasonable, we assume that no progress is made because these are just difficult areas to work in.

But what if the symptoms are actually caused by something no one had ever thought of?

Well, before you start looking for the tinfoil hats, let's see what would be required for a radically new model. First, it would have to be in agreement with existing experimentally-derived biological principles. (Or if not, be able to identify overlooked, inaccurate, or incorrectly extrapolated observations.) Second, it needs to be able to address all of the data, not just 'cherry picked' cases or observations – no ignoring "inconvenient truths". Third, it needs to be able to treat problems existing techniques either cannot, only do partly, or do with great difficulty. And last, it hopefully explains everything in an elegantly simple way, resolving the confusion in existing data and models.

And yes, there is just such a solution, in an area of biology that no one ever associated with psychological symptoms - inside the cell itself.

This desk manual, written for practicing psychotherapists who have been trained in our techniques, focuses on a variety of subcellular problems, their symptoms and their treatments. And gives you an introduction into one of the most exciting new fields of science ever discovered – that of subcellular psychobiology.

This chapter is a brief review of background material relevant for therapists who are diagnosing psychological problems from a subcellular perspective. There are several new, fundamental biological models that need to be understood before working with subcellular problems. An in-depth coverage of these models, how they were derived, and their applications are found in *Peak States of Consciousness: Theory and Applications*, Volumes 1-3.

Trauma and Trauma Therapies

Biographical trauma (and its more extreme case Post-Traumatic Stress Disorder) was considered incurable by mainstream psychology until relatively recently. In 1996, four very different therapies that actually could eliminate trauma symptoms were described in the first peer-reviewed article in *The Family Therapy Networker*, which opened the way for their legal use by licensed therapists in the USA. Unfortunately, acceptance of these methods has been very slow and is still not taught in most university curriculums. Regardless, trauma-healing techniques are incredibly important, because it turns out that most issues clients have are either directly or indirectly due to trauma. Currently, the two most popular techniques are EMDR and EFT.

The Institute's own trauma-healing technique Whole-Hearted Healing (WHH) is based on regression. Developed in the early 1990s, it was designed both as a healing modality for trauma, and to allow easy access to prenatal experiences to investigate the origin of peak states of consciousness. However, practicing therapists taught by the Institute generally use a faster and easier one-point meridian tapping technique. They usually only use WHH or other techniques if the tapping does not work; or use WHH in combination with tapping when doing regression to key prenatal developmental moments.

During the years of development of the WHH technique, it also became clear that there were several fundamentally different types of trauma: biographical (from one's past), associational (as in Pavlov's dog), and generational (inherited trauma). Each type needed its own technique or approach. This was derived empirically at the time – the underlying subcellular biological basis for trauma was not discovered until quite a few years later. Chapter 7 goes through these trauma types in detail, along with illustrations of their biological causes.

The Primary Cell Model

In 2002 we made an extraordinary, fundamental biological discovery. It turns out that consciousness is found inside only one cell of the body. This cell, which forms during the forth cell division after conception, we called the 'primary cell'. All other brain and body structures are extensions of the organelles found inside this cell. It is as if this one cell was the microprocessor, and the brain was a peripheral device designed for pre- and post processing. Problems in this cell echo out into the rest of the body; it *is* the master pattern. In hindsight, the primary cell model makes sense from an evolutionary perspective. We live in a 'cell-centric' world; multicellular organisms are just single cells that have figured out how to extend themselves into a larger environment, very much like a person wearing a giant robot suit.

With this discovery, we soon realized that all psychological trauma types were caused by inhibited gene expression inside this primary cell, involving damaged histone proteins on genes, stuck mRNA strings, and ribosomes. Our model was published in 2008 in Volume 2. Unknown to us, during the same period Dr. Marcus Pembrey discovered the same mechanism by looking at an isolated community in northern Sweden. His work, albeit applied only to epigenetic inheritance, nicely validated our results by using a totally different approach. However, what is not yet known to mainstream biologists is that the same epigenetic mechanism also applies to all trauma types.

The Transpersonal Biology Model

One of the most significant parts of the primary cell discovery was that a person's awareness of the interior of this cell is overlaid over their awareness of the world and their body. It is like a special effects movie, with two very different worlds superimposed on each other. This turns out to be key to how psychological symptoms occur. Biological problems inside the primary cell are *experienced* as psychological or physical symptoms.

An extension of the primary cell model also solves one of the greatest mysteries of our times – how to integrate the existence of spiritual, shamanic, and psychic experiences with modern science. The current scientific paradigm rejects the existence of these phenomena, yet many people's personal experiences and an overwhelming amount of fascinating research work in this area has shown they actually exist. Currently, the dominant explanation among researchers in this area is that non-ordinary experiences cannot be explained by standard science, and so need to be studied as a separate subject with its own rules. Fortunately this conflict of worldviews can be resolved with an understanding of our 'transpersonal biology model'. It simply says that these sorts of experiences always have a physical, biological basis, but one *inside* the primary cell. People are actually 'seeing', experiencing, or accessing biological phenomena that are occurring inside the cell; that's why they cannot be found in the physical world or by medical examinations.

This model also applies to other really hard to accept, unusual phenomena like out-of-body experiences, experiencing oneself as another person or animal, schizophrenic voices, etc. Similar to how you need a physical mobile phone to connect to 'invisible' radio waves, biological subcellular structures in the primary cell allow a person to have these strange sorts of experiences.

'Biological' or 'spiritual' views

People can observe regression events or primary cell phenomena in two fundamentally different ways: from a 'biological' view or from a 'spiritual' view. The biological view is what you would generally expect if you were using your eyes or looking through a microscope. (This includes the 'out-of-body' perspective seen in traumatic memories, because they are still views of 'the real world'.) The spiritual view is far stranger – the person sees images of the intensity and distribution of awareness in the area that corresponds to the biological structures (a bit like an X-ray film), rather than an image of the structures themselves. This mode also includes views of 'spiritual' phenomena (such as hell realms, kundalini experiences, cords, and so on) that correspond to a biological function or substrate.

Although it is possible to switch between the spiritual and biological views, people stay in the spiritual view for a very simple reason – it avoids physical pain. If they switch to the biological view (and go 'in-body'), they will feel pain from any injury or damage there. Unfortunately, staying in the 'spiritual view' has major drawbacks – underlying biological problems cannot be recognized or healed.

Peak States

One of the outcomes of our work with the primary cell is the discovery that the psychological sensations of a peak experience or state occur because a given biological function in the cell is working optimally. To repeat, *biological* subcellular functions correspond to *psychological* experiences or states.

Of particular importance to our research work is a peak state that allows us to 'see' inside the primary cell to look at biological processes and dysfunctions. The full state does not give vague or imaginary visions – it is as clear as looking around in your own house. This is how we were able to make sketches of the subcellular problems for this manual. (As an aside, it took a couple of years after its discovery for us to realize that we were looking inside a cell; at first, we thought it was some kind of strange spiritual experience. This ability, which to some degree is relatively common, is suppressed or misunderstood in virtually everyone who has it.)

However, for research this *deus ex machina* ability is not quite as useful as it first sounds, albeit it saves a tremendous amount of time and money in comparison to electron microscopy or more modern live cell techniques. The primary cell is packed full of unusual stuff in different places and sizes. Finding the source of a problem can be very difficult. For example, we often don't even know if something is supposed to be there or not, or if so, how to tell if it is working properly. To get an idea of just how tough this can be, imagine a gigantic cruise ship. Now, where to look for a problem the size of a house cat, when you don't even know you are looking for a cat, nor would you recognize one if you saw it? Thus, it took us a decade of making observations, working out techniques, and testing them to create the material in this manual. And there is still a tremendous amount of work to be done.

Another important therapeutic area involves 'spiritual emergencies', where a client has unusual religious or spiritual experiences to the point of being a crisis. These problems can often be treated quite simply using an understanding of the corresponding subcellular or developmental causes. For example, kundalini awakening is a subcellular case in this manual; it causes huge problems for many people, but it can be eliminated with a simple healing technique. See our *Spiritual Emergencies - Peak States® Therapy, Volume 4* for a complete coverage of this topic.

Subcellular (Psychological-like) Techniques

We 'live' inside the primary cell – psychological symptoms (emotions and sensations) are just how we experience subcellular biological problems. These primary cell problems also echo out into our bodies to cause medical issues. However, there is a two-way street of information transfer; sensations from our physical bodies also go back into the primary cell. It turns out that we can use this pathway to create 'psychological-like' techniques that interact directly with subcellular structures and problems in the primary cell. In fact, this is how all of the empirically derived, effective trauma techniques actually work. (For example, meridian therapies work by interacting with fungal structures in the primary cell, as covered in Chapter 2.) Fortunately, we can now observe how a technique works inside the cell to figure out its limitations, to improve it, or to find how it gets its effect – does it eliminate symptoms by repairing or by damaging the cell? What is even more exciting about this is that we can also derive never-before-seen techniques now that we know we are interacting with the inside of a cell. A really good example of this is our Body Association Technique. Knowing that we wanted to remove ribosomes imbedded in the rough endoplasmic reticulum, we came up with a simple visualization and a few minutes of instruction that allow a typical client to eliminate the sorts of associations that, for example, create addictive cravings, withdrawal symptoms and a host of other problems.

It turns out that there are many different kinds of dysfunctions inside the typical primary cell. As the WHH process was being developed in the early 1990s, it became clear that there were physical and emotional issues that could not be healed by using our own trauma regression technique, or in fact, by any other trauma techniques we knew of. As ways to heal these other issues were worked out empirically, they became part of a growing list of 'special cases' that a therapist had to learn when using the WHH technique. It wasn't until the next decade that we realized that these psychological cases corresponded to biological, subcellular problems. In this manual, we no longer refer to most of these 'special cases' as part of Whole-Hearted Healing, because the techniques that treat them don't involve use of that regression technique. Instead, we now call these subcellular cases and the techniques used to heal them part of 'Peak States Therapy'.

Subcellular Case Naming Conventions

Unfortunately, we don't use a consistent naming convention for each of the subcellular cases – the names evolved over time as we slowly worked out this material. Thus, some have names that fit standard diagnoses (like 'brain damage'); some that identify their psychological effect (like 'copies'); some that describe the subcellular damage or structure (like 'shattered crystals'); and some are hybrids (like 'ribosomal voices'). We apologize for this confusion!

Subcellular Parasite Infections

As is discussed fully in the next chapter, one of the most disturbing discoveries we've made is that human beings (as well as mammals and birds, and probably eukaryotic celled organisms in general) are host to various kinds of parasites *inside* their primary cell. These subcellular parasitical organisms come in four main classes: bug-like organisms (probably prions); fungal organisms; bacterial organisms; and viruses. In fact, the presence or actions of these organisms is the direct cause of many of the subcellular dysfunctions in this manual. And they are also indirectly the origin of virtually all subcellular problems; for example, the damaged histone mechanism underlying trauma is due to one of these organisms.

As just one example, there is a phenomenon that seems like fantasy from a conventional viewpoint – that of 'past life' trauma. Whether one believes in it or not, it is clear experientially that this causes symptoms in some clients, and several techniques by various people have been empirically developed to deal with this problem. But an application of the 'transpersonal biology model' says that there has to be a subcellular biological basis for this phenomenon – and there is. It is a byproduct of a fungal organism that lives imbedded in the inner surface of the primary cell membrane. Damage to this organism result in free floating structures that connect to stuck mRNA trauma strings and act as 'gateways' to past life experiences. Once this biological problem is understood, another approach becomes possible for global elimination of all past life traumas; either repair the fungal organism, or eradicate it.

From a *therapist* perspective, working with client problems involving the various parasitic organisms in some cases is *potentially* dangerous – training is required to use the techniques safely. From a *research* perspective, investigations involving these organisms are *extremely* dangerous; based on our experience, permanent injury or death is possible and even likely.

Prenatal Trauma and the Developmental Events Model

As previously mentioned, the WHH regression technique developed in the early 1990s was designed to eliminate trauma, although its primary purpose was to see if there was a connection between prenatal trauma and exceptional states of consciousness (what is now called 'peak states'). This hypothesis turned out to be correct; but we also found that trauma in general was irrelevant. What mattered were traumas at key moments in prenatal development, when the organism suddenly becomes more complex. If all goes well, we have a corresponding peak state sensation or ability in the present. If serious trauma occurs, especially generational trauma that inhibits correct structural formation, the peak state is reduced or blocked. This concept is called the 'developmental events model for peak states, abilities and experiences'. Volume 2 of *Peak States of Consciousness* has a chronology of many of the key developmental events.

What is also truly significant about this model is that only a relative handful of specific moments in development matter. This means that the same process can be used on anyone by targeting these unique moments, rather than needing to work with each client as a totally unique problem (as is the case with general therapy). After struggling with this issue for a number of years, in 1998-9 a method to target these events was developed that used specific phrases and music to trigger people into these moments. We call these 'Gaia command processes' using the 'phrase regression technique'.

These key prenatal traumas can also be critically important for understanding and treating many psychological problems. Sometimes the connection between the developmental event and the present day symptom is not at all obvious – but like seeing the trick to solving a math problem, a therapist can quickly eliminate the problem if it is from a known case. For example, suicidal feelings are primarily from cord cutting trauma at birth – the cord is usually cut too soon and causes massive PTSD to the newborn.

To emphasize the point, the developmental events model describes how *past* biology effects the *present* primary cell biology. Like two sides of a coin, these two models describe the same problems either from a lens of current subcellular damage, or from the lens of past causes. Thus, therapy techniques either work on present dysfunctions in the cell (*à la* meridian therapy), or eliminate the cause in the past (*à la* regression), or are a hybrid of the two approaches.

Medical Applications

It turns out that the primary cell and the developmental events models are also vital for another important reason. They explain many medical problems, especially ones that simply don't seem to have any obvious cause and don't respond to antifungals, antibiotics or antivirals. Unfortunately, from a research perspective we've found that figuring out causes from symptoms is no easy task; subcellular biology is often quite complex. The good news is that after these problems are solved, some serious diseases can usually be eliminated quickly in office visits with a therapist without needing drug interventions. This manual lists two such diseases, the 'ribosomal voices' of schizophrenia (a fungal issue), and Asperger's syndrome (a bacterial issue). Volume 3 of *Peak States of Consciousness* covers more diseases, and also gives our current techniques for finding out causes and developing cures.

These models also solve a rather baffling observation in both psychology and medicine – why do different people respond differently to the same problem? For example, given similar people who experience the same severely traumatic event like a bank robbery, why some get PTSD (post traumatic stress disorder), yet about a third will usually be unaffected? It turns out that there are two factors – some already have a damaged histone on genes that are triggered during the event, which causes PTSD to form; or the person has a peak state that makes them immune to trauma. Similarly, impacts to the head affect people differently. We were also able to track this problem down to a very early developmental event that makes (or does not make) the brain resilient to physical trauma.

Most exciting for us, we believe that in the long run we will find processes where individual disease treatments will no longer be necessary. Our models indicate that it is possible to make people immune to whole classes of diseases simultaneously. Given the rapid loss of effectiveness of antibiotics, this may be a critically important application in years to come.

The Triune Brain Model

One of the first fundamental discoveries we made in the early 1990s by using WHH on prenatal trauma was the existence of the 'triune brains' (colloquially, the mind, heart and body awarenesses). Although the triune brain structure had already been discovered in primates by Dr. Paul MacLean years earlier, its application to the psychological concept of the 'subconscious' was new at the time. More importantly, its connection to subcellular biology was (and still is) completely unrecognized.

Over the next decade, we tracked the origin of these brain structures' awareness to the earliest possible developmental stage: block-like structures that are experienced as 'sacred beings' first form inside the mother and father close to the time of their implantation into the grandmothers. There the 'genesis cell' stage is initiated; each block gathers sacs of RNA, which are then enclosed in vesicles to form seven different types of prokaryotic (bacteria-like) cells. They then experience what is very likely a recapitulation of the endosymbiotic origin of eukaryotic life on earth; they coalesce to form a primordial germ cell, with each one becoming a different subcellular organelle. These blocks with their surrounding structures then move through the parental primary cell and into the ovaries or testes area in the parental zygote.

Returning to and again expanding on the example of trauma using this new model, these bacteria-like cells are also the origin of why there are different trauma types. Each contributed their own specialized genes to the new germ cell nucleus, and each organelle still uses those same genes for its own purposes in the cell. All trauma types have the same underlying cause; when a protein needs to be made, a damaged histone coating on the gene causes the mRNA copy to stick to the gene instead of floating out into the cytoplasm. However, the corresponding psychological experiences differ radically. Stuck mRNA strings for the peroxisome organelle (it experiences itself in the perineum area) create generational traumas; ones for the endoplasmic reticulum (it experiences itself in the belly) create body associations; and ones for ribosomes (they experience themselves in the heart area) create biographical traumas.

In the present, the awareness in each of the tiny sacred being blocks extends outwardly into the primary cell organelles. From there, awareness continues to extend outwardly into corresponding multi-celled organs and brain structures. Incidentally, although we usually talk about three brains – the body (reptilian), heart (mammalian) and mind (primate) – in actuality there are seven pairs, with one set from each parent.

Many of the problems people have are directly or indirectly due to damage or conflicting agendas in these triune brains, and several of the subcellular cases reflect this. The opposite is also true - the 14 brain awarenesses are supposed to be fused into one; different configurations of fusion among the brain awarenesses result in different peak states.

The Center of Awareness (CoA)

The triune brain model neatly explains the existence of the subconscious. However, this begs the question, then what is consciousness? Rather than try and use one of the many confusing and conflicting definitions in psychology, it turns out that one can use a simple kinesthetic procedure to identify what we mean by the word. Take your finger, point it at yourself (no need for touch with this procedure), and slowly move it down from above your head to find the range of where you experience yourself in your body. This is the location of your CoA. It can be in one place or several, and for most people this place where you are in your body can temporarily move around by using willpower. We call this experiential concept the Center of Awareness (CoA). As the transpersonal biology model says, it turns out that there is a physical substrate to conscious awareness inside the primary cell. This CoA concept is extremely important for therapists as they use it quite often in various healing techniques.

Key Points

- The 'primary cell model' says that consciousness is found in only one cell of the body.
- A person's everyday experience is a simultaneous mixture of normal perception and perception of the interior of the primary cell.
- Subcellular psychobiology is the study of dysfunctions inside the primary cell that cause psychological problems.
- Psychological-like techniques can interact with the primary cell to repair problems.
- The 'developmental events model' says that peak states are blocked by trauma at early, key developmental moments.
- Disease states or the susceptibility to them also occur at key developmental moments.
- The 'transpersonal biology model' says that all spiritual, shamanic, and psychic experiences are based on physical biology inside the primary cell.

- There are three kinds of trauma: generational, associational, and biographical.
- Trauma is indirectly caused by damaged histone coatings on genes.
- The 'triune brain model' explains the phenomenon of the subconscious, as well as many problems and several peak states.
- The organelles inside the primary cell have awarenesses that extend outwards into organs and the (triune) structures of the brain.
- Parasites inside the primary cell are directly or indirectly responsible for subcellular dysfunction.
- Working with subcellular parasites is potentially dangerous – specialized training is required.
- Consciousness can be defined using a kinesthetic procedure that locates the 'center of awareness' in the body.

Suggested Reading

- *The Basic Whole-Hearted Healing™ Manual* (2004) by Grant McFetridge and Mary Pellicer MD. A how-to manual for therapists on this regression technique.
- *The Biology of Belief: Unleashing the power of consciousness, matter, and miracles* (2005) by Bruce Lipton Ph.D. A good introduction to subcellular biology for laypeople, although it lacks the concept of the primary cell.
- *The Ghost in Your Genes* (2005) by British Broadcasting Corporation (BBC) Horizon. This video does an excellent job of explaining Dr. Pembrey's discovery of epigenetic damage via data from families in an isolated town in Sweden.
- "Going for the cure", *Family Therapy Networker* (July/August 1996), 20(4), pgs. 20-37 by M. S. Wylie. This was the first peer-reviewed article about four psychological techniques that could actually eliminate trauma symptoms.
- "Inner Life of the Cell", Harvard University (8:11 minutes, 15MB) – An excellent video on extra and intra cellular animation with dialog. It can be found on YouTube or on Harvard's website. It is also very useful for understanding the simple sketches in this handbook.
- "Molecular Machinery of Life", Harvard University (2:09 minutes, 19MB) – An excellent video on subcellular functions using state of the art animation. This can be found on YouTube or from Harvard's website. It is very useful for understanding the simple sketches in this handbook.
- *Peak States of Consciousness*, Volumes 1-3 (2004, 2008, 2015) by Grant McFetridge *et al.*
- "Transgenerational epigenetic inheritance: how important is it?", *Nature Reviews Genetics* (March 2013), 14, 228-235 by Ueli Grossniklaus,

William G. Kelly, Anne C. Ferguson-Smith, Marcus Pembrey & Susan Lindquist.

- *The Triune Brain in Evolution: Role in Paleocerebral Functions* (1990) Pleunum Press by Paul MacLean. The definitive work on triune brain biology (written for specialists) from his research at NIMH.
- *Spiritual Emergencies - Peak States® Therapy Volume 3* (2015) by Marta Czepukojc and Grant McFetridge.

Chapter 2

Primary Cell Parasites - Symptoms and Safety

Although I already had a successful career as an electrical engineer doing research, design, consulting and university teaching, at 30 I began a project that I was much more passionate about: how to bring fundamental health to humanity. By 2008, 24 years later, I was starting to feel defeat and despair; that I simply was not smart enough to solve the core problem. True, I'd solved many essential biological issues, like the triune brain origins, the existence of the primary cell, the subcellular biology of trauma, and so on, but I was still unable to understand the really basic issues of our species.

Even worse from my personal perspective, a few Institute therapist trainees had triggered themselves into long-term pain that I could not stop, in spite of the endless hours I spent. Because of this and my feeling that I had failed the core project, in 2009 I cancelled all further trainings and started to shut down the Institute. This turned out to be one of the best decisions I have ever made. Many people dropped out; the few staff that stayed were genuinely focused on the core purpose. This gave me the time and space to just be with these issues, instead of being overwhelmed with management tasks. Slowly, one at a time, we made breakthroughs: first, how to safely eliminate the long-term pain those students had (the class 1 parasite problem described in this chapter); the unique biology of the Beauty Way and Optimum Relationship peak states; the subcellular cause of all negative emotions and that of trauma itself; and in the early spring of 2011, in one of the best days of my life, the source of the fundamental, core problem in our species (and in fact in all mammals).

Although as of this writing we don't yet have solutions for these core species-wide problems, finally understanding the biology allows us to continue our work. The deaths of so many of my close friends and colleagues during this research had not been wasted.

Therapy and Subcellular Parasites

The most dangerous issue in our research into new therapeutic processes is one that the Institute was unwilling to explain to the public until now. This was for a very serious safety reason: knowledge of the problem can stimulate some people into focusing on it in such a way as to cause themselves long lasting pain, injury or potentially even death. The problem is simple – human beings are host to different kinds of parasitical organisms inside and around the primary cell itself. Unfortunately, because of the nature of the primary cell, our consciousness can interact with these organisms in a far more profound and damaging way than we might assume is possible. This effect is *not* similar to our experience with the usual types of disease organisms in our gut or bodies that doctors routinely deal with.

This parasite issue is in everyone, albeit people generally establish a kind of homeostasis to minimize the physical and mental symptoms. Unfortunately, spiritual practices, psychotherapy, and even life events can trigger problems with these organisms. Thus, these problems occur with any therapy, not just our own; the difference is that we recognize the cause of the problems that can occur when doing inner growth or healing work, and have ways to treat many of them.

There are four key problems with these parasitic organisms that the subcellular cases in this manual cover. (See Appendix 8 for a summary list of subcellular parasite cases.) First, the parasites live inside us, and their structures and functions disrupt our own. Secondly, most people interact or unconsciously communicate with them, leading to various physical and emotional symptoms. Third, and probably the most disturbing, one can lose one's self-identity by surrendering one's consciousness into them. And finally, contrary to our cultural assumptions, some species of parasites act like mobile phones, allowing interactions at a distance between people, giving rise to widespread interpersonal and cultural problems.

Unlike usual diseases, these parasitic organisms infect virtually the entire human race and are transmitted from parent to child without the need for external pathogens. And they cause profound problems for our species in terms of mental and physical health. (For a complete discussion on this topic, see *Peak States of Consciousness*, Volume 3.) These parasites can be divided into three classes, with each class exploiting a different mechanism to fool the human immune system. (Unusually, the core parasite species also infect all mammals and birds.) Interestingly, parasite species in a given class are radically different in size, apparently so they can exploit different environments inside the cell. They range from some that are tiny in relationship to a histone-coated gene to ones that are a significant percentage of the size of the entire primary cell.

From a therapeutic standpoint, many of the cases in this manual use treatments on the level of an individual parasite presence. Thus, the techniques are designed to make a client's symptoms go away by eliminating the parasite; by changing the client's interactions with a given parasite; or by healing the parasite and indirectly helping the host. (This single parasite approach is adequate for most psychological issues, but some diseases such as Asperger's syndrome are caused by more complex interactions between developmental event traumas and parasites from different classes.) However, there are more global treatments possible for these parasite problems. For example, the peak states process called the Silent Mind Technique works by making a person immune to the borg fungus (described below); this simultaneously eliminates all of the various problems that the fungus causes in a person. Our current research is primarily focused on finding global processes that will make a person immune to each of the different major classes of parasites.

DANGER

Working on parasite issues can cause long-term pain or serious injuries. In extreme cases it can result in death. This type of problem should only be addressed by a trained, certified therapist who has both experience and backup from the Peak States clinics staff. Do NOT experiment in new ways to heal this, as you can easily cause sudden overgrowth and extreme or life-threatening symptoms.

A cultural blind spot

Oddly enough, the existence of subcellular parasites that can communicate with each other both inside the person and between people is something that most of our students can accept. Perhaps this is because the model allows them to easily treat problems in clients that they have not been able to before.

However, one problem that we've encountered with therapists and in research is due to our cultural assumption that each of us is completely alone; and that what we feel is just due to only our own inner experience that is shaped after birth. Yet nothing could be further from the truth, both in terms of prenatal trauma and the existence of parasites that affect behavior. Unfortunately this assumption causes an interesting blind spot. Therapist (and researchers) generally act as if a subcellular parasite's actions are due only to the client's trauma or issues. Although in a sense this is true – our traumas allow them to be there, and can limit the scope of their actions, or increase them – the problem is that *parasites have an agenda of their own.* This agenda can cause problems that the client has absolutely no direct control over. In the extreme, the parasites can harm or even accidentally kill the human host, something that the person obviously does not want to happen. Trying to heal every parasite activity as if they were the client's own issue does not work. It would be like trying to heal someone who shot up the neighborhood by only working on their spouse – yes, they did marry and live in the same house, but this does not make them the sole cause of the other's behavior.

In a similar vein, not only do people experience the parasite's consciousness as if it were their own, but people also interact with parasites as if they were other people. This can also cause a variety of problems, because the parasite is *not* another person, and it may react in unexpected or harmful ways to the host. What is also hard to realize is that we want them in us because they make us feel safe or comfortable, powerful, and so on - even if they harm us. Continuing the previous analogy, it is like having a bunch of abusive spouses. Understanding this dynamic is important because it may change the way we work with a client; for example, we may start treatment by eliminating the reason why the client feels that a subcellular parasite is someone they know.

Research at the Institute

At first, we didn't realize what was causing various short or long-term, often incredibly painful or debilitating symptoms we were seeing in a few of our staff, therapist trainees and clients. Sometimes they already had symptoms; sometimes therapy (of any kind, not just our own techniques) would trigger their problems. We spent tremendous numbers of man-hours working on this puzzle in ourselves and with the affected people, trying to figure out what was going on. At first, we had an unconscious bias that work on peak states, spirituality *and* psychological healing was intrinsically safe. Over time, this view started to slowly shift as more and more problems surfaced that we didn't understand. Over a period of about five years, we slowly began to suspect that there existed different kinds of parasites in the primary cell. But it was not enough to have a hypothesis – we were simultaneously testing our understanding by inventing new experimental treatments, which in turn took endless hours of effort, frustration and failure. During this period, many of our research team were seriously injured and two died while working on the parasite issues. Because knowledge of this problem could cause symptoms in susceptible people, we felt we had to find treatments that were both safe and effective before we could ethically and safely share this information with the public.

As an aside, we've seen that when some people read about the dangers and risks in doing research they worry that doing therapy is similarly dangerous. However, this is the same situation in something we all take for granted – the development of new medical drugs and procedures. We normally never hear about the mistakes and problems of their research phase (nor do we care), and only think about the product when we go get it at the drug store or doctor's office.

Fortunately, in our early planning in the 1990s we had designed the future structure of the Institute to specifically deal with possible safety problems, because we did not know what to expect when we developed new, never before seen techniques for peak states of consciousness. By the early 2000s the Institute had grown enough in size to implement this safety structure and its protocols. As with all of our research projects, our testing starts with the research team. Once we believe we have a potential treatment, we then expand the testing to our Institute staff. If this goes well, we then expand our testing again by have our licensed Peak States certified therapists test on themselves; and finally, after having tested on enough people, we cautiously release the process for use with clients. However, our testing and safety net does not stop there: our advanced clinic staff are a backup for the certified therapists in case they encounter problems with clients. This also gives us the feedback we needed to long-term test our processes. And since all our certified therapists only work on a 'pay for results' basis, we also get good feedback if the process is not fully effective.

Many of our students have had a natural impulse to want to do research on their own. It is hard for most people to believe that this could be dangerous. Either they have the same sorts of beliefs we once did, like "inner exploration is beneficial"; or like teenagers driving a fast car, they think bad things can't happen to them because they're smarter, more able, luckier, and so on. It is especially hard for people to get out of the isolationist mindset of our culture to emotionally realize that they are dealing with more than just themselves – that the parasites have their own consciousness and actions separate from their own.

Especially in the case of the parasite issues, we tell our students to *not* try and find alternative or better ways than the ones we teach. This is because there are several (what look like obvious) ways to eliminate parasites. Unfortunately, we found by bitter experience that these obvious ways were unsafe. The biggest problem is that the body believes at a fundamental level that it needs these organisms. If you start to disturb homeostasis, the body will respond by making the problem much, much worse to compensate. Unfortunately, we're also talking about organisms that have their own agendas; our survival is not one of them. To an individual parasite, it is not obvious what major repercussions their actions can have to the host.

The Humanity Project

One of the hardest things for anyone to do is to look at the world and see inconsistencies with their own paradigm. Normally, we take things for granted – that is "just the way things are" – and perhaps work within that framework to improve things. But one of the most important discoveries that the Institute made was that the world around us is not supposed to be like it is *at all.* That what we consider normal at almost every level of the human species - personal, interpersonal, socially, culturally, physically, medically, and environmentally – are the outcomes of widespread pan-species parasitic diseases.

The Institute was founded to try and solve just one problem – how to heal the human species. Our early work had shown us that it was possible to have fundamentally better states of consciousness that would automatically solve a host of planetary and species-wide problems if most people had them. This includes environmental destruction, population excess, social injustice, mental problems, physical disease, bacterial and viral immunity, bodily regeneration, and a host of other issues. By 1998 we realized that our species needed only three key states of consciousness (out of over a hundred that we had identified), but it wasn't until 2011 that we discovered that these key states were blocked by developmental damage from parasitic organisms inside the primary cell. (In fact, these organisms have infected all mammals, which is why we don't see any significant differences between species.)

The three different classes of parasites listed below each block a key 'humanity project' peak state. These organisms are listed in the order of approximate overall severity; this is also the chronological order that they originally infected our species. Now that we understand the nature of the problem that has crippled humanity, our Institute's efforts are focused on finding ways to make people immune to these three parasite classes. (For much more detail on the derivation and biology of this problem, see *Peak States of Consciousness,* volume 3.)

Bug-like Parasites (Class 1)

These parasites live inside and on the primary cell, and share one common characteristic; they all look like various hard-shelled insects, and usually 'taste' metallic. These organisms can cause feelings of stabbing pain, burning, and sensations that something is on the skin or burrowing in the body. Putting attention on them, consciously or unconsciously, causes them to react like wild animals: they can freeze in place, emit toxins to hide, burrow into membranes, or attack with claw-like appendages that cause stabbing or ripping pain. We observe that these parasites are extremely common in the cell. They come in a huge range of sizes; ones that are a significant percentage of the nuclear or cell membranes are particularly dangerous, as they can rip the primary cell membranes open, causing death to the client.

One particular species in this class causes the primary block to fundamental peak states of consciousness, including the ability to regenerate. Partial healing or suppression of this infection results in various major states, such as Beauty Way, Optimum Relationships, and others. Work with this species is beyond the scope of this manual.

Surprisingly, this 'bug-like' class of parasites is not described in standard biology texts; however, it is very likely that this is because they are actually prions. These bug-like parasites appear to be a primarily non-carbon based form of life; some, and perhaps all species of this class are rapidly destroyed by ATP (the oxygen equivalent in cells) if their protection is breached.

Subcellular cases that are caused by different species of this class of parasites are soul loss, resistance to having altruistic positive feelings, and bubbles.

Risks involving work with these organisms include extreme pain (intermittently or continuously), underlying fear, delusions, psychosis, loss of self-identity, severe irreparable injury to cell membranes, several serious diseases and body dysfunctions, loss of peak states, and sudden death.

Fungal Parasites (Class 2)

Fungal parasites all share two characteristics – they have a crystalline material inside themselves, and feel nauseating (like vomit) when sensed fully. However, different species have radically different forms, ranging from fixed structures, to masses of white or black cotton candy-like filaments, to squids or jellyfish. Many of the subcellular cases in this book are the result of actions or problems with different fungal species inside the primary cell. For example, various structures identified in Volume 2 of *Peak States of Consciousness* inside the nuclear core (the empty area inside the nucleolus) are all fungal: the ring that creates the 'column of self' that is the basis for multiple personality disorder and other issues; the 'merkaba' that creates problems with triune brain interconnection and a type of ADHD; the 'chain' that is responsible for the existence of 'core traumas'; and the 'pinecone' that creates the bubble and time loop problems.

Far outside our cultural beliefs, several of the fungal parasite subspecies also share 'group minds' (sometimes called 'collective consciousness' or 'composite awareness'); they experience themselves as one organism living in many human bodies simultaneously. Because most people also experience these organisms as part of themselves, this creates havoc at both the interpersonal and societal levels. Probably the best example of this problem is with the subcellular, squid-like 'borg' fungus (so-called because of its horrifying functional similarity to the borg species in Star Trek). At an individual level, the borg act to interconnect people's trauma sensations, giving rise to the real-time, sensed experience that others have a characteristic 'personality'. Various psychic traditions describe these connections as 'cords'. Surprisingly, this is not a metaphor; it is a misunderstood perception of tentacles from a borg fungus. In therapeutic terms, this phenomenon of 'cords' is the primary cause of transference and counter-transference. A worse problem is due to this parasite influencing people's actions and behavior in an effect we call the 'tribal block'. This unconsciously gives people the 'rules' of their culture, and creates cultural conflict. Most people sense when someone from a different culture is present – what they are actually sensing is the antagonism one borg subspecies has with another. Thus, the large scale, bloody history of mankind with its nationalisms, racism, and wars is actually caused by this fungus in its competitions to increase its living space into more humans. It doesn't just influence behavior; a large percentage of our species merge their consciousness into the borg's to feel powerful, compensating for feelings of powerlessness and inadequacy; but they lose their humanity when they do so.

Many of the various different fungal organisms are misunderstood as 'spiritual' or 'energetic' structures of the body by various spiritual or religious traditions. For example, 'chakras' with their connecting 'meridians' are actually the body of a fungal organism that lives on the outer nuclear membrane. Other examples: the 'life paths' on the inside of the nuclear membrane are part of a fungal organism; the past-life network on the inside of the cell membrane is a different fungal species; the 'oversoul' structure inside the nuclear core that is experienced 'above' the person is yet another fungal species; and s-holes.

Risks involving work with these organisms include loss of personal identity, triggering schizophrenia, feelings of weakness, tiredness, blocks to awareness and body sensations, physical numbness, extreme fear, mild to debilitating fatigue, severe nausea, corrosive acid inside the cell, parasite injuries initiated by other people, memory loss, and sudden death.

Bacterial Parasites (Class 3)

These single-celled bacterial parasites have the characteristic look and feel of water balloons – they generally have soft surfaces, are very flexible, can range from rather amorphous to perfectly globular, usually 'look' translucent or transparent, some have filaments (fimbriae), and some have attached structures at the end of filaments. These organisms all share the quality of feeling intrinsically 'toxic' to the observer (if the sensation is not blocked from awareness). They can also emit toxins – when they do, the bacterial cell 'looks' grey to black. Different species in this class come in a huge range of sizes, and can be found in the cytoplasm, in the nucleus, and outside the primary cell. During regressions, they are also found inside and outside the sperm, egg and zygote. Regardless of the species, organisms in this class all exploit the same underlying cellular vulnerability that allows them to be in the cell.

People can sense each bacteria cell as having an emotional tone that can be neutral, negative, or fully evil. Some are experienced rather like passive 'people' or presences, but with an underlying negative or evil sensation. One species found in the nuclear core in virtually all humans and mammals is experienced 'below' the person, and gives rise to the experience of an 'underground hell realm' if a person puts their CoA into it. Most importantly, damage from these organisms in the earliest developmental stages is the underlying cause of the mechanism of trauma, as well as the reason people can even have 'negative' emotions.

The body brain often uses these 'water-balloon' bacterial parasites as a sort of patching material, to seal damages like breaks or holes in other subcellular structures. Hence, one generally can't eliminate these bacterial patches from these areas unless the underlying damage is healed first.

Subcellular cases that are directly caused by different organisms of this class are copies, sound loops, e-holes, trauma bypasses, the presence of negative 'ancestors' in the present, and the presence of the grandparents in one's awareness. They also cause other serious problems in people, such as mild autism (inability to connect emotionally), tiredness, pressure pain, nausea, emotional numbness, paranoia, and many specific psychological issues. More rarely, they are sometimes used in an unconscious defensive reaction against another person - it giving the sensation that the person is 'in your space', with the sensation of filaments inserted into your body, causing reactions that range from anxiety (or fear) to annoyance (or anger).

Risks involving work with these organisms include triggering horrifying sensations of evil, extreme exhaustion or fatigue, paranoia, negative thoughts and feelings, feelings of pressure, autistic (Asperger's) symptoms, sensations of electric shock, extreme feelings of cold, suffocation, numbness in part or all of the body, and other serious problems. One can become partly or fully identified (i.e., the CoA is inside it) with a bacterium, making people feel paranoid, negative or evil, numb (suppressed body sensations and positive feelings) and tired, and can involve complete loss of self-identity; the motivation to surrender awareness into these organisms is to feel safer and more comfortable, in spite of the resulting aggressive and negative feeling and thinking.

Viruses

As of this writing, our models and some preliminary experiments strongly suggest that viruses are present in the cell's cytoplasm or nucleolus due to developmental problems caused by bacterial parasite damage at early development. Thus, viruses appear to be opportunistic rather than exploiting a direct biological vulnerability themselves. (Interestingly, some people do have a state of complete immunity to viral and bacterial infections. Acquiring this state is one of the goals of our research efforts.) Since viruses can sometimes cause psychological symptoms (as well as an incredible number of diseases), we include them in this discussion of parasite classes.

Viruses use signals to trick the body brain of the human host. For example, the cause of viral pneumonia is a virus that looks a lot like a soccer ball as it moves through the cytoplasm. To the host, these viruses 'feel' like childhood friends and family. Thus, when a person feels deeply lonely, their body may pull in and support this virus to assuage the loneliness (giving rise to a potentially lethal lung disease).

We've also seen psychological issues related to viral action. In some people, a viral net (looking a lot like a fine lace handkerchief) is constructed about halfway between the nuclear membrane and the nucleolus. This viral net can partly or fully surround the nucleolus and causes a squeezing pressure in the head of a person who has it (usually diagnosed as a migraine headache). Surprisingly, people who have this problem and who wish to evoke a negative group dynamic will actually trigger the viral net formation in other susceptible individuals.

Ameba

As of this writing, it is likely that there may also be amebic organisms inside the cytoplasm of the primary cell. These would be protists (eukaryotic, with a nucleus), rather than bacterial (prokaryotic, without a nucleus). As of this writing we have not identified an amebic subcellular case; there may be one we haven't yet seen, or we may have misidentified an amebic parasite as bacterial without realizing it.

Regardless, our biological model predicts that any amebic parasite can be in the cell only because one of the three main parasite classes indirectly allows it to be there.

Key Points

- The three classes of primary cell subcellular parasites are bug-like, fungal, and bacterial.
- Different subcellular parasite species cause different emotional, psychological and physical symptoms.
- There are many sizes and species in each subcellular class of parasite; some mobile, some not.
- Each class of parasite exploits a different vulnerability in the cell.
- Viruses appear to exploit vulnerabilities created by the bacterial parasites.
- For client safety, therapists must use only tested techniques.
- Research into this issue is extremely dangerous.

Suggested Reading

- "The Life of a Dead Ant: The Expression of an Adaptive Extended Phenotype" in *The American Naturalist*, Sept 2009 by Sandra B. Andersen *et al.* Available online. Describes the ability of a fungus to control ants, and gives other examples.
- *Foundations of Parasitology,* 8th edition, (2008) by Larry Roberts and John Janovy Jr. Undergraduate textbook for biology and/or zoology students.
- *Host Manipulation by Parasites* (2012) by Richard Dawkin. Excellent summary of this new field.
- *Peak States of Consciousness*, Volume 3 by Grant McFetridge.
- "Parasitic Puppeteers Begin To Yield Their Secrets", *Science Journal* (Jan 17, 2014) by Elizabeth Pennisie. Short online description of this new field of parasitic influence.
- *Parasite Rex: Inside the Bizarre World of Nature's Most Dangerous Creatures* (2001) by Carl Zimmer. Excellent summary book for non-professionals.
- "Suicidal Crickets, Zombie Roaches and Other Parasite Tales". Presented by Ed Young in the online video series *Ted Talks*, March 2014.

Section 2

Diagnosis and Treatment

Chapter 3

'Pay for Results'

When we talk about our work with clients or professionals, their first reaction is often "where's the proof?", or from academics, "where are the evidence-based studies?". When we reply that we have a 'pay for results' policy so there is no need for it, there is a momentary pause, eyes glaze for a second, then they usually repeat themselves as if we hadn't spoken. Apparently the leap to results-oriented treatment billing is simply too foreign a concept to comprehend at first.

Why is this? Well, clients sometimes confuse this concept with some kind of scam, where people 'guarantee' a product, don't deliver and then keep the money. Or they simply don't believe that you are serious, because this is so far outside their previous experience. Academics tend to have a different issue, one that strikes at the heart of the practice of psychology and medicine. Currently, a great deal of statistical tools are used (often incorrectly) in research because investigators are not designing for a binary solution set of 'it worked, or it didn't work'. Instead, test outcomes are usually so vague or contradictory the best they can hope for is often only slightly above the threshold of the placebo effect. This mindset can also lead to completely bizarre situations like I saw in my own doctoral training, where we were taught measurement scales that ignored the specific client problem we were treating, and instead rated 'overall improvement' – sadly, because there really were no effective treatments for specific problems.

When Frank Downey and I designed the structure of the Institute in the 1990s, we fully expected that our first generation techniques simply would not always work (or work partially) for some clients. We were developing something entirely new, there was a lot we didn't yet understand, and people's problems are often very complex. However, we were only interested in full elimination of symptoms (note that we use this phrase because is socially and often legally unacceptable to talk about 'cures'). Partial successes were valuable from a research viewpoint, but with 'pay for results' the only meaningful outcome is "what we agreed upon is done". This means that therapists have to actually deliver; and if they can't, that they are not financially penalizing clients because of their (or the Institute's) own limitations. This also has the tremendous advantage that we don't have to do extremely costly third-party studies – after all, the client is the one who really knows if the problem is gone and stays gone.

What is 'Pay (Charge) for Results'?

The Institute for the Study of Peak States is pioneering a way of charging clients that is different from the one used by most all conventional therapists (although it is already used in many other professions). When talking to clients, we call it 'pay for results', and when talking to therapists, we call it 'charge for results'. All therapists who license our processes and use our trademark agree to abide by this condition in *all* the work they do, whether it is using our techniques or anyone else's.

How does it work? In the initial session, the therapist and client come to a written agreement of what is to be worked on and what criteria would constitute success. The fee is negotiated at this time (although most therapists use a predetermined flat fee that makes this step much simpler). Open-ended fees such as by the hour are *not* acceptable – the client has to know exactly what he is agreeing to and what he is going to pay as part of the contract. Obviously, some people won't choose to become clients, but there is no fee for this initial consultation since there were no results. After treatment, if the predetermined criteria for success are not met, the certified therapist does not get paid, and does *not* charge for the time spent. Clearly, some clients won't generate income and, in cases with dishonest clients, the client will get the service but the therapist will not be paid. However, this fee structure is not unusual – it is standard for most businesses, and the fees are adjusted to take these problems into account. Appendix 10 shows a simple way to calculate what a therapist's minimum fee needs to be when using a single 'fixed-fee' billing.

In some cases, the Institute sets a non-negotiable criteria for success for some licensed, specific processes used by our certified therapists – for example, someone who hears voices no longer does; the addict no longer has cravings; peak states processes have to actually give the client the sensations of the state; and so on. Another example of this pay for results principle is in research. Although we on occasion do contract with a client for a specific outcome that we have to do research to solve, the Institute never writes a contract with clients charging them for the hours spent on investigating treatments for new diseases.

The Rationale Behind 'Pay (Charge) for Results'

The 'charge for results' principle solves a number of serious problems in the medical and psychological healing profession.

In this chapter we'll discuss a number of practical reasons why charging for results is a good idea for therapists. However, from our perspective the primary problem with current billing by the hour is an ethical one. It is simply morally repugnant to require money from clients you don't help. The principle of the 'golden rule' describes this clearly – 'do to others what you would have them do to you'. Many clients come to therapists in desperate need of help, and often they are the people who have the least ability to pay due to the nature of their problems. These people need their resources to get real help, not support a sense of entitlement in the therapist. This is very much like taking your car in for repair, and having the mechanic tell you he can't fix it, but that you now owe him thousands of dollars for the time he wasted.

Probably the most serious practical problem 'charge for results' addresses is the (hopefully) unconscious incentive for failure in the current system. When we charge by the hour we get rewarded for our failures. The payment reinforces the failures and as you know, what we reinforce we get more of. This principle is well described by Kylea Taylor in her book *Ethics of Caring*, where she displays a chart of the traps therapists can easily fall into with clients. Thus, standard billing practices where you are billing by the hour, not based on performance, has several potential problems:

- The typical therapist unconsciously wants to keep his client coming in to therapy so that the therapist continues to be paid.
- The typical therapist is again unconsciously resistant to learning new, faster techniques because this would interfere with his income stream.
- The therapist has to suppress their own instincts and buy into a system that denies the ethical issue against charging people when nothing is accomplished.

From our perspective as a teaching and certifying organization, 'charge for results' also solves the major problem of how to verify a therapist's competence. Normally, therapists and other health professionals take exams to show competence. Unfortunately, this measure does not actually work well, as anyone who has taken high school or college exams can well testify! By using pay for results billing, we find that therapists either are or quickly become competent or they simply don't earn a living. Thus, this system itself is automatically self-correcting - our therapists are financially motivated to become better healers and seek out better treatment techniques. (Of course, we do check their knowledge and skills before licensing to help them through the transition as a new therapist. And we support them in becoming better therapists for the first year; but the problem of competency quickly solves itself without financially penalizing clients.)

'Charge for results' also solves another common problem – rejecting newer therapies simply because the therapist is comfortable with what he already knows. As the Nobel physicist Max Planck, the founder of quantum theory once famously said, "A new scientific truth does not triumph by convincing its opponents and making them see the light, but rather because its opponents eventually die, and a new generation grows up that is familiar with it."

Fortunately, with the 'pay for results' principle therapists are forced to actively seek out newer, more successful techniques, rather than simply avoid change or rely on organizations that have a vested interest in promoting obsolete or ineffective techniques.

In summary, the Institute's 'charge for results (success)' fee structure means that the therapist charges for performance, not for time. It has many advantages:

1. It encourages therapists to be as capable as possible.
2. It encourages the therapist to make clear and realistic criteria with their clients.
3. It minimizes the problem of unrealistic client expectations.
4. It discourages the problem of the therapist becoming a 'paid friend' and so unnecessarily prolonging the client's suffering.
5. It encourages therapists to refer clients to therapists who can heal the client.
6. It minimizes the problem of the client forgetting that they ever had the problem after it is gone (the apex effect).
7. Is ethically satisfying.

With the 'charge for results' format, the therapist is automatically supported to reinforce results, more focused on the client's issues, and faster when working with clients. It is ethically satisfying, and is also an almost unique feature in the therapist or medical marketplace.

Therapist Fears About 'Pay for Results'

As part of our regular therapist training, we have our students practice healing on their fears about using 'charge for results' in their work. Because these issues (often involving survival fears) unconsciously drive the therapist, we've found that rational discussion of the issues involved is often a waste of time till the underlying emotional issues are eliminated. Some common triggers are:

*   I feel guilty that I charge so much for such a simple/ fast process.
*   I feel guilty charging extra to compensate for clients I can't help.
*   What if the client gets healed and says they didn't?
*   I don't understand what the client really wants – I am missing the real issue.
*   I am afraid the client will have a too high expectation of me.
*   This is too complicated.
*   I am afraid of legal actions.

Writing the Contract - Negotiating Outcomes

As we will be showing in the next few chapters, the 'charge for results' principle has a major impact on exactly how you diagnose and do treatments with clients. Rather than offering some sort of emotional support or helpful advice, the therapist now has the job to accurately define the client's real problem and succeed in healing it.

We've found that initially most of our students have a very difficult time writing the 'pay for results' contract with the client. Often this is because the techniques and practices that they've learned in the past get in the way, be it conventional therapy, breathwork, or other modalities. Although diagnosis can be difficult, identifying the desired *outcome* is far, far easier than people realize.

Simply ask your client what the major problem is. Clients are in your office for a reason, and usually it is fairly straightforward. Generally the client has only one major problem, even if they have trouble putting it into words. A major mistake made by most therapists happens at this step. If they are not careful in the wording of this question, they will get a laundry list of problems. It is exactly the same as if a car mechanic asked about the problems in your 15 year old car – a general question gets a reply that the door squeaks, the trunk latch doesn't work, there is rust on the body where you banged it, and so on. But the real reason you are there is because the car is belching smoke out the tailpipe!

Sometimes there really are several issues. Never write a single contract for multiple issues, because any one failure means you won't get paid for any of your work. Instead, you offer to work on and bill the issues separately. Put in these terms, the client immediately prioritizes and identifies what they are really there for. They decide what is financially important to them.

When writing the contract, less is better! If you've focused down to the real problem, usually an agreement to eliminate the emotional pain around a single phrase that evokes the maximum suffering (what we call the 'trigger phrase') is all that needs to be put in the contract. Again, new therapists mistakenly put a laundry list of symptoms into the contract, but all this does is include unrelated problems into their agreement that they are now obligated to also heal. Keep the contract simple, and keep it focused. (Appendix 2 gives examples of several different types of 'pay for results' contracts.)

A new therapist can write a results contract without even a clue on what is causing the problem. This is fine, and any failures will become a learning experience for the therapist. However, with experience the therapist will now sometimes recognize an issue they know they cannot heal. In this case, they let the client know this, and offer to work on issues surrounding the problem. For example, a client has OCD that the therapist doesn't yet know how to eliminate. So once they let the client know this, they ask if the client would be satisfied if they eliminate an issue connected with having the disease, such as stress or embarrassment. In another more extreme example, a client was dying of cancer. Although the therapist could not heal the disease, he found that the client's secondary issue was fear of death, which he was able to successfully heal (the cancer-triggered fear of death was caused by a near drowning as a boy).

One problem we've seen come up with therapists doing contracts is 'overselling processes'. By this we mean that they know some treatment, say the Silent Mind Technique, and instead of really figuring out what the client needs, they suggest that the client should do a (usually expensive) treatment instead, implying that it would probably fix the client's problem. This only ends in disaster; even though the client agreed to the contract, they will be unhappy afterwards because they still have their problem. This is in contrast to a therapist who actually figured out what the client wanted and realized that he would be unable to provide it, so offered other options around the problem. In this latter case, the client is treated as an ally, rather than as an income source.

Take clear notes on what you have agreed to! Let the client read what you wrote and see if he/she understands it. Use the client's wording exactly; don't try to paraphrase. This helps make sure that the expectations are well defined (the 'criteria for success'); this will be necessary to avoid the apex problem after you've finished.

In summary, stay focused on what you can do, and if needed break the problem down into its key elements, and offer choices for them to decide on what is important for them.

Example: The client wants a divorce

The client has a painful issue – problems with a partner – and wants to learn the therapy so that he can help himself. You know that there are usually dozens of issues with a partner, so you focus on what the key one or ones is. In this case, the client basically wants to be with another person. You don't make a judgment but explain what therapy can do (get him to calm around his feelings). The client realizes that the key problem is about his anxiety about talking to his spouse on this issue. And he wants instruction on how to do EFT as part of the package (this assumes that EFT works on this client's issues).

In the contract, you could include EFT instruction or bill it separately. In either case, you need to determine criteria for results. It may be that results in this case is just exposure to the technique, and there are no explicit goals, or it could be a certain level of proficiency. Defining which you are comfortable providing is up to you, and you can negotiate with the client to determine what works best for both of you. An experienced therapist would not include EFT instruction in the primary contract, and might simply take some time to show the client the process as part of the treatment, along with advice to watch free videos on YouTube.

Example: The client can't feel

The client was unable to remember her past, or feel emotions or body sensations. This is typical in cases of extreme sexual abuse at an early age, and in fact this turned out to be the case with this client. Determining what the client wanted as a result had to be tempered with a recognition that regression therapies would not be effective. (This assumes that the therapist does not cord with the client to suppress the extreme feelings of the abuse in the client.) Thus, the therapist would have to evaluate whether the client was a good candidate for healing issues, or whether they should just write an agreement for coaching and support on specific issues. Or whether the client should simply see a conventional therapist or peer support group for emotional support.

With more experience, the therapist might recognize the client's numbness is from a bacterial parasite interaction problem and refer the client to a clinic for that treatment. In this case, once the numbness was gone the traumatic emotions could now be felt and follow-up treatment would probably be needed. The issue might also involve a trauma that blocks memory, or an MPD issue where the current dominant personality was not the one that experienced the trauma. The client would have to decide if they wanted treatment for this, as the trauma or the splitting was allowing them avoid the traumatic memories.

Setting Fees and Estimating Treatment Time

In the 'pay for results' approach, the contract includes a predetermined fee. Appendix 10 shows a simple, low risk and effective way for therapists to set this fee. In this approach, the general practice therapist simply offers one fee for any client problem. This is typically how most 'pay for results' therapists do their charging (although some specific disease treatments may use a different predetermined set fee.) Because we know that there is a certain percentage of clients who the therapist can't help, the therapist has to know when to give up trying. Fortunately, this optimum 'cutoff time' minimizes client costs while maximizing therapist income. This cutoff point is typically in the 3-6 hour time frame. Clients who take longer are not charged, but are sent to more advanced or specialized therapists, such as ones who work in our clinics.

It is possible to use other methods of billing, such as estimating how long therapy will take and billing on this basis. Or perhaps use some sort of combination of approaches. However, these increase the financial risk to the therapist, and increase the cost, sometimes dramatically, for about half the clients. We don't recommend these other approaches unless you specialize or are very experienced. If you are interested in the formulas for these other fee methods, we refer you to our Institute website.

The 'rule of three'

Therapists need to plan on including the time for two brief client follow-ups after the issue has been fully healed: one a few days after the issue has initially been fully healed, and another about two weeks after treatment is optimum. This should be scheduled with the client as a normal part of treatment. But why? This follow-up is due to the epigenetic cause of trauma and the limitations of most healing techniques. Waiting after 'successful' treatment allows relevant 'hidden' or untriggered traumas or traumas that weren't fully healed to become activated by daily circumstances in the client's life. This can also be due to 'time loops' that put the problem back into the client. This problem is not simply a client's attention moving to a new issue, although that can obviously happen and cause problems of its own.

We don't have a good estimate for how often these additional healing sessions are actually needed, but assuming it happens with a third of the clients is probably reasonable. Planning for this with the client is simply good business practice and an assumed part of 'charging for results'. Some therapists pre-book and cancel the extra appointments if all goes well; others add appointments as needed.

Duration of conventional treatment

The time a typical client will actually spend doing conventional psychotherapy is quite short. Oddly, it is very hard to find any studies defining exactly what these times are, especially in the last 10 years. In one summary article from 2000 (without any supporting references): "In reviewing the data about psychotherapy utilization and outcome, it is increasingly well-known that there is no such thing as brief therapy because there is no such thing as long-term therapy. About 90% of all psychotherapy patients come for less than 10 visits with the mean treatment episode being about 4.6 sessions and the modal number of visits being just one." In a large 2011 study of major depressive disorder: "The modal number of sessions for any treatment in the community mental health system was one in both 1993 and 2003. The median number of psychotherapy sessions was 5.0 in both 1993 and 2003. The average number of psychotherapy sessions was 8.5 (SD = 10.0) in 1993 and 9.4 (SD = 10.6) in 2003."

Fortunately, our approach to therapy fits this typical client pattern. As Gay Hendricks, the developer of Body Centered Therapy has said in his trainings: "The client should be healed in two sessions. If it takes more than three sessions, the therapist doesn't know what he's doing." We agree. Thus, basic certified therapists should try to fully treat as many clients as possible in the first session, heal the typical client in two or three sessions (about 2 to 4 hours), or, at worst, end treatment at about three or four sessions (4 to 6 hours).

Results Criteria and Time Duration Guarantees

When you work with a client, you need to determine exactly what the criteria for *results* are. In many cases, it may mean that you write down something that can be checked on the spot. In other cases, the client may need to actually go somewhere or meet someone to test if the intervention was successful. As a therapist, it is up to you and your client to decide what is acceptable, and for how long you are willing to wait to see if the results are stable.

For example, the Institute clinics offer specialized, often expensive treatments for various conditions or disorders. We generally require payment from the client after three weeks without symptoms. (Two weeks would be adequate to verify stability of the treatment, but that third week generally makes the client feel more secure because of the large fees involved). After that period, if the symptoms came back for some reason we would simply refund the money (and/or try to help the client). In a therapy situation, a much shorter time would be adequate and more prudent unless you had made an agreement with your client otherwise. You may also need to determine if you want to have the client agree to more treatment before you do a refund, or just do a simple refund. (Note that if you give more treatments, this data goes into your running tally of income and total client contact time for estimating future fees – see Appendix 10.)

Client Satisfaction and the Apex Problem

When you heal a client's issue fully, you'll quickly encounter the problem of clients forgetting that they ever had the issue you healed. This is because when they try to recall what the problem felt like, there is no feeling left and so the client simply 'can't remember' what the problem was. (This is like forgetting which arm you hurt when there is no pain left to guide you.) This may mean that they won't want to pay you – "it was never a problem" - and worse, will tell others that the therapy session was useless or a waste of time. As far as they are concerned, their *real* issue is the new one that they're feeling at the moment.

You can deal with this problem in several ways. First, education: the apex problem is addressed in the client brochure, and you will have to explain it to them up front. Explaining the nature of the latest generation of therapies and how they work is important. Second, make a record. One way to do this is to have them write down exactly what the issue is, how bad they feel, give a SUDS (subjective units of distress) rating, and particularly focus on the parameters of the 'charge for results' you've agreed on. Writing is ok, but a far better way to do this is via video or audio recordings. This captures the immediacy of their suffering, and later the clients are almost always surprised that they felt that way – they simply no longer remember.

The other advantage you have is in charging a predetermined, fixed fee that they have agreed to in a contract. How you collect fees is up to you – and obviously may vary from client to client – but one way to address this apex problem is to have them write a check for the amount you've agreed upon, and simply hold it for the duration of the therapy. Since they were willing to do this, at some level the clients decide that this must have been an important problem since they wrote the check!

Some Situations Don't Allow 'Pay for Results'

In some circumstances, the 'charge for results' fee structure isn't possible or isn't appropriate to implement. For example:
- For health insurance company payouts (and they won't allow a performance based fee structure);
- The client wants to try out one of the techniques that you know and doesn't have any particular success criteria;

- The client is your student and the session is part of or supporting a training program.

As long as particular circumstances really inhibit 'charge for results' criteria, and this is clear to the client, the therapist can put an exception rider on the client agreement on a case-by-case basis. However, outside of teaching situations, this situation rarely arises – you can generally figure out success criteria for almost any activity.

Unfortunately, we've also seen that therapists are reluctant to approach insurance or other organizations to suggest they switch to this type of billing, either generally or in their particular case. As this financially benefits the company involved, it will be interesting in the future to see if the insurance companies themselves end up pushing for this change.

Disputes with Clients

In spite of your best efforts, there will be clients that you have problems with. Hopefully most of these people will decide not to work with you after the initial interview, but some will. Accept this as a fact of life, and not as some sort of personal failing on your part (We assume you do take it as an opportunity to look at your own issues, though).

If the problem is that a client feels he didn't get the results agreed upon, and you can't come to a quick and amicable agreement, the response is simple. Remember, "The client is always right". You're in this business for the long haul, and word of mouth is critical to your success. You simply don't charge (or refund the money). Obviously, there will be some people who will take advantage of this – but that happens in every business. You simply plan for it in your fees. Fortunately, in our experience dishonest clients are very rare.

As far as Institute certified therapists are concerned, their client brochures (and our websites) also tell clients that they can contact the Institute if there are disputes. This is part of our licensing agreement, and it makes it obvious to clients that these therapists are part of an exceptional professional organization. Over the years, we've rarely have problems with these licensed therapists but it sometimes happens. As part of their license agreement, we retain the right to end their license and their use of our licensed tools, trademarks and logo.

Trademarks, Logos, and Affiliate Organizations

When one of our trained therapists signs a license agreement with the Institute, they receive the right to use our processes for specific diseases or problems, have clinic backup for difficult clients, and get access to new discoveries and safety updates. They also get the privilege to use a certified therapist Institute logo on their documents and websites for advertising purposes. But this logo means more than using   cutting edge therapeutic tools - it means that they have agreed to use only 'charge for results' in all their therapy work.

These unusual therapists are leading the way to a fundamental change in the way therapy and medicine is done in the world.

The Institute also lists affiliate organizations or individuals from around the world on our websites. Aside from being cutting edge organizations that do excellent work in various areas, they also use the 'charge for results' (or donation) principles in their work. We feel privileged to have met and known these different individuals and groups who also work to make a difference in the world.

Questions and Answers

Q: "Do you have any suggestions on how to advertise 'pay for results'?"

One therapist found that saying 'No Result – No Fee' in his advertising worked well.

Note that offering a 'guaranteed' healing is not appropriate (as in 'guaranteed or your money back') as many places have laws against such wording when applied to psychotherapy. Note that these laws were designed to combat fraud, not forbid the use of the 'pay for results' billing model.

Q: "I'm still unsure on how to set the criteria for results. Do you have any advice?"

Some therapists tend to think this step is much harder than it is, even though they already unconsciously do it in their practices anyway. You are in a partnership with your client - you are making an agreement that both of you feel is desirable and possible. It doesn't have to be huge and difficult - it is just whatever you both want it to be. For example, if you both agree that a 30% reduction in a symptom is the result, that is fine - you don't have to make it some kind of perfect healing.

The key here is that your client agrees that what you contract to do is worth the money he will pay. The agreement can range from just a willingness for the therapist to listen to the client, to an agreement to get partially or fully get rid of a chronic, long-standing problem. There are no set rules, other than it is what you both have agreed to.

Q: "How do I keep from going broke while I still can't do diagnosis well?"

We recommend you use the fixed per contract fee from Appendix 10. It won't take long - probably 20 clients or so - before you find that you are much more confident of your ability to diagnose and set the results criteria.

Q: "I'm a therapist using a variety of techniques. If I get certified by the Institute, do I have to charge for results even though I don't use your techniques with the client?"

Yes, your whole practice would have to change to incorporate 'charge for results' (where possible). Being certified is a license, as if you got a McDonalds franchise. You can't start serving burritos while having the Golden Arches and McDonalds name on your door. To some therapists, this feels like too big a change in their comfort zone. Thus, they don't become certified but use the publicly released techniques like Whole-Hearted Healing as just another technique, and just don't use the non-public-domain material they learned in class.

Q: "My big problem is getting clients who are just a bundle of problems, and I don't know how to clarify their issue to get an agreement on results. The client doesn't recognize that he has separate issues, as he just feels bad and wants it to stop."

Some clients really are a bundle of problems, and in that case, you would isolate the worst ones and offer to work with them either separately or as a group, depending on what you negotiate with the client. A person like this might be a good candidate for Inner Peace state. There are also certain disease processes that can cause this effect, such as the s-hole problem or the addiction bugs. You may also want to bring in a specialist or advanced practitioner/mentor right from the start if it is big and bad enough.

However, clients like this are the exception. In our experience, the real problem is that the therapist has gotten 'lost in the client's story'. Thus, as one tries to unravel it, the client moves from one problem to the next. Having them staying focused on the emotion and feeling that is the dominant sensation for them is the key to getting to the core issue. Remember - you can offer calmness and peace about their issue.

Some clients simply want to talk and feel connection. You are basically a paid friend. Identifying this and coming to an agreement about what constitutes results for this person can be done. However, you are generally more expensive than standard therapists in this situation. However, since in this case no healing is needed, you might want to lower your fee because there is no risk of not being paid. You are basically charging just a talking fee.

Paula Courteau writes: "Some clients, and this includes most people with depression, and people with a history of abuse, will need regular sessions in order to maintain decent functioning; in the case of depression this is because we don't know the root cause of every type of depression; with abuse there are often several triggering events. If you're very clear about this state of affairs with these clients, and they still want to work with you, then a teaching or coaching model with a per-session fee might be more appropriate than a per-issue system." However, if the client has an explicit or implicit expectation of healing, then a series of brief, pay for results contracts is the correct choice.

Q: "I have a client with very complex problems, and it will take a long time to unravel them. How do I charge?"

You also identify major issues and offer to charge for each separately. This causes the client to evaluate what is really financially important to him, rather than you trying to make the decision for him.

Setting a maximum time you can work with a client keeps you from getting into a financial bind with him when charging for results. However, this doesn't mean you don't have to help the client - it means that you work with your specialist/advanced practitioner/mentor to deal with the client in a more efficient fashion.

Respect your own limitations - you can't be everything to everyone.

Q: "I'm frustrated with this system and its limitations. I will just go back to what I already know."

Unfortunately, learning and actually using new skills often involves discomfort. One of the problems here is that many therapists have never had to do a charge-for-results approach for their livelihood. However, if you'd ever done consulting, worked at a car dealership, or had your own business you would probably think it was perfectly normal. The people at those jobs all work for a fixed fee and don't always know if it will work or not for any particular client either.

Interestingly, we've had a couple of therapists notice that they didn't have a feeling of calm underneath their sense of frustration with this new system - a key indicator that the feelings are from past trauma - so they healed their issue, and to their surprise, found themselves feeling very comfortable about it.

Q: "There are lots of other therapists out there doing excellent work. I don't see how the Institute's certification stuff is significantly better. After all, your material is now mostly in the public domain."

Yes, there are many therapists with the same skill and success rates as Institute certified therapists. What you have that is different is: 1) charging for results; 2) Institute clinic backup for your practice; 3) the chance to do peak states work with some clients; 4) hopefully an eventual name recognition with the Institute: and 5) after you become comfortable with the basic techniques, the possibility of working at one of our clinics.

Q: "I feel there are too many rules by the Institute. I want to be trusted to use my own judgment, because I'm an honest, ethical, competent person. I'd like to move forward slowly into these new ways of working. There wasn't anything like this in my old bodywork profession."

Many people in the helping professions have never had exposure to the way a high technology company operates. The certification agreement with our graduates is a license to use the some of the material we've developed, something that many are not familiar with from their own working background. Fortunately, although unfamiliar, it is quite normal and accepted in other professions - including the concept of 'charging for results'.

Because we're backing up our certified practitioners with support and our reputation, the agreements we make are more specific than many are used to from other modalities. Additionally, the material we're developing is experimental, and requires more careful handling for safety and quality control.

Q: "I didn't succeed in healing the client before my 3 hour cutoff time. Now what?"

You have to decide if you want to continue or not. You may have already realized that you can't help this person anyway. If you simply stop right now, on average, you will make your income goals - because you already figured this happening in the prices that you charge people. At this point, you should refer the client – or if you are so inclined, to continue to try and help and accept that your equivalent hourly income will be somewhat reduced.

Paula Courteau writes: " I would also ask: is the person healing anything at all? That is, is it taking a long time because the person can't heal (can't get in body, can't feel, resists the process, etc) or because the issue is complex? If there is good progress and the issue keeps evolving, I might consider spending extra time. If we're spending most of the time being blocked, I'd quit without hesitation and forfeit my fee."

Q: "I've decided to run over my three hour cutoff limit ("I'm almost there!"). Was this a bad idea?"

Obviously, you may gain your fee if you succeed. However, it is wise to plan on failing, which means your income will take a dip depending on how long you continue. Sometimes the learning time is good, as you stretch yourself. However, remember that you have the Institute clinics ready to assist (if you are certified by the Institute).

Q: "There is no way I'll have enough clients if I heal each in just three sessions!"

This is both a problem and an opportunity. For better or worse, the nature of therapy is changing due to the introduction of power therapies. The therapist has to figure out ways to get a continuous flow of clients, such as by working for an institution that finds and funnels them to the therapist. Thus, having something that sets one apart from the competition is important, such as 'charging for results'. Word of mouth might help you, if the apex problem doesn't defeat it - but the best way to avoid this overall problem of client base is to specialize in one problem or problem area, and build your reputation on that, rather than be a generalist.

Q: "How many practice sessions will it take me so I can calculate fees accurately?"

Roughly 10 successful sessions will give you good enough information to compute your standard minimum fee and optimum cutoff time. However, you should keep a running tally as you get better at diagnosis and healing, to make sure your equivalent hourly income rate is still on track.

If you are setting fees by estimating completion times, you are going to need a much bigger experience base! We only recommend this for very experienced therapists, or therapists who specialize and are familiar with most of what can happen.

Key Points

- 'Pay for results' addresses ethical problems by making explicit agreements: (1) you are paid only if all the predetermined success criteria are met; (2) the client knows how much treatment will cost before it starts.
- The 'pay for results' billing system is standard for many industries. With minimal practice it is simple to incorporate into therapy.
- The 'pay for results' principle automatically requires the therapist to identify the key client issue and determine the outcome of therapy (criteria for success) that the client wants.
- The simplest billing system for 'pay for results' is a fixed fee for all clients. It incorporates a predetermined 'cutoff time' for when to give up on trying to heal a client issue.
- With 'pay for results' the client determines the results they want, except in the case where they are using a specific process that has predetermined outcomes.
- The use of subcellular psychobiology and modern trauma therapies means that the client is usually healed in a few sessions. This fits well with the actual amount of time that typical clients are actually willing to put into therapy.
- The apex effect causes many clients to forget they had a problem after it is fully healed. You need to plan on this happening by keeping written or recorded material of the client's difficulty before treating them.

Suggested Reading

- *The Ethics of Caring: Honoring the Web of Life in Our Professional Healing Relationships* by Kylea Taylor and Jack Kornfield (1995).

Chapter 4

The Initial Client Interview

When we train therapists in subcellular psychobiology, prenatal events and trauma techniques, we also have to train them in new ways of working with clients. Our requirement that therapists *always* 'charge for results' and *not* charge by the hour means they have to be able to quickly and effectively diagnose the client's problem, as well as recognize what they cannot treat. This shift from a traditional 'paid friend' orientation into one more like a highly skilled auto mechanic, engineer or physician is a huge relief to some therapists and a struggle for others. We've found that even therapists who are already using cutting-edge trauma therapies still need to be retrained in how to quickly identify the client's problem and write an effective 'pay for results' contract.

The material in these chapters is taught in our therapist training – rather than being some sort of theoretical or academic exercise, it is used by practicing therapists seeing paying clients in countries all over the world.

The Initial Interview Steps

When we do our initial interview of a new client, we usually have to do the following tasks:
1. Client history (usually done before meeting with the client);
2. Empathy building;
3. Explaining the typical course of treatment;
4. Discuss and sign the liability and informed consent forms (Chapter 6);
5. Clarifying the issue (and getting the 'trigger phrase');
6. Establishing the 'pay for results' criterion and writing the contract (Chapter 4);
7. Diagnosis (Chapter 5);
8. Treatment (if there is time).

These different activities are usually done somewhat simultaneously, although for teaching purposes we break them out as separate activities. The order can also vary from client to client and from therapist to therapist. If these steps are done sequentially, one finds that it is usually necessary to iterate a bit to get adequate results. For example, diagnosis and setting 'pay for results' are usually interactive – one should do at least a minimal level of diagnosis on the problems you identify, so that you have some confidence that you can likely help the client. This means that you choose problems and results that you believe you can actually accomplish. Note too that with the 'charge for results' system, therapists don't charge for the initial interview and diagnosis stage. Instead, that time is accounted for in the fee amount that is part of the initial contract with the client.

With experience, the various approaches and tricks we're giving below will simply become automatic; or you'll find your own way of doing things.

Tip: How long should the initial interview take?

With practice, the typical client can be interviewed *and* diagnosed in usually 3 to 10 minutes; figure up to 20 minutes total to finish all the other aspects of working with a new client before starting treatment. To speed this process, most therapists have the client fill out their history, and if appropriate have them review the liability and informed consent forms *before* the first meeting.

Taking the Client History

Getting the initial history on a written form is usually done before the face-to-face meeting, saving your time and allowing the client to think more carefully about their answers. We are not going to include sample history forms for this handbook, because what you need to know can vary greatly with the type of clientele you see. For example, clients with addiction problems usually need a much more detailed history than more typical clients.

Regardless, we recommend taking a history not only for your own bookkeeping records, but for several other very practical reasons:
- In terms of safety, you need to know if the client has a weak heart or other medical issue like diabetes that would make trauma therapy dangerous or difficult;
- Are they currently or have they been suicidal;
- It can save you time, as it can be used to help the client focus on their issue before your office visit.

Diagnostically, it can also be very helpful:
- If the client's ancestors or family also have the complaint, this immediately simplifies diagnosis to either generational issues or copies, both of which are easy to heal;
- A history can help you separate the current problem from other pre-existing conditions, whose symptoms might confuse you when you were trying to come to an endpoint with the current issue.

- A description of other treatments already done for the issue can help you diagnose. For example, if the client also saw a trauma therapist, this might mean the client has time loops around the issue.
- Knowing if they are using legal (or illegal) psychoactive drugs can also help clarify your diagnosis.

Empathy Building

Part of working successfully with clients is the skill to quickly establish a rapport so that they will trust you to guide them through sometimes painful processes. And it can also help to later get referrals from them (if the apex effect does not cause them to forget they even had an issue after you treat them.)

However in our training we emphasize that you are not a 'paid friend' and the time you spend just chatting with clients is generally more effectively spent actually diagnosing and curing them. Remember, you are not being paid by the hour, you are being paid to successfully heal the client's issue. In class we stress learning the ability to quickly do diagnosis and treatment – after the therapist is proficient at this, they can get a feeling for how much time they want to spend chatting in their office. By analogy, it is like a car mechanic speaking to a customer – being helpful and friendly is important, but you also have a job to do.

You should accept that some clients are simply not going to respond well to you – or your own gut may be telling you that there is some kind of problem with the client that will sabotage your work with them. Whatever the reason, you should quickly decide if you want to continue with the diagnostic interview. Remember, you don't charge for the diagnostic interview - it is a waste of your time and effort if the client simply walks away after you spend that time with them.

Paula Courteau writes: "Empathy building is an essential aspect of your interview, but it isn't necessarily a separate component. Good communication skills throughout your interview will build mutual empathy while you stay on task."

Explaining the Typical Course of Treatment

Because many therapists don't have experience with trauma therapies, below are some 'rules of thumb' for typical client sessions. Sessions usually last between 1.5 and 2 hours – the client may get too tired to continue if it goes longer – but a fixed amount of time, like the standard 50 minute office visit just doesn't work. (If you explain this to your clients ahead of time, they are usually understanding when a session for someone else goes over the allocated time.) The typical client will take between one and three sessions to eliminate the issue – and then you need to expect to briefly see the client two more times to make sure the treatment was stable and lasting. We call this the 'rule of three' (see below).

To save time, we suggest that you have a standard list of questions and answers ready for your clients in a handout, brochure, or online. It covers obvious questions a client would want to know:

- What do I need to do before the appointment? (Such as read and fill out the forms, write down the issue, etc.);
- Do you work in person, or via skype? (This can depend on what you are treating and your own preferences);
- What type of problems do you treat, and what you don't. (For example, specialized training in addictions, suicide, etc.);
- How long do sessions last, and how many can they expect;
- Questions about using or changing their medications;
- How you arrange billing, the 'pay for results' policy, etc.;
- What happens if I quit treatment before finishing?

Depending on the client's needs, you might have to explain the difference between trauma healing and simple counseling (for example, help in finding jobs, etc.). Depending on your skill set, you might need to refer the client out, or you might be able to do both as needed – but the 'pay for results' criteria still need to be identified. This also helps you to be sure that the client isn't expecting you to solve some difficulty with counseling that really require trauma therapy.

We've often seen that therapist trainees want to explain too much to clients. They forget that most clients are there to get rid of their suffering, not to understand the material the therapist has learned. Clients assume you are an expert in your field – and will do what you tell them to do, even if it doesn't make much sense to them. They view you the same way you might view a tax attorney or car mechanic – after all, you don't want the details either, you just want the job well done.

As obvious as it sounds, therapists need to have had enough practice to feel confident in what they are doing. This doesn't mean that they are going to be perfect, but rather they know what they know and what they don't know, and can figure out any mistakes they made in treatment if things go off track. The client can feel your confidence, but can also feel if you lack it. Again, do you want to work with a tax attorney who seems nervous about doing your return?

If a session has to end before the client is finished, they may be feeling an extremely negative feeling, so having them focus on a positive emotion like gratitude can bring them back into the present moment. And be sure that at the end of a session, the client can drive safely. For example, the client may be so relaxed from the tension that they were under that they fall asleep while driving. And remind them that during treatment to refrain from making big life decisions, if possible, until they've finished treatment – stimulated trauma feelings from incomplete therapy can drive a person inappropriately. Even after treatment is finished, encourage them to take some time to let things settle out before making major decisions (such as jobs, relationships, etc.).

Tip: The 'rule of three'

Remember, after a client has had their symptoms fully eliminated, we've found empirically that you still need to schedule *two more (usually short) follow-up sessions*: one in a few days, and one in about one and a half to two weeks. Sometimes trauma material around an issue that was not activated in your office gets triggered later; sometimes the client has a time loop problem that resets the trauma. Let the client know ahead of time that this is a standard part of therapy, and that they can expect the symptoms that are gone in the office may come back. This radically changes the ongoing relationship you have with the client - instead of being in a panic or despair if the problem comes back, the client calmly expects this and plans for it.

Since you are doing a 'pay for results' service, the time for these extra two visits or phone consultations need to be included in your original price.

Tip: Session lengths

In traditional talk therapy it is a lot easier to find a point where you can leave the session and restart the process during the next one. In our work once you've started a regression or other intervention, it is usually important to finish it. This is for several reasons:

a)   New problems may arise in between sessions, and it is difficult to reconnect with the original issue. The client can get confused about what they started originally.

b)   To get back to the old issue may require that you eliminate the current one. Valuable time gets spent on other - now dominant - issues that have no relevance to the criteria for results you agreed upon.

c)   The client might continue to suffer after the session. He may have impaired driving and coping skills when he leaves your office in spite of any 'Band-Aids' you use to pull him out of the trauma because the time is up.

On the other hand, trauma work takes energy and the client can become exhausted after a certain point, so spending more time with him becomes counter-productive. This varies from new to old clients (old clients already know the processes to some degree), and from client to client. A reasonable maximum time would be around 1.5 hours, although some therapists do plan on 2 hours maximum.

As a certified therapist, you'll need to decide how you want to set up your session length. However, there will be some clients who will need more then the allotted time, even if someone else is waiting. Telling clients ahead of time that this may happen, in our experience, usually defuses any problems, especially if you point out that they may be the one needing more time in the future. Another strategy is to arrange your 'non-contact hours' in between clients, so you are more flexible. Therapies like breathwork and TIR recognize this issue and build it into the practice. Therapists using EFT tend to be able to stick more to a typical '50-minute hour' per session.

Liability and Informed Consent

To save office time, we recommend that the therapist give the liability and informed consent forms to the client ahead of time online, or when they are waiting for their session. But regardless of whether you do this in your office or in advance, you will still need to verify that they have read and understood the documents, and get their signatures. These documents are legally required in most countries.

Going through these forms has an interesting effect on most clients. It lets them know that you really understand the problems that can arise – that you are an extremely competent state-of-the-art professional - and want them to know what to look for in case problems arise.

Chapter 6 goes into these legally required forms in great detail.

Before seeing clients, have you prepared for any unexpected problems?

- Do you know what to do if the client becomes suicidal? Do you know where to take your client if they need around-the-clock monitoring?
- Do you know how (and why) to treat for severe trauma abreaction? (For example, which sometimes occurs when sexual abuse memories are triggered?)
- Does your client intake form explicitly ask about any heart or other life threatening physical conditions? (This identifies clients that are at risk when using potentially stressful techniques, and also addresses liability concerns.)
- Does the client have any conditions that could complicate the work, such as a history of psychiatric treatment?
- If you activate a problem in your client that you can't heal, have you arranged with someone more qualified to take them on in an emergency?

Note: Unless you specialize in working with suicidal clients, we recommend that you not work with clients who have a history of suicidal attempts or suicidal ideation. This should be one of the first screening steps you do with clients, both to protect the client and to minimize their disappointment around not being accepted for treatment. If you do work with suicidal clients, doing so remotely (via skype or phone) is a very bad idea – they need to be supported locally with people who can physically intervene.

Clarifying the Issue

Up to this point, the interview steps have been fairly standard for a trauma therapist. Here is where our students need to start changing the pattern that they know from other therapies - and here is where the trainees start to make mistakes.

Find the single problem: Clients typically have lots of problems. Most people are like old cars that have seen a lot of miles. As a therapist, you have to keep the client focused on their major issue, the one that drove them to your office, that they really want eliminated and are willing to pay for. And this is where many therapists make their first mistake. They immediately ask the client to describe their problems - a question that is far too general - and the client will try to comply with a laundry list of symptoms and issues. It's like taking your old car to the mechanic. Figuring he's going to fix everything for free, you tell him about the sticky doorknob, the squeaky suspension, the wheel shimmy... The real problem, that the engine misses, is just another item in your list.

The therapist does not realize that many clients have no idea what you can or cannot do. Sometimes their expectations are too high, sometimes too low. Sometimes they believe that all their problems are tied together. Your job is to get them focused on the item that really matters to them, the one that they are happy to pay for. Continuing the car analogy, you need to find out what they really want fixed. And note, this may not be what you think they should fix. If they really have more than one problem, write the next one up as a separate contract. Do not try and do more than one problem at a time!

Sometimes the client describes a single issue but doesn't realize how many individual, unrelated parts it has in it. Again, having the client find the most important aspect of their issue for treatment is critical for their satisfaction and your success. Often, after the key part has been healed, they don't care about the rest of the issue.

Focus on the symptoms: Some of your clients will try to 'explain' to you why they have a problem and what causes it. Especially with therapists as clients, it can be very difficult to get them to actually use sensation words about what is bothering them. (Because of this, we generally recommend that our therapists charge up to three times more for therapists as clients due to the amount of time that will be wasted in this way.) The most common problem we see here is that the trainee loses control of the interview – and this can go on for hours! The therapist must firmly cut off this sort of thing, get the client back to symptoms, and keep them there. Remember, you need to have symptoms in order to diagnose the problem and write a contract. (Of course, some clients actually do know what is the cause of their problem, but this is rather rare.)

A related issue is when the therapist gets caught up in the client's tale – it's called getting 'lost in the story'. As entertaining as this can be, it wastes time and doesn't matter to writing your contract, doing diagnosis, or treating the problem.

Others avoid sensation words because of embarrassment or religious issues. For example, even these days many people have a hard time talking about their sexual issues. When they talk about their relationship, they circle around the topic and avoid any sexual words. We've also seen people in conflict between what they feel and their religious teachings, needing more gentle inquiry than one would expect.

Client-directed treatment: The client comes to you, the therapist, because they are suffering and are willing to pay for relief. This does *not* mean that the therapist decides what problem needs treating (except for court mandated clients). The client is in control here, even if it is obvious that the client needs help in other areas. For example, it might be clear the client is paranoid and needs help – but this is usually not what the client wants eliminated. Nor should you try, unless it is part of an issue that the client does want to have healed.

There is another ethical problem we've seen around this issue – where the therapist tries to sell their favorite (or financially lucrative) treatment process. True, with 'pay for results' the client gets what was agreed upon, but this is *not* what they came in for. For example, just about everyone needs the Silent Mind Technique – quality of life for most people improves greatly. But this is usually not what the client has come into the office for. It is unethical, and obviously creates unhappy clients to act in this way.

Predefined Disease Criteria: Unlike general therapy, if the therapist identifies for treatment a specific disease that doesn't have a medical lab test (such as Asperger's Syndrome, Chronic Fatigue Syndrome, schizophrenia, ADHD, and so on), the Institute predefines the criteria that will be used to check if the problem is gone. This is because most DSM or diagnostic manual categories give lists of symptoms without any idea of their cause, so they often include a wide variety of symptoms irrelevant to a given disease process – essentially, they are lumping different diseases in the same basket. Thus, our processes are optimized for a given disease and its defining symptom(s). Secondly, some clients have symptoms from multiple diseases or conditions, and mistakenly expect all their symptoms to disappear with treatment. And third, if there is a disagreement after treatment, we can check to see whether that the agreed upon condition is gone or not after our certified PeakStates process is used.

The Trigger Phrase – a 'Pay for Results' Criteria

"Clarify the issue" – "focus on the presenting problem" – "get the symptoms" – all this sounds like good advice, but therapists have a hard time actually doing it in a way that makes the client confident that you understand what they are asking for. And this doesn't even begin to describe the trouble therapists have with writing the 'pay for results' contract. Beginners soon have several pages of symptoms on their contract, something no therapist could actually do in a reasonable time frame, or even fully accomplish given the current state of the art. Fortunately, we've come up with an elegantly simple and direct trick to solve this problem – we call it the 'trigger phrase'.

This is a phrase that triggers the maximum symptoms and discomfort in the client, *not* a description of the problem, story or symptoms. For example, to get the trigger phrase you might ask the client, "Give me a phrase, or a couple of phrases that captures what about this situation really, really bothers you?" Hence, a trigger phrase might be "She left me" or "The bastard!" rather than a short description of symptom or story. I'll emphasize this one more time: the trigger phrase is *not* a description of the problem or the symptoms, but rather what triggers the worst emotional pain into the present.

The real trigger phrase is obvious to the client, once they put it into words – the SUDS rating is a 10 or almost a 10, and the client will say this exactly captures the essence of their pain. Other possible trigger phrases will have a lower SUDS rating. The client might give you a couple of phrases, but this means the therapist hasn't quite gotten the worst, most painful trigger phrase. With a little practice, it is obvious to a therapist when the client has hit the real core of the problem – their suffering hits a maximum. You can easily see it in the client's body language with a little practice.

Once you have the right trigger phrase, virtually all clients will agree that this is what they want you to heal. If they don't, this generally means you didn't get the best trigger phrase. You just simply write the trigger phrase into the contract, along with a SUDS rating by the client, and put the 'pay for results' criterion as being able to say the phrase with a SUDS of zero.

Thus, when working with the client to clarify the issue, the therapist listens to the story for a few minutes, and then usually moves quickly into getting the trigger phrase.

The other key use for the trigger phrase is to help us find relevant trauma during the healing process. By saying the phrase, the client automatically triggers their symptoms into consciousness.

Exceptions: Some subcellular problems don't have or need a trigger phrase. For example, a mitochondrial vortex has a fixed symptom, so trying to get a trigger phrase doesn't make sense. By contrast, a trigger phrase is especially useful for trauma-caused issues.

Tip: Note-taking

When listening to the client, jot down the client's words around emotionally charged phrases. It is important to get their exact wording, not use your own wording for what you heard. You may need some of them to help trigger the client when getting the trigger phrase, for writing the contract, as well as during the healing to be sure the issue is resolved. You will find that this can also help you learn to spot key words that are from subcellular cases.

The other important use for note taking is to record the traumas and other cases that you healed during your sessions, so you can check your healing work in the follow-up sessions for reversals or other problems.

Incidentally, when repeating back material to the client, don't switch perception modes. By this we mean stay with kinesthetic words if the client is obviously kinesthetic, visual words if the client is obviously visual, and so on. This avoids having the client confused and having to translate into their own terms what you've said to them, interrupting or derailing the interview.

Diagnosis and Treatment

Chapter 5 covers several ways to do diagnosis, with the bulk of this handbook covering specific subcellular cases. Treatment methods are only listed in this handbook; see Appendix 9 for the manuals where they are explained.

Certified PeakStates therapists generally work alone as private practitioners. However, unlike most therapists, they are tied into a network of highly skilled Institute clinic staff, in case of any problems or they need diagnostic guidance. We've found empirically over time that most therapists go through about a yearlong learning curve with this material, but then find that they rarely need help or assistance with clients.

Tip: Therapist networking

Oddly, in our experience very few therapists network with other therapists, either in their local area or in their specialization. This is the exact opposite of what you should be doing! Perhaps this is due to financial worries; but remember, you can't heal everyone, and trying to only wastes your time, as you are paid only if you successfully complete the job. Not only can networking make being a therapist a lot more fun, but you can send clients to them if you are not qualified to work with their issue, or simply have bad chemistry with a client.

Working as a team in a clinic can also act to attract clients, especially if your clinic has a theme that is relevant to your area. This builds up your presence in the community, as well as your reputation and clientele, because you can handle a larger stream of clients in co-operation with other practitioners. Additionally, it can be more fun than working alone, and gives you the opportunity to increase your skills and discuss problems with your colleagues.

Tip: Specializing

We stress the next point over and over in our training – therapists can be 'general practitioners', but it is *far* better to specialize. Not only can you become far more competent in your ability to diagnose and treat, but by choosing a specialization that you are genuinely interested in, you wake up every morning looking forward to your day. And there are other advantages:

- Clients generally want a specialist for their problem, not a generalist.
- You can often attract clients globally, not just in your local area.
- Other therapists who don't specialize in what you are doing will be more comfortable in sending you appropriate clients.

Specialization is one of the best and easiest ways to increase clientele – being known as an expert in a particular problem really attracts clients, and is generally far easier than being a generalist.

In addition, specializing allows you to charge more than your competitors, especially if you are providing a service that cannot be found elsewhere. As many of the Institute's treatments are unique, they offer scope for increased revenue. For example the Institute's clinics charge a premium on this basis, as we specialize in problems that either have no or at best partial treatments elsewhere (and it recoups some of our research costs).

Key Points

- The initial interview typically takes 20 minutes, with the diagnosis part taking about 3 to 5 minutes.
- Keep the client focused on telling you their symptoms; their own analysis and detailed story is usually not helpful.
- The 'rule of three' says that after you have successfully eliminated the client's problem, you need to check two more times over a two to three week period to verify or reinforce the treatment's stability.
- Identifying a 'trigger phrase' that evokes the client's worst suffering about their issue gives you a simple criteria for the 'pay for results' contract.
- When writing the contract: keep it short; specific; write several contracts if there are multiple problems; get enough experience to know what you cannot treat; don't contract for something you can't verify or give the client (like a date with a supermodel).
- The contract can be written without diagnosis, but it can be helpful to do them somewhat simultaneously, as it might change what you offer the client.

Suggested Reading

On how to be a trauma therapist:
- *The Whole-Hearted Healing™ Workbook* by Paula Courteau (2013). This updated book is designed for people working on themselves.
- *The EFT Manual* by Gary Craig (2011).
- *Traumatic Incident Reduction* by Gerald French and Chrys Harris (1998). Excellent source on non-judgmental listening and the TIR trauma therapy.
- *The Basic Whole-Hearted™ Healing Manual* by Grant McFetridge Ph.D. and Mary Pellicer M.D. (2004).

- *Eye Movement Desensitization and Reprocessing (EMDR): Basic Principles, Protocols, and Procedures,* 2nd edition, by Francine Shapiro, PhD (2001).

Chapter 5

Diagnostic Approaches

In our therapist trainings, we spend a lot of time teaching techniques and having students practice on themselves and their classmates. In the early years, we tried to cram everything into a 5-day, and later a 9-day training to minimize the cost for the students. We assumed that the students would be self motivated enough to practice what we'd taught. Unfortunately, we found that very few therapists would practice, use, and actually master this new material after the training – it was just too big a hurdle to do on their own. In 2010 we changed to a month long training format in response to this problem, and our certification rate went from around 5% to around 70%.

Now with more teaching time available to us, we saw that it was absolutely vital that each student have the opportunity to have supervised practice with three or more real clients, doing the initial interview, diagnosis, and treatment. It was surprising how many students only wanted book learning – actually having to face clients and apply what they knew would almost always stir up huge resistances (actually, mini-revolts!) in most of the students, even in therapists who had already been seeing clients for years. It was always fun to tell these unbelieving students that their feelings were typical, but by the end of their practice sessions diagnosing and treating new clients would be a fun experience that they would actually look forward to. We also found that their enjoyment greatly increased during sessions by having other students watch and offer suggestions if the student therapist in the hot seat so desired – it becomes a fascinating and supportive community activity for everyone, including the clients!

Generally, the teacher could diagnose the practice client in the first minute or two, but students would take up to 30 minutes as they mastered the skills. It became a fun challenge to stop the client interview after the first three minutes to ask the students for their diagnosis. Partly this speed difference was simple familiarity with the subcellular cases; but also because diagnostic skills had become second nature in the teachers. To try and pass on these skills, in 2013 Paula Courteau published an excellent workbook on the Whole-Hearted Healing regression technique that gave a pattern for diagnosis that covered many of the subcellular cases in this handbook. The methods in this chapter are a bit different; both approaches are useful.

I hope you will find the methods in this chapter helpful in your own practice.

A New Orientation for Therapists

If you only get one thing out of this chapter, what you're about to read in this short paragraph is the most critical. When doing diagnosis with a client, in the back of your mind you must *always* have ideas about what the client's problem might be – starting even before they open their mouth. You *cannot* be just a passive listener!

This is very, very different orientation than most therapists are trained to have. Generally, therapists learn compassionate listening skills, which is fine – but in our experience, this training gets in the way of their ability to do diagnosis. The therapist has to be proactive, not reactive when doing diagnosis.

This new orientation changes everything. It does not mean your initial ideas will be right – but it immediately allows you to ask the correct questions so you can rapidly and accurately diagnose your client. We cannot stress this enough – over and over we see therapist trainees asking completely meaningless questions, in a vain attempt to get the client to say something that they might recognize, or simply so they can emotionally connect. When you ask the wrong questions, or ask general questions like 'how are you feeling?", the client will try to comply. This leads to confusion, discussions of random symptoms or problems, and derails the entire diagnosis process.

In our experience with students, they err on the side of being too undirected when doing the assessment. Instead, because you have all the subcellular cases in your mind, you will want to really direct your client to describe what is bothering them, and ask directing questions to find out if it is simple trauma, a subcellular case, or structural issue. Of course, the therapist needs to thoroughly know the subcellular cases so they can ask relevant questions as they diagnose. Again, asking random questions (or empathetic questions that are not diagnostic) is *not* a good idea. That approach should be considered a very last resort.

As we said in the introduction to this chapter, as practice our students are given three minutes to do the initial diagnosis. If they are not sure of the cause, we have them list the possible subcellular problems, review relevant differential diagnostic questions, and so on – but 9 times out of 10, the client's diagnosis is obvious and any additional diagnostic questions just verify it.

In Appendix 4 are short symptom examples that we use to give trainees practice in recognizing subcellular cases – and in Appendix 5 is a list of real case stories that we use to get them thinking about diagnosis in this new way, before they start with real clients. Appendix 1 lists some of the standard emotional issues that students encounter when they try to do diagnosis. We have students run through the list, or have them think about doing diagnosis to find the ideas that trigger their emotional reactions; and for practice we have them heal them so they no longer have any emotional content.

Focus on actual symptoms

The other key point is that you need to keep the client focused on describing their actual, experiential symptoms, not their story about their problems, or their explanations, or their previous therapist's, physician's or their own self-diagnosis. Again, this goes against standard talk therapy training; but once you really start to understand subcellular psychobiology and developmental trauma, you realize that most problems started in the womb and persist because of damage inside their cells. Once you really emotionally accept this principle that symptoms are not a logical result of the client's present circumstances – rather, those are just triggers for underlying biology - you realize that talking about their problems not only wastes time but actually interferes with the diagnosis process. These sorts of discussions only bring in extraneous problems that cause the client to lose focus on their real issue.

Although occasionally you'll need to have the client tell their story for a while longer to figure out what the issue really is, for most clients story telling is actually a very bad idea. They will simply add more problems to their list as they try and give explanations for why they feel the way they do. (Of course, occasionally the client really does know what is wrong, so be watching for that.)

Much more rarely, some clients can't describe physical symptoms or settings for a very different reason – they are having a 'spiritual emergency' and their descriptions are experientially 'spiritual' in nature. (These are not issues of religion or faith, which are treated using standard techniques.) In these cases, the client has switched into a mode of seeing and experiencing we call 'spiritual view'. This complicates diagnosis, because the underlying biological cause of their problem is not recognizable from this viewing mode. The therapist diagnoses the underlying biological problem either from their description, if it matches a standard case; or by having the client switch to the painful but more useful 'physical view' so the underlying biological issues can be seen. Chapter 13 goes into these problems in more detail.

The fear of being wrong

Another common problem with therapists new to this material is a fear of making a mistake in their diagnosis. Of course, this is partly created by their past experiences in the test-heavy academic environment, but some of it is genuine fear of harming the client. It usually takes a while for the therapist to learn it is ok if they make a diagnostic mistake. If their treatment is not working, they can simply stop to assess why – perhaps the client simply doesn't understand the treatment directions; is it due to an interfering traumatic issue; or is it an actual mistake in the diagnosis? Whichever the case, the therapist can just calmly re-evaluate and start over. In our training classes, we always let the students make errors in diagnosis so they get comfortable with starting treatment, realizing that the problem is not going away, and restart.

Occasionally, the therapist may come up with several alternative diagnoses for the client's issue. Although they might choose to continue asking diagnostic questions, it is often quicker to pick the most likely cause and start treatment; or eliminate one of the other possibilities if its particular treatment is very rapid (for example, as in the case of a simple biographical trauma). This trial and error approach will quickly show the therapist whether they are on the right track or not.

Other common mistakes doing diagnosis

The most common mistakes new therapists make doing diagnosis is by talking or asking questions to fill up the silence when they are uncertain about their diagnosis. It is far, far better to say *nothing* than to ask random questions! If you ask a question (or tell them to do something they don't understand), the client will usually try to be helpful to the best of their ability. So choosing the wrong question will send you off into unrelated problems in their life or cause them to become confused. We can't stress this enough – only ask a question if you have a good reason to, and be aware that you might have to help the client get back on track after you ask it.

In addition, during this diagnosis phase be careful that you don't ask questions that make the client have to think! (These are the kind of questions that make the client pause before answering.) If you do, clients often go off on a tangent, introducing new problems that are irrelevant to the real issue the client wants to fix (and is willing to pay for).

The therapist also has to be very careful in how they word their questions, so the client does not become confused. Asking a kinesthetic-oriented client a visually oriented question is likely to cause misunderstandings that will take time to sort out. The client will do what you say – even if it just adds confusion. Watch out what you say!

As we've said, the therapist is active, not passive. Always have an idea of what the problem might be caused by and check what the client says against that. This is the opposite of typical therapy. It can take a while to train yourself in the new way of working. Let's restate this in a different way – when the client enters your office, just looking at them you should already have diagnostic ideas in mind. Or at least have the most common cases in the back of your mind. Although this seems like it would lead to error by prejudicing the interview, the opposite is the case. Instead, it allows you to ask appropriate questions and really, really listen to what they are saying to see if it matches your ideas.

Another common problem we see in new therapists is not checking for pre-existing symptoms. This means the client has a current problem and also an older, generally continuous symptom that is not related. This can both mess up diagnosis and confuse the subsequent treatment as the client won't discriminate between the two sets of symptoms unless you make sure they do. Remember to check for that!

Again, we often see new therapists lose control of the diagnostic session for long periods of time when the client gets into story or explanations. Most of the therapists need practice in gently cutting this off; perhaps by explaining that they need actual, physical symptoms to help them diagnose.

Finally, when diagnosing and interviewing, don't let the interview drag on. Keep your client focused on the issue that needs healing, i.e. be somewhat actively directive with most clients (but don't make the mistake of directing their attention to other issues – stay on task). For the most part, there are just a few things you should pay attention to right at the beginning:

- Is it a medical problem? (Therapists often forget that some issues are caused by bodily injury or disease.)
- Is it generational? Do other relatives have it? Healing these traumas has a huge impact on the clients.

Understanding Trauma, Structural and Parasite Symptoms

Because we work with subcellular cases, it is very important that you have an understanding of the difference between simple trauma issues, structural issues, and subcellular disease issues. As we've said, simple biographical and generational trauma can and do cause a host of problems with people. These traumas have feelings in them that get temporarily triggered into awareness by outer circumstances or thoughts; or are there continuously. Body associations are also created during traumatic events and most notably drive addictive behavior.

Subcellular structural issues are different. Here, the client's emotional symptom is caused by a structural defect in the primary cell, and is not due to some similar-feeling trauma. Physical and emotional symptoms from structural problems in the primary cell are due to cell damage, *not* from the feeling of the trauma that caused the damage to occur in the first place. By analogy, a structural issue would be like having a hole in the roof that causes furniture to get wet and moldy. Structural problems are indirectly due to generational trauma. To help the client, you have to be able to recognize symptoms of structural damage and learn how to find the causal traumas. Many of the subcellular cases or situations in this handbook, or in the Whole-Hearted Healing manuals are due to structural problems. In addition, most of the peak state processes we teach work by fixing structural problems in the primary cell.

Subcellular disease issues are yet a third type of problem. They can be broken up into two parts: the obvious one is where a symptom is due to a parasite causing problems in the cell. For example, when a bug-type parasite causes pain as it rips a cell membrane. Looking for a trauma with the same feeling of pain in it is a waste of time, as the symptom is not directly related to trauma. The second type of parasite issue is more common but far creepier. In these cases, the client experiences the parasite as themselves. Any problems or injury to the parasite is experienced as if it were the client's own issue. These two effects can also overlap, where the client's symptoms are both from damage the parasite causes and from the parasite's own suffering. To diagnose and treat these problems, you have to be able to recognize the relatively few symptoms that these parasites can cause and learn what to do. This may involve the destruction of the parasite; get the client to stop unconsciously provoking the parasite so it quits harming the client; or make the parasite healthier and symptom-free.

Assumptions about the therapist's background

In our training, we assume that the therapist already had experience using trauma therapies: EMDR, TIR, meridian therapies like EFT, and so on. In fact, most therapists who take our training are already using those techniques professionally, but simply want better tools so they can heal more client issues than they can currently. We do recommend therapists know as many techniques as possible – *not* just our own - in case a particular technique does not work well or at all on a given client. As part of our courses, we teach our own efficient techniques that specifically target the different trauma types, but other's techniques usually get the job done.

Differential Diagnosis and the ICD-10

No matter what diagnostic approaches you use to diagnose your client, you will need to memorize all of the current subcellular problems that we've identified so far. At about this point our students give a heartfelt moan in chorus – but really, there is no way around it. Unfortunately, different cases have different treatments, so the therapist usually needs to figure out what the cause is to treat it properly.

For many clients the diagnosis is obvious, as the symptoms really only fit one particular subcellular case. Surprisingly this happens quite a bit of the time.

However, with some clients you will have several possible subcellular cases come to mind as you do your diagnosis. You will then need to do 'differential diagnosis' to figure out which case actually fits. Sometimes this will involve checking for other symptoms that identify the particular case; sometimes it will require you to start an actual treatment to test your hypotheses and see if there is any change to their symptoms. As you will see, there are also various diagnostic approaches that help you sort through the possibilities to reduce the list of possible causes. For example, we teach students to start with the most common case first if there are several possibilities when working with typical middle or low functioning clients. Fortunately, the diagnostic approaches can all be used simultaneously – like using Venn diagrams, this greatly reduces the number of cases to just the ones that overlap from each of the approaches.

Each subcellular case entry in this handbook lists the other cases that share similar symptoms, and gives brief steps for doing differential diagnosis. Below are two examples to illustrate how this works. We've arbitrarily selected two common emotional symptoms and listed their most likely subcellular causes;

included are quick ways to differentially diagnose and hence identify which case is actually the cause. These possibilities are roughly ordered from most common to least common. Students are expected to be able to derive this kind of list on the fly while diagnosing the client in the initial client interview. Chapter 12 covers standard symptoms and their differential diagnosis in much more depth.

Example: The client has long lasting, severe sadness
- Soul loss – are they sad because they are missing someone or longing for them?
- Biographical (simple) trauma – is there a trauma image or moment that matches the feeling?
- Copy – test by asking if the feeling is partly outside the body; does the feeling have a personality (watch out that they don't ignore parent personality); or tapping doesn't work on the feeling.
- Generational trauma – the feeing is personal; a lot of their family has it.
- Tribal Block – the client actually feels 'heavy', not sad.

Example: The client has long standing fear or anxiety
- Holes – is there a location inside the body? This is a very likely cause.
- Trauma – does simple tapping work? (Watch out for psychological reversals).
- Copy – is it partly outside the body? Does the fear have someone's personality?
- Tribal Block – is the fear response to what emotion is coming in the navel?

On the other hand, sometimes you will be simply clueless on what is causing their problem. This is where skill and experience comes into the practice of therapy. In a later section we give some of the common reasons why a therapist doesn't recognize a standard case, and what to do about it. But sometimes you just have to guess – and the best guess is to start by using trauma-healing techniques. Fortunately, our Institute certified therapists have another resource available to them: our highly-trained clinical staff is available to assist them as needed in diagnosis and treatment.

The current state of the art

But there is more to diagnosis than fitting the client into one of the particular subcellular problem boxes in this handbook. Unfortunately, this is a new technology, and there are many problems that we don't yet know how to treat. As part of your training, it is as important for you to know what you *don't* yet know how to treat as it is to know what you can treat. The ICD-10 (International Classification of Diseases from the United Nations World Health Organization) list in Appendix 11 shows what the likely subcellular causes for various problems are – and shows all too many areas where we don't yet have solutions. When you know your limitations, you can offer the client what you do know how to do and let them decide if it is worth the cost, rather than fail at what you don't.

But change is very rapid in this field. To stay current, please check our PeakStates website for updates. That list is constantly changing as we develop new techniques and find the causes of more diseases. In fact, one of the best reasons to become certified by the Institute, aside from the pleasure of associating with other cutting-edge therapists who also 'charge for results', is to get our steady stream of new developments and techniques.

The subcellular psychobiology approach allows us to understand and treat various 'untreatable' or unknown etiology problems, because it straddles the zone between psychology and biology. For example, we now understand the cause and have a treatment for Chronic Fatigue Syndrome, which you can read about on our website. After enough testing, and if there are no safety or improvement issues, we eventually publish these processes for the public. The as yet unpublished *Peak States of Consciousness*, Volume 3 will cover the theory, analysis methods, and treatment methods for a number of significant diseases. For those interested, we also list a number of our research projects on our website; but we have many other unlisted projects that we work on as we have time and opportunity. For example, currently three of our high priority research projects are:

- Severe autism, which is a listed project;
- Type 1 diabetes – we believe we've identified the cause and are working on a treatment for it.
- OCD – we believe we've identified the cause and are working on a treatment for it. This is an unlisted project.

Diagnosis – Fast Functional Assessment Approach

One of the tricks we use is an almost instant assessment of the client. We put clients into one of three categories:

- High functioning – thoughts, emotions and actions are consistent. The client feels stable, with just one or two issues that affect them. They are fine in the rest of their life. Good candidate for peak states.
- Average (or medium) functioning – a typical person, they have lots of emotional drama in their life, but can function. Most private therapy clients and most therapists are in this category.
- Low functioning – has many problems, may be diagnosed as mentally ill.

The reason for this rough, and virtually instant categorization is that high functioning people generally are very simple to heal, almost always with only one issue that is bothering them in an otherwise easy life. They are automatically great clients, and you can jump into a contract virtually immediately. These people are relatively rare as clients; but they may come to you for peak states, and for this they are ideal. Their usual problem is from tribal block, with heavy or resisting feelings coming up in their lives as they try and live more fully than an average person. This categorization trick usually takes the new therapist some time to learn, because they generally lack exposure to high functioning people in their practices or in their own lives.

Average functioning and low functioning people are usually *not* good candidates for peak states. If they come to you for one, they almost always want it to 'self-medicate' – to cover or block some painful feeling or problem in their lives. From experience, we've found that you need to find out what they are trying to cover up with the state and treat that instead. After it is healed, they won't have any interest in the peak state. If instead you go ahead with the peak state process, their problem will usually still be there and you will have a dissatisfied customer. (Note that a few peak state processes, such as the Silent Mind Technique or the Inner Peace Process, get their effect by eliminating a specific problem; the therapist needs to be able to recognize when they are needed for their client's particular issue.)

The low functioning people are ones that you need to be very careful when writing contracts with. Since so much of their life is a problem, you have to specify exactly what you are agreeing to heal. It is unlikely that they will feel significantly better when you are done, as they have so many simultaneous problems that eliminating one won't usually make them feel that much different. However, there are exceptions – some mental disorders caused by a disease process (such as ribosomal voices, s-holes, or the addiction bugs) may have cascaded into other parts of their lives to cause other problems. Eliminating the disease sometimes can significantly improve their lives in many areas.

Key questions
- If the client asks for a peak state, are they really just trying to treat a problem? (If so, healing the problem will eliminate the desire for the state. Giving them the state *won't* make the client satisfied with the outcome, as it is unlikely to help their problem.)

Diagnosis – Symptom Keywords Approach

The first diagnostic skill we teach therapists is to listen for key words and phrases as the client talks. This can quickly identify the problem as a simple trauma or a particular subcellular case. Obviously, this assumes that you've really learned and internalized the subcellular cases, so that you can recognize the possibility of one as the client speaks. In the handbook we include many of the ways that a client will describe a case; and when possible we get the therapist to experience the cases in themselves, so that they can still recognize one even if the client describes it in a different way. Of course, the therapist may need to ask more questions to be sure that the case they have in mind is the right one; but watch out for leading the client into an unrelated problem!

This keyword approach is far from foolproof, but with practice can often be used to almost instantly diagnose a problem. Here are some common examples from this handbook:

Example: Simple stuck gene trauma cases
- The problem is very personal; it is about who I am, how I'm defective at my core – generational trauma
- Family members have the same problem – generational trauma
- Addictions – body association
- Positive feeling problem – positive trauma
- Pulled in two directions – dilemma

Example: Subcellular structural or parasite cases
- Tapping therapy has no effect on the symptom – copy
- Feel heavy, resisted, want to change my life – tribal block
- Anxiety/fear – holes
- Loss, longing, lonely, sad – soul loss
- Pain when I move – crown structure
- Voices, sex addiction, demonic possession, channeling – ribosomal voices
- Several people I know radiate the same problem – projection
- Sharp pain, tired, heavy – curses
- Lose ability to form judgments; people as objects – brain shutdown
- Narrow emotional range – flattened emotions

Diagnosis - Likelihood of Occurrence Approach

The subcellular cases in this handbook are organized specifically for general practitioner therapists. Since these therapists will see virtually every problem in their career, the three groups of cases are roughly in order of how common they are in a random client population. The most common cases are in chapter 8, and student therapists are expected to be able to recite every aspect of these cases in their sleep. Chapter 9's cases are less common, but we still expect the therapist to also know them well. Chapter 10's cases are on average even less common. The therapist still needs to know they exist, but we expect they will look them up when they need more specific treatment or differential diagnosis details. However, therapists who specialize usually work specifically with one or more of these uncommon subcellular cases.

Simple trauma is by far the most likely cause

During diagnosis, new therapy students often jump to rare subcellular cases when the cause is just the usual sort of simple, ordinary trauma they are familiar with. (And like first year medical students, they also mistakenly diagnose themselves as having these unusual cases too.) If you do no diagnosis at all, you can still use only a trauma technique and expect to fully heal a client over half the time (assuming that they have not already tried trauma therapies before on their issue and failed). That's the good news. Get the SUDS rating, fill out the charge for results criteria, get the trauma phrase, and you're set to go.

The bad news is that many of your clients have come to you because they've tried everything and have not been able to get rid of their problem. This doesn't necessarily mean the problem is not still just simple trauma, as they may be struggling with time loops (see chapter 11) or a hidden causality problem (see below). Or perhaps the trauma techniques they used were not able to adequately target their biographical, generational or body association issues. But it does mean that it is more likely that they've got a subcellular disease issue (such as a copy) or a structural problem.

In this handbook we won't go into the many different techniques and diagnostic methods for simple trauma that have been developed for other therapies (like EMDR, EFT, TIR, etc.) – we expect that you already know them adequately. However, we will focus on the problem of hidden or suppressed trauma because our students generally have difficulty with in their diagnosis sessions with practice clients. At a rough guess, this issue comes up about one time in 15 or so clients. There are also a number of subcellular problems that undo or falsely mimic trauma healing. Chapter 11 covers them in detail.

As a final note, if diagnosis is not going well and you can't figure out what is causing their problem, the odds are in your favor if you simply try a trauma therapy to see what happens. In fact, for some complex clients, you may end up diagnosing the real cause by actually simply attempting to heal the client one possibility at a time.

> *Tip: Copies look like simple traumas that won't heal*
> If what looks like a simple trauma just won't change after two minutes from a 9-gamut tapping therapy, the most likely reason is that it is actually a 'copy'. They do not respond to *any* trauma therapy because the feelings are not from a stuck ribosomal trauma string. Instead, a bacterial organism in the client was used to make a 'copy' of another person's emotion or sensation during a moment of trauma. Although it is possible that this blocking effect is due instead to a 'guarding' trauma (i.e., psychological reversal), this is less common than the problem of copies. You can quickly do a differential diagnosis by asking if the feeling has someone else's personality with it, or if the feeling actually extends outside their body.

Key questions:
- Have you used tapping on your problem? (If so, it is likely not simple trauma.)
- Have you done other therapies on your problem? (This may or may not be relevant, but may help you eliminate possible causes.)

Which trauma type do I heal first?

Say you've diagnosed the client, and found they have a trauma issue that you can treat. Is there an optimum order for the trauma type you should address first? The answer is 'sort of'. Thus, as a rule of thumb, if it is *not* already obvious what you need to heal, you start with generationals, then do body associations, and do biographical trauma last.

We have students remember this simple idea by noting that this is the same as saying 'heal from the bottom of the body up'. The bottom of the body, the perineum, has the triune brain awareness that contributes the genes that create generational traumas. These in general have the most impact on the typical person and in fact, generational traumas are often the source of the client's problem. If the client feels the problem is about how they are defective at the deepest level, or it is an issue that feels very, very personal, then you should strongly suspect that a generational trauma is either the cause or contributing to the problem. If so, heal this first. Generational traumas not only feel 'personal', they determine how your primary cell is actually made, hence they also have a huge impact on structural problems. Many people can heal generational issues by simply feeling the emotion and tapping – others need to become aware of the generational line before the tapping (or regression technique) will be successful.

The next brain going upwards is the body brain at the belly; and it contributes genes that make body associations, which can have the next most impact on a typical person. However, if the client's issue is an addiction or they continuously recreate a symptom, then of course you would start with this type of trauma, not a generational trauma.

Continuing up the body, the genes from the heart brain create biographical traumas; they have an even lesser impact on a typical person. We are not saying that they have no impact – far from it, as abuse survivors can well attest - but rather the relative effects are proportionally lesser. This type of trauma causes stuck emotional feelings that are usually the presenting symptom; but their other effect, creating stuck beliefs and decisions, sometimes causes great havoc in the client. Obviously, if a stuck belief is the client's issue, you would start by healing the biographical trauma and ignore the rule of thumb.

Key questions:
- Do other people in your family, especially ancestors, also have this problem? (If so, this is probably a generational problem and generational healing would be used. Note that most clients don't think in these terms, and do not think to include that information in their history forms or descriptions – you have to ask.)
- Does the problem feel like it is about you at your core? (If so, look for a generational trauma.)

Diagnosis – Type of Issue Approach

We can often immediately categorize a client issue as a physical, emotional, mental, relationship or personal problem. This gives us a small group of likely subcellular causes to check out with specific, directed questions. Student therapists find this approach to be extremely useful during their diagnosis sessions. Obviously, the list of causes below is just a guideline, as the same symptom can have several different possible causes; and it does not cover all the possible cases, just the relatively common ones. For more detailed material, see Chapter 11.

Physical Issues (be sure it is not a medical problem)
*   Back pain: Simple trauma causing the spine muscles to stay tense and pull the spine out of alignment.
*   Pain when the client moves: crown brain structure.
*   Feel heavy: tribal block.
*   Burning/stabbing/ripping feeling: bug-type parasites.
*   A constant sharp pain like a nail in the body: curse.
*   Tired in some areas of the body: blanket curse.
*   Can't sleep well: kundalini, anxiety (trauma, holes), or voices.

Emotional Issues
*   Trauma (generational, associational, biographical)
*   Sadness, loss, loneliness: soul loss.
*   Feelings that won't go away: copies
*   Traumas constantly being triggered: body association, or the mRNA anchor problem.
*   No emotional range: flattened emotions or enveloping bacterium.
*   Extreme emotions: treat with the Waisel technique.

Mental Issues
*   Fixed or dogmatic beliefs: biographical or core trauma
*   Mind chatter or obsessive thoughts: use the Silent Mind Technique.
*   Can't get songs out of your head: treat for sound loops.

Relationship Issues
*   Issues with spouse: cords most likely; projections; e-cords less likely.
*   Problems with how others feel: usually a cord problem, or less commonly projection.
*   It feels like others are blocking ones life: tribal block.
*   Missing someone: soul loss.
*   Other cultures are scary, a burden: caused by the borg fungus (and treated with SMT).
*   Now feel the same as someone else did: copies.
*   Inappropriate sexual attractions: ribosomal voices.

Personal Issues
*   Identity was lost (homemaker, job, etc): column of self void problem.
*   Death/ annihilation/ suicide: placental death trauma.
*   Suffering groups of humanity: projection.

Diagnosis - Inside or Outside the Body Approach

One way to do differential diagnosis for a number of conditions is to have the client become aware if the symptoms are inside or outside the body. Paula Courteau came up with this useful approach to diagnosis; we refer you to her *Whole-Hearted Healing Workbook* with its diagnostic flowcharts for a better description. The subcellular cases of problems felt as outside (or partially outside) the body include:

- Copies (half inside, half outside the body).
- Ribosomal voices (at fixed locations in space around the body).
- Tribal block (the manipulative feelings are from outside the body).
- Blanket curses (on the surface of the body).
- OBE images from trauma (like watching a play or movie).
- Projections (people or objects radiate a feeling).
- Cords (personality issues sensed in others).
- Bug emotions (although they can sometimes be inside the body).

Other subcellular case symptoms are generally felt inside the body.

The Endless Problem or Incurable Client

Over the years, we've seen a small percentage of clients come in with a never-ending series of problems. No matter what you successfully heal, they are not satisfied and soon return and claim you did not help them as promised. Each time they say 'this is my real problem'; but once it is gone they are soon back with a new one. Sometimes these people are middle functioning, or more often low functioning. In some cases, this problem is mixed in with obvious serious mental illness or 'borderline' behavior; in others, the client can function adequately in the world. As some of these people were actually therapist students, we had the lengthy opportunity to try and figure out what was going on in them. As of this writing, it is clear we still don't have all the subcellular mechanisms that can cause this behavior, but here are the ones we've seen so far (in approximate order of occurrence):

- S-holes: The client feels they have to have attention from others or they will die. Clients with this problem often don't notice the driving feeling in their body without help; they may also use parasites that 'drain' others so they can suppress this underlying feeling. This is a very common problem.
- Addiction bugs: The client is addicted to feeling negative feelings. No matter what you heal, they soon return to this default negativity. This is also very common.
- Body associations: For some reason the client has associated death or suffering with one or more positive feelings. Their body will continue to serve up an endless supply of traumas to avoid 'dying'.
- Kundalini: The client has a never-ending series of traumas triggered. They also usually exhibit ego inflation and deflation, as well as sleep disorder. The body brain causes this problem.

- Triune brain conflicts: The symptoms result from a triune brain attacking another at a physical and/or emotional level. Symptoms show up in a triune brain's area of the body (for example, in the head, the heart, etc.). Symptoms can include different kinds of pain; strange parasite issues; etc.
- Full body holes: The client does not usually actively complain, but they never feel ok after treating other issues. In essence, they don't really have a body – it is mostly a hole. Commonly they feel hopeless and 'grey', and that they will never be well.
- Global paranoia: In this case, the client cannot accept that they have been helped – they feel that the therapist must be at fault no matter how successful treatment is.

Hidden causality and suppressed trauma

For simple traumas, the client's presenting symptom is the same as the trauma symptom. Since this is the usual situation, trauma therapy works well for many clients.

However, with some clients it is necessary to find when the problem started, because the symptoms they complain about are *not* causing their issue; trying to eliminate them won't solve the client's problem. It turns out that many people use defense mechanisms that allow them to successfully suppress their own major emotional (or physical) traumatic feelings. As hard as this is to believe, they are often completely oblivious to the extremely painful feelings that drive their actions and create other emotionally painful experiences in their life. Thus, checking on the origin of an event is sometimes a smart thing to do, *especially* when the client complains of a number of feelings, rather than just one core problem.

The therapist soon learns to recognize these hidden causal traumas. The therapist can see there must be an originating moment for the client's issues; but the client will unconsciously try to avoid that painful decision point and painful feeling. Getting to it can be a bit of a struggle, because they will resist going to that moment in time when it first happened to avoid the painful emotional content. Perseverance is the key; it helps when you know there must be a suppressed, causal trauma moment creating subsequent client symptoms. If needed, we highly recommend using the TIR approach when dealing with these suppressed types of trauma. This problem is even easier to see if the client's issue is cyclic; they go through a period where everything is ok, then the issue gets triggered again and the subsequent painful symptoms that the client is complaining about re-appear.

A student writes: "I guess it's difficult to move forward in diagnosis when the client is not able to feel. We both stayed with it for a while, not going anywhere, until she started to feel what was bothering her. So we talked about you, the staff, her reaction, etc. From there on, the discussion slowly revealed more key words that helped me recognize what this case is."

In the example below is a graph of the sequence of the client's feelings over time. The hidden causal trauma, which has both a painful feeling and an unconscious, trauma-driven decision, is at the moment when there is a shift from ease and simple enjoyment to the start of various painful feelings.

Example: A client in debt
A client came in wanting to heal his feelings around constantly being in debt, having to borrow money, and feeling rather underhanded with how he treated people because of his financial circumstances. It turned out that this was a repeating pattern for many years. Trying to get him to back up to the moment where he decided to not seek work and so start the cycle of poverty over again took some work, but finally he got to the moment where he felt afraid and inadequate about what he was doing for a living, something he was ignoring and avoiding when he spoke about his issues. Once this moment was identified, simple tapping on the feelings that arose not only eliminated the trigger, but all the subsequent feelings he had from making this bad choice.

Essentially, we had to keep the client focused on the moment that his situation changed – the cusp moment from positive feelings to negative feelings - until the traumatic feeling driving the behavior came to awareness.

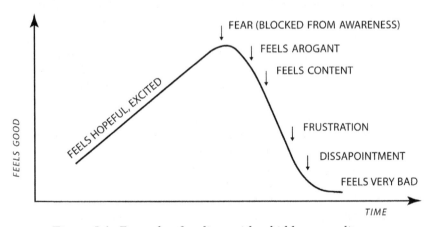

Figure 5.1: Example of a client with a hidden causality –
a cause blocked from conscious awareness but obvious in its temporal location.

Key questions:
- When did the problem start? What symptom happened at that point? (You use trauma healing at that moment; or see if it is the start of a subcellular case.)

Compensating with parasites

Fortunately, the following problem is not common in randomly chosen clients, but is often found in clients who just can't seem to be helped on a specific issue. This can be quite baffling unless you understand the mechanism and ways to identify it. In this problem, the underlying cause is again a traumatic feeling that the client is unwilling to feel. But rather than avoiding or suppressing the trauma sensations, they find a way to compensate for the feeling. For example, the client feels inadequate, but avoids this feeling by staying in situations where they constantly get praise. Or perhaps they feel afraid of being poor, so continue to accumulate money and objects to try and offset the fear. By analogy, the client is like an oyster that forms a hard pearl around an irritating grain of sand.

Unfortunately, people's awareness is simultaneously inside the cell and in the outer world. What they do in the real world is also what they do inside the cell – more accurately, what they do in the cell feels the same as what they do in the world. Thus, the client will try and find ways to compensate for their feelings by also simultaneously interacting with parasites or other disease organisms inside the primary cell. Thus, you have more obvious actions in the outer world and hidden actions inside the cell. In some cases the subcellular compensation works so well that they don't also act out in the real world.

> *Example: a viral lung infection*
> One client had a long-term chest cold. She wanted this chronic problem to go away. However, this disease was compensating for a hidden, painful emotion. Trying to heal the virus issue directly would not work, because the client would unconsciously resist any healing so she could hang onto her compensation. The initial trigger for her problem was feeling alone. This loneliness was a feeling she knew she was desperate to avoid in her life, although if you asked her, she would say she was fine with actually living alone. It turns out that the virus felt like childhood friends to her body. The virus was such an effective compensation that the client did not feel lonely in the present. The solution was to heal the initial, underlying loneliness and feeling of not being loved. Addressing these feelings directly made the secondary need for the viral feelings end, and the lung illness was immediately gone.
>
> *Example: feeling powerful*
> The client had a chronic, underlying feeling of powerlessness until age 19, when he suddenly found a way to feel powerful and suppress the

powerlessness. What he had done was surrender his awareness into the borg parasite. The tradeoff was losing the ability to feel a gentle humanity with others; rather he now saw them as just objects to mold to his will or push out of his way. The client also used this fungal connection to manipulate and harm others. Sadly, we estimate that this very common mechanism is in about 20 to 30% of the general population. Treatment was the Silent Mind Technique with follow-up treatment for the traumatic feeling of powerlessness.

Sensate substitutes as addictions

Another way clients compensate for a traumatic feeling is to use a 'sensate substitute'. Here the client was in some kind of traumatic experience (almost always pre- or perinatal). At a body level, the client has associated survival with whatever surrounded them during the trauma moment. Later in life, they seek out substitutes that *feel* the same as those prenatal surroundings, or have as close to the same feeling as they can find. Because to the body 'more is better', the person unconsciously holds onto sensate substitutes in the real world and also finds ones inside their cell.

Example: Sexual attractions
This extremely common problem is caused by *in utero* injury to the fetus. During injury moments, the fetus desperately tries to connect to the mother for help to survive. The traumatic feeling is similar to drowning, where the person is desperately trying to reach air. During this moment they automatically associate survival with being surrounded with the *emotional* tone that their mother had as they were injured. After birth, the client then surrounds themselves with people who have the same emotional tones. After puberty, they find themselves sexually attracted to people with those emotional tones, although they rarely realize this is the driving force. In this case, the sensate substitutes are sexual partners. Likewise inside the cell, they acquire ribosomal 'voices' that also match the emotional tones that the mother had.

This unconscious sensate substitute drive is a catastrophe at many levels – the client will also unconsciously attempt to induce the feelings in the people around them. This causes relationship problems, and in children is often the cause for temper tantrums.

How can a therapist identify the hidden feeling? Fortunately, they may not even need to. If the therapist can identify the sensation or feeling that the client is attracted to, simple body associations will get rid of the underlying drive and eliminate the whole problem. But sometimes it is not at all obvious what the target feeling is – as shown in the previous example, it is not obvious that sexual feelings have anything to do with the other person's emotional tone!

The simplest way to find one of these hidden driving traumas is to have the client feel what happens when they imagine that the substitute is no longer available. This may or may not work, depending on how strongly the client is avoiding the underlying feeling. However, a trick that often works is to have them imagine someone else who no longer has the substitute and see how they would feel. This distancing usually allows the client to recognize in another the feeling they are avoiding in themselves.

A variation on this trick of imaging that the client no longer has the substitute is to try and imagine the extreme opposite of the substitute. For example, if the client has a fear of having no money, you could have them imagine that they don't have their savings account, but the opposite would be that they are in debt and penniless on the street. However, this has to be done with care so as to avoid stimulating unrelated issues. In a similar vein, you can block the compensating activity or feeling. For example, if the client is desperate for a coffee, you would have them imagine that they could never have another cup of coffee again. This examination of the extreme case can often help the client recognize the more subtle feeling that they are avoiding.

These approaches usually flush up the underlying drive force or traumatic feelings that are pushing them to have a compensating feeling or sensate substitute. It can also flush up 'guarding traumas' that cause psychological reversal and a desire to block any change on the issue. Regardless of how you do it, once the driving feeling is identified, healing the trauma with regression or by directly eliminating the body association does the trick.

Trigger events and parasite interactions

Another way to find the originating, compensated feeling is to look for hidden causality. In a previous section, we said it was a good idea sometimes to look at when the problem started. This can help us find the traumatic cause of the client's issue; or identify it as either a subcellular case or simple trauma from a description of what happened. When dealing with simple trauma, the originating feeling is going to be severe, since the client is doing their utmost to avoid it. However, when you include structural and parasites into the mix, the originating cause can be much, much milder. The subsequent sensations and problems can be far more extreme than the cause.

Students often confuse severity of symptoms with causes. They forget that the symptom, no matter how bad, might be the indirect result of a parasite or structural issue. Checking for when this happened (and seeing if it is something that is also in their relatives to identify generational causes) may allow the therapist to pinpoint the originating trigger. Once identified and healed, the subsequent symptoms vanish. However, therapists need to remember that some disease processes won't respond to this approach - healing the triggering trauma does not undo the cascade of problems it started. Like shooting a gun, the bullet won't return to the barrel if you release the trigger. These problems generally involve parasites and need a deeper level of healing; some of the subcellular cases in this handbook cover these sorts of disease issues.

Tip: Ignored symptoms

When the client has a major symptom that is not responding to treatment, they may also be feeling much milder symptoms elsewhere in their body. These milder symptoms may actually be the cause of the more obvious problem! For example, a migraine caused intense pain in the client's head. But it was the mild, subtle sensations in their solar plexus that were responsible for the headache via a parasite interaction. Once they were healed, the head pain vanished.

Avoiding areas of the body

Although this may seem surprising, most people completely avoid feeling anything in some areas of their body. Fortunately this problem is usually not relevant to their current complaint. However, if healing is not going well, or there is no obvious cause for the problem, the therapist may have to ask the client to check certain regions of their body for missed symptoms. The one that virtually all clients blank out on is their navel area. In fact, even asking them to sense their navel is often not enough; the client has to actually touch it with their hand before they will notice any symptoms there. (This is due to various traumas like cord cutting, or parasite interactions in early development at this location.)

Lack of awareness in a body area is often caused by the MPD problem covered later in the handbook, but can be the result of a parasite issue in that location, especially an amebic one. In this case, the client is using the bacterium like a comforting blanket, or using it to anesthetize the underlying damage or symptom. For example, s-holes often have a covering parasite that blocks the feeling of extreme neediness. Blanked out or numb regions of the body can also be caused by traumatic experiences, such as sexual abuse or traumatic injury – they may also have soul loss or holes in those locations that block sensations or symptoms.

Dominant traumas and peak states

Some people have one particular issue in their lives that overshadows everything else. This is usually caused by a major trauma being continuously activated for some reason. For the purpose of diagnosis and healing, it is just treated like any other client problem.

However, we mention it here because it is relevant to contracts involving peak states of consciousness. Dominant traumas cause a very strange effect in some clients – they block the acquisition of peak states using developmental event trauma healing. Even if a peak state process is done correctly, there is no change in the client. Yet strangely, if the dominant issue is later healed the client will suddenly also have that peak state.

Letting the client choose a peak state from a list because they hope it will fix their pain just doesn't work (with the states available at this time), and only leaves a dissatisfied client - even when they get exactly what they asked for in the contract. The therapist has to identify and treat their client's real problem before any peak states work is attempted.

Key Points

- Diagnosis requires the therapist to be pro-active in identifying possible subcellular cases while working with the client.
- Memorization of the various subcellular cases is necessary for therapists to do diagnosis.
- Diagnosis is usually very fast, usually just a few minutes for experienced therapists.
- Simple traumas are the usual cause of client symptoms about half the time.
- Many ICD-10 diagnoses are not yet addressed by current subcellular cases. However, more treatments and discoveries are constantly being made in this new field.
- There are several different approaches that can be used simultaneously to help identify or speed subcellular case diagnosis:
  - o Fast functional assessment
  - o Symptom keywords
  - o Likelihood of occurrence
  - o Kind of issue
  - o Inside or outside the body
- Some clients have a never-ending series of problems. There are currently several known subcellular cases that cause this phenomenon.
- The cause of some client issues is hidden simple trauma. Suppressed causal trauma, parasite compensation, mild trigger symptoms, loss of awareness in parts of the body, and other mechanisms have to be understood to correctly diagnose these clients.

Suggested Reading

- *Peak States of Consciousness*, Volume 3 by Grant McFetridge (not yet published). Goes into the theory behind finding treatments for various diseases that cause psychological and physical illnesses.
- *The Basic Whole Hearted Healing ™ Manual* by Grant McFetridge Ph.D. and Mary Pellicer M.D. (2004). The manual describes the treatments for many subcellular cases without explaining their subcellular origin.
- *The Whole-Hearted Healing ™ Workbook* by Paula Courteau (2013). This book, especially designed for self-help, contains an excellent systematic approach to diagnosis for many of the subcellular cases.
- The World Health Organization ICD-10 mental and behavioral disorder categories (F00-F99) online at their website www.WHO.int.

Chapter 6

Risks, Informed Consent, and Ethical Issues

"I'm here so that I might become a better human being."

This quote was from one of my students during a 2012 therapist training. To put this in perspective, out of nearly a thousand students his response to the question of what they wanted to get out of our training was unique – yet it is the real point of the Institute's research.

As I originally came from a completely different field, electrical engineering, I naively expected high ethics and altruistic motivations in therapists, spiritual teachers, technique developers, and other kinds of healers. And I have had the wonderful pleasure to have met many amazing people exactly like this. However, probably the most disturbing problem I've seen over the years is a complete lack of moral or ethical behavior in many of the therapists who have come to me for training, or who volunteered to work at the Institute.

Worse, this problem permeates the entire field of therapy and personal development. For example, we occasionally discover problems in other developer's techniques because we understand the underlying biology. The first time this happened, it was with a process that got its effect by harming the client. When I contacted the technique developer to discuss the problem and what we'd found, it quickly became clear that he simply didn't care – instead, only his income and social position mattered. Sadly, after this and a few other bad experiences, our policy is now not to discuss problems in other people's work because it is simply a 'no win' situation. In another example of systemic ethical problems, one of the finest women I knew of in this field had finally made headway in nurturing and introducing new techniques in conferences she founded. Once it became profitable, a small group of outsiders then deliberately used lies, emotional manipulation, and deceit to sabotage her reputation in order to take control of her work. What was bizarre to watch was how easily so many people went along with this! This crushed her so completely that she quit the entire field.

In the attempt to understand what drove these types of behavior and what made other people susceptible to it, we discovered several new subcellular cases. For example, a need for attention so strong that harming others just doesn't matter is often driven by the s-hole case. Similarly, people who surrender their awareness to the borg fungus also exhibit a total willingness to harm others for their own ends (or more accurately, the parasite's ends). However, it turns out there is a deeper, more fundamental problem in our entire species. This problem, which is outside the scope of this handbook, is the focus of our work at the Institute.

Conventional Training for Client Safety

One of the biggest problems we have in training therapists is to get them to understand emotionally, not just intellectually that there are real risks with healing, meditation, and other spiritual practices. Over and over we've seen students who don't believe that they or their clients will encounter serious problems using powerful trauma therapies. This can be due to simple lack of personal experience (they've never seen or felt a serious problem in themselves, so cannot emotionally believe that it is possible); lack of professional experience (no crisis intervention, rape or suicide hot line training); or religious beliefs, training or convictions ("We never get more than we can handle", "Meditation is always beneficial" are examples of this sort of erroneous beliefs.) Worse yet, they are completely oblivious of the danger they are exposing their clients or themselves to. When problems occur, these students are totally unprepared and tragedy can result.

Obviously, conventional training as a therapist usually covers client safety issues. However, even this isn't enough – in my opinion, many therapist training programs don't give adequate training. For example, about half of the psychotherapy Master's programs surveyed don't give *any* formal training in suicide prevention whatsoever (American Psychological Association, 2003). If you intend to use the material in this manual, we *strongly* recommend that you get training as soon as possible in the topics listed below. They are offered in most locations as continuing education for therapists. If you intend to become certified by the Institute, for your safety and the safety of your clients, you are *required* to have completed these areas of specialized training.

- Suicidal intervention.
- Crisis intervention/ sexual and physical abuse.
- Identifying psychosis or other mental illness.
- Spiritual emergencies.

Suicide

There are several excellent training courses on recognizing and dealing with suicidal people. As we said earlier, we require all Institute certified therapists to be trained in this topic. This is because trauma and other types of therapy can uncover suicidal feelings; or a client may have it when they come in your office. You need to be able to recognize it, be able to refer the client the support resources available, and know the relevant legal requirements in your location.

The reason trauma or other types of therapy (or spiritual practices) can activate suicidal feelings is because they trigger placental death trauma from birth, or trigger a copy or generational trauma with the suicide feeling in it. We know from bitter experience that these trauma memories can activate the overwhelming drive to commit suicide. This gives a body sensation that one must kill oneself immediately. This feeling doesn't need any emotional reason to exist, as it isn't from a desire to escape. Instead, a person with this feeling simply wants to obey this often overwhelming compulsion. This problem is deadly, partially because the client may act on it immediately, or worse wait till they won't be observed and stopped.

The traumas that induce the compulsion to commit suicide are:
- Placental death traumas during the birth sequence. There is usually more than one of these traumas.
- Cord cutting at birth almost always stimulates suicidal feelings.
- And less common events like the placental cord wrapped around the neck during birth.

This problem can occur in clients who have *never* felt this sensation before. These clients in particular don't have any coping strategies, as the experience is new - and so can be at even more risk than clients with a history of suicidal impulses. Worse, you can heal the presenting trauma but the client might trigger another from this time zone and still kill themselves. This is an area for trained and licensed experts, not amateurs.

If your client has a history of suicidal feelings, we strongly recommend that you do not attempt to induce any peak states with them, even if you are a qualified therapist. This suicide issue needs to be dealt with first, as doing work that makes the client feel better or have more energy can simply give them the energy to kill themselves.

Chapter 11 has more on this issue, as well as other subcellular cases that can also cause suicidal feelings.

Psychosis and other severe mental disorders

Unfortunately, *any* powerful therapy or spiritual practice can stir up repressed material that results in severe emotional and physical crisis. Some clients can actually trigger a major psychotic break. As therapists, we can tell that some clients are obviously fragile and clearly are not ready to face painful or difficult issues. However, even clients who have no history of these kinds of problems, and who are clearly stable and mentally healthy can be triggered into severe mental illness of different kinds.

Even something as straightforward as simple regression can sometimes trigger psychopathology. For example, one can trigger bipolar (manic depressive) disorder by accessing birth contractions in some people – even in clients that have never before had a problem with it. (Dr. Stanislav Grof has also made this observation.)

Another example is the problem we've seen with multiple personality disorder (MPD). MPD is a much more common problem than we'd ever believed – we estimate that approximately 70% of the general population has it to some degree. It usually isn't obvious because the client manages to switch between personalities rather smoothly, and because the client is unaware that this is occurring. Unfortunately, effective healing modalities can make this problem worse in susceptible people by removing problems that tended to mask the issue.

For these reasons, we highly recommend that therapists who use power therapies or use regression techniques take conventional training in psychopathology and treatment, so that they can learn to recognize it, and know when their training is inadequate and their client needs to be referred elsewhere.

Spiritual emergencies

Regression, trauma therapy, spiritual practices, or peak states work can deliberately or accidentally trigger states, experiences, and abilities that are considered 'spiritual' in our culture. Unfortunately, some people experience these events by going into crisis – the origin of the phrase 'spiritual emergency'. There is a huge range of problems that can occur. Students who certify with the Institute are required to take more coursework in this area.

Some examples of this problem that you will probably encounter in your career:

• Feelings of grandeur and mania.
• Absolutely terrifying experiences of evil or God.
• Kundalini awakening.
• Inability to moderate psychic abilities.

Many other problems exist, and should be reviewed in the texts on spiritual emergency. Two excellent books are Stanislav Grof's *Spiritual Emergency* (which defined this field) and Emma Bragdon's *A Sourcebook for Helping People With Spiritual Problems*, which is more oriented towards helping and intervention. Our Institute certification test in this topic is from the material in these books. Recommended but not required are Dr. David Lukoff's web based courses "DSM-IV Religious and Spiritual Problems" and "Ethical Issues in Spiritual Assessment" at www.spiritualcompentency.com.

Note that spiritual emergencies are usually mistaken as psychosis by conventional therapists and psychiatrists. The drugs that clients are given in this case simply slow down or stop the integration that has to occur, and can leave a beneficial change blocked by a lifelong assumption that they are psychotic.

Chapter 12 goes into relevant subcellular cases in more detail.

Risks with Standard Psychotherapy

Most of the newer generation of powerful therapies can accidentally uncover or evoke traumatic material that may cause your client (or yourself) harm. *Trauma therapies are not intrinsically safe, nor harmless.* This harm can range from short-term distress, accidents due to incapacity after a session, long term mental and physical symptoms like pain or incapacity, bipolar disorder, psychosis, spiritual emergencies, death by suicide and other problems. These problems can occur even in people without *any* previous symptoms. Fortunately, these problems are relatively rare and usually treatable; in most cases the benefits far outweigh the risks.

These types of problems occasionally occur even with the extremely mild talk therapies used by most therapists. However, trauma therapies can quickly and *accidentally* uncover suppressed material that may not be able to be healed in a session, or even at all with the therapy being used. This fact is not stressed in most of the therapy literature, but it is a fact nevertheless. For example, this is one of the reasons why EMDR is taught only to licensed therapists, who have already received training in how to handle these types of issues.

In this chapter we won't be repeating all of the information you should have already gotten from your training in the various trauma techniques in recognizing and treating these sorts of unexpected problems. Instead, we'll just focus on a few problems that are often omitted, or ones that can be better understood from a biological perspective.

Prescription drugs and trauma therapy

Oddly enough, one of the problems that clients have who are using prescription psychoactive drugs is when the therapy actually works and they feel better. They then have the temptation to change dosages or simply throw out the medication when they feel the first improvements. So why is this a problem?

First, many of these drugs cause severe physical and mental withdrawal symptoms when they try to go 'cold turkey' from them. You have to keep reminding your client, "If your condition improves, please ask the prescribing physician for a reassessment before discontinuing medication. *Do not discontinue your medication without medical supervision.*"

The second reason can be just as grim. You may have healed the presenting symptoms, but the drugs may have masked a secondary problem that had been hidden or controlled by the medication. It may be one that you don't know how to treat (like manic-depressive disorder or OCD); or it may be one that causes serious issues with the client, like psychosis, paranoia, or suicidal feelings. Slow tapering of the dosage can reveal this issue and allow you to stop further decreases.

Another surprisingly common problem with psychoactive drug use in the last decade is due to the sheer number of clients who are under medication. This is a problem because of drug side effects - there are a large number of psychological (and physical) conditions that can be triggered by these drugs that many clients don't realize are due to their medication. This can completely throw off your diagnosis unless you realize this is happening.

What can be even more confusing is that there are many prescription drugs that are not supposed to be psychoactive but may cause psychological symptoms, such as confusion, depression, paranoid delusions, visual and auditory hallucinations, and psychosis. "Drugs that cause symptoms of psychosis as a side effect almost always do so when they are first started. The psychotic symptoms will go away, sometimes immediately and in other cases more slowly, as soon as the drug is stopped." (quoted from *Surviving Schizophrenia*). Thus, the therapist needs to check exactly when the client's symptoms started to diagnose this problem.

Remember, unless you are an MD you are not legally permitted to give advice about a client's prescription drugs.

> *Example:* The client had been unable to sleep adequately for many months, and was very frantic and disabled as a consequence. It turns out that this was caused by an unusual reaction to her new, expensive vitamins; not realizing this, she would take more to try and help her fatigue. Simply stop taking them eliminated the problem in a couple of days.

Re-traumatization

Because so many therapists are unfamiliar with trauma therapies, they often trigger problems that they are unable to understand or deal with. For example, they may be empathetically listening to a client's problem, but instead of helping, it simply activates the client's painful memories and adds yet another layer of suffering. For therapists trained in several trauma therapies, this problem is unlikely to happen, although it might take a while to get to the root of their suffering.

At this point in time, in our opinion if a therapist does not know several effective trauma therapies, we strongly feel that seeing clients should be considered malpractice. This does not necessarily mean that they need to use them; but rather that knowing these techniques is a minimum level of competence for a therapist.

Destabilization or decompensation

Rarely, you are working on a client and you heal something, but the symptom you eliminated was actually being used unconsciously by the client to keep themself functional. In terms of typical trauma therapy, the presenting issue may have been hiding much more painful abuse or other PTSD experiences. Or the presenting problem was keeping a subcellular case out of awareness. For example, a client had issues about losing his job, but healing trauma around this only caused him to feel the much worse feeling of annihilation underneath. Fortunately, these problems can be treated, albeit the client is often shaken by what has happened – this is when having the client actually read the informed consent forms really helps them view this just something that can happen, rather than some kind of crisis or betrayal by the therapist.

In some cases, the client becomes completely disabled with a more serious psychopathology problem. This is extremely rare in average functioning clients, but is more of a possibility in low functioning clients who have a history of mental illness.

Risks with Subcellular Psychobiology Cases or Developmental Event Processes

In previous sections we identified some of the common risks with trauma therapies. Subcellular psychobiology cases (involving structural or parasitic problems) usually use trauma therapies for healing and so will have the same risks associated with those therapies. The cases also add new risks because there is the greater range of issues that can be addressed; but overall client risk is actually *reduced* by training in subcellular psychobiology. This is due to a better understanding of what standard therapy is actually doing biologically to the client. This is a bit like saying that a conventional therapist only has a hammer, so every client symptom is treated like a nail; and so potential problems from banging on them are not recognized.

In this handbook we won't be listing developmental event trauma safety issues. For more on this we refer you to our textbook *Peak States of Consciousness*, Volume 2, Appendix A; and our manuals on the Whole-Hearted Healing regression technique.

Underlying unconscious assumptions about healing and risk

As we've said, when we teach therapists, we find that in spite of everything we say, demonstrate in class, or have them experience themselves, many students simply don't emotionally believe that healing (or meditation and other spiritual practices) can cause problems. This becomes a safety issue both for themselves as well as their clients – and it causes them to skip needed precautions or avoid discussing safety issues with clients. This problem absolutely has to be addressed in their training.

Some of their beliefs about safety are from simple trauma; they feel they have to believe this so that they can pretend that nothing bad will ever happen to them (or more fundamentally, that they will never grow old and die). For example, "I'm so evolved that I won't have any problems", "It's just the lesson I came to this life to learn", and so on. In Appendix 1 we list some of these trauma-driven beliefs, and we have students heal them as part of the class. This has the added benefit that it makes the teacher's job easier in this part of the training.

However, there are also other reasons why people feel this way in spite of contradictory evidence. The simplest reason is that the therapist has never encountered this idea, or more often they've been taught just the opposite, either from their academic instructors, their religious upbringing, or their social circle. As you probably know, unlearning ideas from a trusted authority takes much more time and is much harder to do than learning ideas in the first place. This conflict causes unavoidable inner confusion and distress in students, but after a few weeks of exposure to training material the students generally internalize the new information adequately.

Another, much trickier but very pervasive problem are the unconscious underlying models that therapists use when trying to understand new material around therapy or medicine. Essentially, people unconsciously use simple, familiar analogies when trying to understand new information or how something works. In this case many therapists imagine that healing is like having a cracked bowl, perhaps with a piece that has come off. So the underlying assumption is that they simply have to know how to find the piece and what glue will hold the piece once they put it back in place. Another commonly used analogy is that of cleaning a bowl. The therapist's job is to help the client wash out old food remains. These analogies often work, but are examples of what an engineer would call 'linear small signal models'. This means that as long as the changes made are small with respect to other parts of the psyche, the psyche remain relatively stable, and the client can heal their issue in a relatively straightforward way. If you think of the bowl as the psyche, the rest of the bowl stays solid and the scrubbing or gluing works well.

To get closer to the truth, let's look at our trusty model of the person like an old beat up jalopy. When it is time to fix things, you start to unbolt a part and the rusty bolt snaps inside the engine block. Or an old electrical relay is actually the cause of the intermittent starter problem. Or the new shock absorbers you just put in causes other worn out parts to become overstressed and make noise or break. In terms of therapy, symptoms can be from indirect causes, or fixing one problem can cause another, or healing an issue can reveal another problem. This is the model that experienced trauma therapists might use if they had a difficult client.

Unfortunately, some problems or issues that we treat in clients are not at all like either of these analogies. In reality, the psyche (the primary cell) in the present is more like the bottom of an avalanche. This model is actually pretty close to reality, as early developmental problems snowball into bigger and bigger problems (subcellular damage and parasite activity) later on in life. Some lucky people just have a small snow pile; others had an avalanche that squashed the ski lodge. What happens in an avalanche also depends on the terrain, as some stable areas can minimize damage downhill. The impact depends on where things went wrong, not just the amount of snow involved. Most healing is like reaching into the snow bank to pull the dog out. But when we heal some big issues, it is like we're digging into a collapsed building looking for survivors. If you move too much stuff, the room caves in and you are worse off than when you started. Engineers would call this a 'nonlinear large signal model', as they would like to be able to predict where to shore up the roof before digging. From a subcellular viewpoint, perhaps you got rid of a parasite, but this left room for a more aggressive species. Or you got rid of a symptom that your body felt was needed for survival, so it found a new way to make the symptom that was even more damaging.

Finally, the analogy of a 'landmine' or 'pulling the trigger on a gun' fits some issues. These are usually prenatal problems that lurk quietly until some life event triggers them – and then serious problems erupt in the present. A number of diseases (such as diabetes, chronic fatigue syndrome, and schizophrenia) and psychological problems (such as suicidal feelings) are like this. A common trigger is any event that felt life threatening to the client, like an illness or childbirth; other times it is something more unique to the individual. Usually the client comes in because they triggered one of these problems; sometimes they get triggered during therapy. If the therapist is lucky, just healing the triggered trauma reverses the problem. If the therapist is unlucky, the trigger event started an avalanche or cascade of problems and healing the initiating event has no effect. This latter case is like expecting the bullet to return to the gun by releasing the trigger, or your leg to reattach after the land mine exploded. Part of the therapist's training is to know about issues like this, and to either avoid them (as in the case of placental death) or hopefully know how to treat the resulting problems.

Part of your training with subcellular psychobiology is to be able to choose the best model for your particular client and their problem: are you working with a pottery bowl, an old rusty car, an avalanche or a landmine?

Safety and the Primary Cell state

One of the biggest risks with working with subcellular biology is not immediately obvious. If the client (or the therapist) gains the ability to work inside their own primary cell, it is unfortunately possible to damage themselves by accident. This is because the person can now 'see' and 'touch' the interior of their cell. The temptation to meddle seems to overcome some people, especially ones who believe that they are so capable or 'spiritually advanced' that nothing could ever happen to them. Unfortunately, it is exactly like giving a 15 year old the keys to a new Ferrari and expect them not to have an accident.

Another common risk is that the person can now 'see' subcellular parasites and unintentionally interacts with them. Unfortunately, when the person focuses attention on them, they don't like it. If they respond aggressively, as many parasites do, they cause damage inside your primary cell. This parasite interaction problem is somewhat random – you just don't know when you might trigger it or the degree of injury.

In our trainings, we routinely have a speaker or two who talk about how badly they damaged themselves by playing around with the interior of their primary cell (even though they had been warned of the dangers). For example, one was left in constant, overwhelming pain for years, unemployed and destitute (as we had no idea how to fix the damage he'd done to himself). Thus, to avoid these sorts of problems, we do *not* teach people how to directly interact with their primary cell. Rather, we teach psychological-like techniques that allow them to efficiently interact with the cell without actually using (or needing) the primary cell state. We also have students sign an agreement to keep private certain techniques we teach that we feel are too potentially risky for clients or the public because they interact too directly with the cell.

On the other hand, cell biologists doing research would likely find the primary cell state to be invaluable. The state can be used exactly like an infinitely adjustable, moveable, real-time microscope with slow motion and freeze frame controls. They could use the state to study *in situ* biological pathways, structures and infectious agents in tandem with their standard tools.

Group process work healing developmental events

We generally discourage (but don't forbid) our certified therapists doing developmental event healing work in groups.

This issue can arise if the therapist wants to do a peak state process (for example, doing the Silent Mind Technique) on a group to minimize the clients' costs and maximize their own income. However, we've found from experience that in a group setting, you typically have one out of five or so clients triggered into a problem that can't be handled other than one-on-one. Hence, if a therapist wants to do group work, we only permit it with advanced clinic backup on call, or if the therapist has other therapists to help – plan on another therapist per each additional 5 to 6 clients, to handle any crises. And no matter how many therapists attending, we also limit the maximum group size, again for simple reasons of safety, to no more than 15 people. This also applies to training therapists in groups.

Aside from safety issues, the other issue is simple effectiveness. Doing work in groups does not stop your responsibility for meeting 'pay for results' success criteria. This generally means that therapists will end up having to individually treat a significant percentage of the participants anyway to finish their process; although group work can save some time. However, over time most therapists who used to do group work abandon it because it just is not as cost effective as it used to be when they did not guarantee results, or were only doing some other type of mild process or activity.

There are circumstances where group work makes much more sense, as in some fairly straightforward healing treatments such as eliminating vortices.

Working with clients remotely (via Skype or phone)

Many of our certified therapists do work remotely via skype (or an equivalent) quite safely and effectively. Some screening is required; for example, clients with a history of suicide attempts, or worse, ones who are actively suicidal should not be worked with because of the risks of triggering a problem. Remote work with suicidal clients should only be done by therapists who are specifically trained for it, and only if the client has a safety structure and a therapist *at their location* who will take responsibility in case of problems. For more typical clients, simply make sure that there is both a support for the client during and after treatment, such as a family member in the house, and preparations for emergencies such as extreme emotion, overwhelming pain, or sudden suicidal feelings. (This is in addition to explaining the possible problems the client might encounter in therapy and the liability form signed so they know what they are getting into.)

There are still some problems that therapists who use remote therapy may encounter. Rarely, a client may say they have some symptom, but in reality they are experiencing something else that they don't want to admit. You can usually see this problem in their body language when you are physically with these sorts of people, but on skype it is easy to miss.

Risks with spiritual or 'distant' healing

Our society and most therapists consider the variably named 'distant', 'remote', or 'spiritual' healing a fantasy – but it exists, and can cause unintended harm because it can trigger exactly the same problems that any trauma therapy can. Because of these risks, we have ethical guidelines for certified or Institute clinic therapists using these techniques. We say that therapists can only use remote healing techniques when all the people involved are present to give feedback and have given permission (along with the usual informed consent and liability agreements). Even aside from the safety and risk problems, this whole area also raises entirely new ethical issues.

Client participation in 'distant healing' sessions is necessary for client safety. The therapist might not know if something goes wrong if they don't have verbal feedback - the client needs to be able to let them know if something doesn't feel right, and to be able to describe symptoms so the therapist can help them or get help for them. Secondly, the techniques may cause major physical or emotional symptoms to suddenly and unexpectedly occur in the client. He or she might be accidentally harmed if they are involved in activities that require undisturbed attention, such as driving or using dangerous tools (saw, knife, etc). Third, because the client would have no idea why a symptom just suddenly appeared, it might cause them needless anxiety and worry, or cause them to seek unnecessary emergency or long term medical interventions.

> *Example:* 'Spiritual healing' is often attempted with cancer patients. Unfortunately, cancer (along with some other illnesses) is a 'psychologically reversed' disease. This means that the client's body feels it needs the disease to survive, even if the disease is in reality killing them. If a treatment actually starts to eliminate symptoms, their body will generally make the disease worse or more aggressive to compensate for the effects of the intervention. When using standard techniques, the client will feel this effect and avoid any more treatment. However, when well meaning 'spiritual' healing is employed remotely without the client's participation, they can't halt the intervention. For the most part this doesn't matter, because remote healing techniques are usually so poor they have no effect anyway. However, if it actually has

a positive effect on symptoms, this can hasten a client's death as the body tries to compensate by restoring or increasing symptoms.

In particular, in 2004 we published a technique we call 'Distant Personality Release' (DPR). Although it can be viewed as just another technique for healing, it actually gets its results by eliminating trauma in another person at a distance by a limited interaction with the borg fungal organism. Fortunately, although the technique can potentially cause problems in the remote person because traumas are being eliminated, this happens very rarely – and the technique only works between two people who are already connected via 'cords' that are causing them both problems. Thus, in balancing benefit with harm, we do permit the use of DPR *when necessary* in those cases where circumstances don't allow both people to be present and give permission.

Another well-known technique for healing at a distance (that is not taught by us) is called 'surrogate EFT'. This technique can cause exactly the same problems that the trauma therapy EFT can. Unfortunately, unlike DPR, it can also stimulate a completely unrecognized problem covered in this manual we call the 'peak state bug' subcellular case. This causes susceptible individuals, either the client or the therapist or both, to permanently lose peak state(s) of consciousness. Even worse, other parasite-parasite interactions can also occur between the healer and the client that can occasionally cause other serious and sometimes permanent symptoms. Assuming the healer can even successfully use these sorts of techniques, these problems tend to occur randomly as a function of trauma and parasite dynamics between different people. However, some healers have systemic parasite issues, internal damage or trauma issues that cause problems to clients much more frequently. By contrast, therapists who have a stable Beauty Way state automatically do not interact with parasites even if they are present, and so don't cause these issues in clients.

In the case of family members using remote healing on each other, parasite problems are rarely a concern because they have already been unconsciously connecting to each other on an occasional basis their whole lives anyway. In other words, all the damage has pretty much already happened and parasite homeostasis established during the time they were growing up.

Example: We saw a very unusual case where a high-functioning son avoided any closeness with his mother because he unconsciously sensed the damage it did him. He was completely baffled by his own feelings around this, because he knew that this mother was a good person who cared deeply about him. All attempts to heal the issue using trauma healing made no difference, because it was not a trauma issue and so did not address the real parasite problem.

The Institute clinics occasionally have clients who come to us for help after having been genuinely harmed by 'healers' attempting 'remote healing'. Trying to figure out what needs repair is often very difficult because the client generally can't give specifics on what was done to them, and it often involves unusual parasite interactions.

Regenerative healing

Almost everyone confuses distant or spiritual healing with regenerative healing, due to our Christian cultural assumptions. Regenerative healing has several defining characteristics: it will heal virtually everything in a person, from teeth to missing organs; and it is fast, in the order of seconds to minutes. A simple and defining test of someone who claims to be able to do regenerative healing is to find a scar on your (or their) body and ask them eliminate it – if they can induce regenerative healing in others, the scar will completely vanish in a few seconds and only smooth skin will be left. However, people with this skill are vanishingly rare – in almost 30 years of looking around the world, we've only encountered three people who consistently had this ability.

Healers who are doing distant healing – if they are legitimate and consistent - are simply doing exactly the kind of healing found in this handbook. What they do is what a normal person could do on themselves with guidance and training. In contrast, regenerative healing uses a radically different approach that does not involve any kind of trauma healing, but rather temporarily bypasses the core problem of our species. Interestingly, this regenerative approach has no risks or parasite issues; all these sorts of problems are automatically dealt with. However, people who can do this are normally only temporarily in the regenerating state. When they are out of it, if they are not in a stable Beauty Way state, harmful parasite interactions can still occur. In our small sample size, two of the people had stable Beauty Way states; the third did not and so caused damage to some clients.

This misunderstanding of the difference between distant healing and regenerative healing can cause a lot of harm. In our experience, distant healers often 'oversell' their ability, claiming that they can heal far more than they actually can to get attention or income. Worse, this causes desperately ill clients to waste money and time they cannot spare trying to get help from these people. All this is on top of the potential trauma or parasite problems we've already discussed when having remote healing done.

Therapist Training and Safety Precautions

In our therapist trainings, the students do and learn far more than they are permitted to do with clients. In addition we may also ask for volunteers to test new experimental processes. Thus, there is potentially more risk involved for our student therapists than there is for clients.

Thus, over the years, we've found that it is useful to use extreme emphasis on safety concerns *before* the training. This both filters out inappropriate students whose fear issues would slow or disrupt class; and gives a clear warning to students that this is new and experimental work. "First, you must recognize that by attending this class you are risking your health and your life. If you and your partner are unwilling to accept that this is potentially dangerous or life-threatening activity, you should *not* take this class. This field is too new to guarantee that you will not have problems – worse, you may encounter problems that you have never experienced before." Fortunately, our understanding and our techniques have improved in the last number of years to the point where these sorts of concerns are much less of an issue; in fact, this is why we are now willing to publish this handbook.

Secondly, our training is for well-balanced people who have no history of mental illness or suicidal ideation. This isn't a statement on your worthiness as a person, but rather a recognition that you came into the world with trauma that causes you problems and should be dealt with first, before continuing. If the state-of-the-art in the Institute or elsewhere doesn't know how to cure your illness, you simply need to wait until one is available. Also note that acquiring various peak states will probably not fix your problem.

After the training

During the workshop, the teachers can handle most situations that arise. However, once you've left training, you need to take precautions for your safety. It is possible that traumatic memories will become active some days after the workshop – by analogy, we removed a part of the dam, and the water can start to flow. In rare cases, the activation of new material can be a flood. (Note that this can occur with any powerful therapy, and isn't just from our work.) To handle possible post-workshop material, we give you our phone numbers – use them if you need to!

We give new students about three months to take their Institute certification exam. After that time, you lose eligibility to become certified unless you take another training course. We have this policy for two reasons: the rate of change in our material is quite fast, so students can become out of date quickly; and this addresses the problem of students who 'never graduate' but who want to continue to use our free support resources.

Practicing at home

If you decide to practice on your own, you need to be prepared for the potential problems that can occur. Nothing will be foolproof – you need to accept that there is an element of unavoidable risk – but you can intelligently prepare ahead of time to minimize this possibility. First, inform your loved ones of the possible hazards, and work out a strategy with them ahead of time. One of the simplest and most useful steps is to make arrangements for someone else to check in with you after new inner work. For example, you may encounter material that makes you act like a crazy person, or you might feel that it is perfectly understandable why you must kill yourself right away, and so on. Your 'buddy' can help you in this situation, or at least call for help. Although spouses should be a part of your network, we recommend colleagues outside of the family be buddies – we've seen situations where the student became uncommunicative and the spouse just assumed everything was all right.

Other practical steps you should take:

- Find a local crisis intervention hotline. (www.befrienders.org/support/)
- Find a local suicide intervention hotline and facility for 24-hour watch.
- Find a classmate or friend to be your 'buddy'.
- Establish a practice relationship with other Institute students. Do at least some of your work with other students who can offer insight into your mental state (perhaps you became manic, delusional, suicidal, etc.), and give 'on-the-spot' advice if you go into trauma that is too severe for you to keep your 'observer' state intact.
- Find a local therapist who works with the latest power therapies.
- Establish a mentor/therapist relationship from a certified Institute therapist.

If problems occur

After a therapist training, issues and problems can show up after you get home. This is particularly a problem with short intensive trainings because there is no in-class time to monitor students after they've done major healing work on themselves. Students may not realize that they are in trouble or that their behavior has radically changed because some traumatic material surfaced. Just in case, your teachers will be checking in with you over the days immediately following the training.

Here are some simple things you can do if you have problems:

1. Contact your training instructor immediately. If they can't be reached, any Institute clinic therapist will do.
2. Contact your 'buddy'. This will be a person that will call you regularly to check up on you, and who you can call to talk to if you start to feel badly.
3. Go to the following website and read about what to do if you start having suicidal feelings (www.metanoia.org).

After Institute certification

Newly certified therapists go through a year of once-a-month mentoring. This is designed to improve your skills by bringing up difficult client cases with your mentor and your colleagues.

We also hold regular teleconference seminars for our certified therapists. We use this to introduce new material that they did not encounter in their training, or go into more depth on material that they did learn. Thus, they *must* have all of the safety steps in place before they participate in these calls. All of these activities have potential risks, and we won't work with them until their 'safety net' is in place.

Informed Consent

An informed consent form simply lets clients know what the risks of therapy are, so they can decide if they want to have their issue treated or not. Many countries now require that clients read and sign an informed consent form before starting therapy. For example, it is required by law in the USA. Some other countries do not yet require this type of document. There are many sample forms that can be found on the web to cover this requirement.

All Institute certified therapists are required to use an 'informed consent' form, whether it is required or not in their country. Our standard form is found in Appendix 3; it covers all the legal requirements for the US and Canada. This does not mean that our certified therapists need to use that particular form; they can rewrite as they see fit to cover their country's particular requirements.

Therapist fears about using an informed consent form

One of the problems we've seen in working with informed consent forms in just about all countries we've been in is a fear in the therapist that if they actually have clients read and sign such a form, they will leave because they will become afraid to do therapy.

In countries that require informed consent by law, this issue is less important because there is no legal choice. In countries that do not require informed consent, the problem becomes more of an issue for some therapists, as they feel their financial wellbeing might be threatened if they were to do so, because other therapists are not telling their clients about these issues. However, even where it is legally required, many 'alternative therapists' feel that they are not bound by the same laws and usually avoid using them, leading to the same conflict with therapists who are licensed.

First, let's look at the moral issue (which in my view is the only relevant one). The golden rule in Christianity is the idea that you treat others as you would have them treat yourself. You would want to know these things before therapy started, and your clients deserve the same honesty. But this unfortunately doesn't address many therapists' survival fears and rationalizations around this issue.

So let's look at the practical issues:

1) Your client might actually have problems in the therapy. They are *not* experts in this stuff, and usually have no idea that problems can even exist. Letting them know ahead of time increases their comfort and safety if there is a problem, and increases the chance that they will respond appropriately.

2) If you do not do a signed disclosure, you might get sued – this can be especially a problem with clients who have trust issues or actually have problems during the therapy. (Incidentally, we recommend always recording your sessions with clients, both for your own legal protection, and to be able to demonstrate change for clients who have apex'ed their memory of the problem away.)

Turning informed consent into a feature

Interestingly, we've found that therapists who have fears around informed consent do not even realize that it can be turned into a powerful marketing tool. Clients want to feel that you are the best therapist they can get, that you are an expert and can help them if anyone can. By explaining that you are an expert who knows about these sorts of problems, and that you simply take them into account in your practice, you increase their confidence. Remember, you are the expert – and if you are calm and matter of fact about these issues, the client will be also. If you are fearful or reluctant, clients can feel that also. We've found that clients simply won't care about the informed consent issue if you don't have an issue with it yourself.

As you talk about informed consent, you communicate that other therapists are either ignorant of these issues – which is often true – making you much more an expert in their eyes; or that other therapists are unwilling to tell the truth - which is also often true. By addressing these risks as a problem with all therapies, you also eliminate the idea that they have to go to another therapist for safety – since you have explained that these issues are just the way it is, like heat in the tropics. You turn your client into an ally who trusts your training, expertise and judgment right from the beginning.

It may be that after reading and understanding the possible problems, the client really does feel that the risk is too great for them – for example, perhaps they have small children and don't want to take any chances that might interfere with their children's care. Whatever the reason, the therapist can either offer to do simple advice counseling (with a very minimal 'pay for results' contract) or recommend another therapist for it. Or perhaps they would benefit from some other service, such as from a licensed social worker. In these cases, having a peer network you can refer these clients to is a real benefit to both your client and to your colleagues.

Ethical Problems

Over the years, we've seen a number of professional ethical issues come up with our research in subcellular psychobiology, in Institute certified therapists, and in our staff. Below are some examples of the problems we've seen that are unique to our work.

To help address safety and ethical issues, we adapted the ethical guidelines used by the International Breathwork Training Alliance to our work. We've added two items to their list that are unique to our work: the charge for results principle, and ethical behavior around the use of techniques that can affect other people without their participation. These guidelines are on our websites and shown at the end of this chapter. As another safety measure, staff and certified therapists also sign employment or licensing agreements that spell out the limits we impose on the use of these new techniques.

In this handbook we are not going to discuss standard therapists ethical issues. There are a number of good resources on the web and in college textbooks, and we refer you to them.

Pay for results

As we've discussed in Chapter 3, this issue of charging for time rather than results is oddly not seen as an ethical problem by most therapists or alternative healers. Unfortunately, because of the historical context and the sense of entitlement that many therapists and healers have, this unethical behavior not only continues but is considered to be acceptable practice by most in this field. This has led to many ethical problems: for example, therapists trying to keep their clients in therapy so that they could continue to get an income, regardless of the service being provided; and resisting new approaches and training because it might actually work and diminish an income source. Essentially, these therapists prey on the desperate and helpless. Fortunately, in the last few decades it is now possible to actually heal clients in many cases. Hence, regardless of past conventional practices, charging for time spent and not results is now clearly unethical. Hence, charging for results is both ethical and automatically encourages competence in the therapist. Charging for results has other important benefits. It clarifies objectives; greatly reduces the potential for legal problems and lawsuits; and can be used for advertising.

Some therapists had always used the 'pay for results' principle in their work. Around 2006 or 2007 this principle was instituted for all therapists certified by the Institute. This change caused many people to quit the Institute, both among staff and licensees. Since then, we've had a few clients call the Institute about charge for results problems, because the therapist ignored or distorted the ethical principles to maximize their personal income. So far, most of the client complaints were valid.

> *Example:* A certified therapist talked about peak states processes with a client, but did not write anything down. The client called the ISPS complaining that the therapist had not delivered what had been agreed upon. Because the therapist had neither written anything down nor recorded the sessions, there was no way to tell if the client or the therapist was telling the truth. Later it came out that the therapist was also 'overselling' peak states processes and not addressing the client's needs, because they got more money for the peak states processes.

> *Example:* Again, another example of not writing down 'charge for results' criterion. The client turned out to be a borderline, so nothing the person said could be considered true. Because there was nothing written down, there was no way to tell what had been agreed upon. The therapist had to return all the money, which was a considerable amount.

Disclosing unsafe or restricted material

> *Example:* Recently, a certified therapist called the central office because she had told her client about the existence of subcellular bug-type

parasites. She had done this because she didn't want to seem incompetent to the client. The client, who had the ability to 'see' in the primary cell, started to try and get rid of them without using our approved techniques. It turns out that we had already tested and rejected what the client was doing because it caused long-term harm. However, once the client had been told about the problem, she would not believe that what she was doing could be harmful to herself.

Example: A volunteer needed to have constant attention. She e-published a restricted document of Gaia commands for various developmental events so that people would give her attention and make her feel important. She knew that many of these commands would harm people, and simply didn't care.

Crises in the therapist's life

Example: One certified therapist had been rendered incompetent by her own emotional drama. Rather than deal with her own issues, she continued to treat clients in a irregular fashion leading to the neglect of several clients who needed help with traumatic material triggered in previous sessions. Ordinarily, it would have not been a problem, but the therapist did not refer the clients to someone else. This situation lasted for months, causing a lot of unnecessary suffering and work-related problems.

Inadequate or non-existent follow-up

Example: We've seen this problem in a couple of ways. We saw it after trainings, when the teacher did not follow-up with the students to see how they were doing. In one case, the student had gone into a spiritual emergency where he felt ok but was unable to leave his home. Because he didn't contact us, it was weeks before concerned family contacted us for help.

Example: In another case, a client had a bad reaction to the Silent Mind Technique, due to the extreme feelings stimulated by the process. Because the client had not been warned of this normal reaction, the client did not call the certified therapist back because they felt the therapist had injured them. This condition went on for months before our staff heard about the rather desperate situation the client had gotten into.

Certified therapists doing research

Our research work has a huge amount of safety issues. To address this, we have a very extensive safety protocol. Typically, it takes a couple of years of testing before material is released to certified therapists. We've had some people come to our trainings so that they can start doing research on themselves. Albeit potentially very dangerous, we certainly understand why some people will want to do this, and for the most part we accept this activity as a personal choice.

However, when a person wants to use our material to start research with a group of people, the chances that someone will be hurt or killed who doesn't understand the risks is almost a certainty. Because of this, we will not certify a therapist in our work who uses our training to do research in a group setting outside the Institute; and we de-certify someone doing this. This does not mean we feel the person is wrong or bad for wanting to do this – but we do want to minimize the possibility of lawsuits against the Institute if (or much more likely, when) injury or death happens to the people who are involved.

Distant ('spiritual') healing

The Institute teaches our clinical and research staff proprietary techniques that can heal clients at a distance. Developed for clients who cannot help themselves, such as catatonics or autistics, they are also used in our research for finding new disease treatments. When we teach these techniques to new clinic staff, they sign an agreement not to use them if they leave the Institute due to safety issues. Unfortunately, experience has shown that some therapists feel that they are entitled to lie, break agreements, and use any technique regardless of the experimental and possibly dangerous nature of the techniques.

> *Example:* Recently, we had a client from the UK call our central office complaining that he wanted his money back because he didn't get the results promised, and worse had been harmed. He had saved for over a year for the treatment. The therapists had used remote healing techniques for their work. Upon investigation, it turned out that the therapists had claimed to be from the Institute, but had never taken any of our classes. They had been taught very dangerous, untested and unreliable techniques by a woman who had been fired from the Institute for embezzlement and harming clients. Like their teacher, these two therapists exhibited the worst of unethical behavior – breaking agreements, lying, theft, and harming the client.

> *Example:* A student therapist decided to see if he could heal at a distance after finding out this sort of thing was possible. He chose to experiment on people he knew even though they had refused him permission to do so; but he ignored this because he believed that God had told him to work on them because 'they needed the healing'. Since any healing technique can trigger problems, to try this on people without their permission or awareness – even if it was just a fantasy and he could not actually do it – is a gross violation of our safety and ethical principles. He was refused permission to become certified by the Institute, and the people he was experimenting on were contacted and informed.

Illegal, unethical or bizarre conduct in Institute volunteers and staff

Ethical problems extend past simple client/therapist relationships. As an organization, we've certainly had our share of problems with volunteer staff. Because of these experiences, we've become much more reluctant to work with new volunteers at the staff level. This is one reason why we only draw from certified therapists for staff positions, to give them time to demonstrate ethical behavior, and to make sure they have adequate training before going further in our work.

> *Example:* A research staff person lied about her actions because of the large amounts of money she could make by completely ignoring safety issues and using or teaching material that was experimental or downright dangerous. She ended up harming well over a dozen people that the volunteer Institute staff had to find and help (which we did for free). This took hundreds of hours and pulled our small team away from research for over a year while we helped these people.

> *Example:* A business person was asked to help write our staff employment contracts. Rather than do this, he tried to disrupt the organization so that he could get rid of the founders and control it himself. When confronted about this, he said "I have to be the boss in any organization I'm in".

> *Example:* After a staff volunteer was trained in advanced techniques, he became very negative about the Institute and its founder, and convinced several people to leave the Institute to join with him. He also violated his agreement not to teach experimental and dangerous material to other people, apparently because it paid well to do so. Years later we realized that he had severe s-holes that drove him to this behavior.

The Institute Code of Ethics

Trainers, practitioners and trainees in the Institute for the Study of Peak States agree to observe the following code of ethics: "I agree to accept and aspire to the principles of the ISPS and to uphold the following code of professional ethics described below."

These guidelines are the result of years of work by Jim Morningstar and his colleagues at the International Breathwork Training Alliance. We have modified the guidelines slightly to adapt them to our Institute for the Study of Peak States. The original text can be seen at http://breathworkalliance.org/form_1.htm. Our thanks to Jim for his kindness in letting us use and adapt his work.

Institute certified therapists use many state-of-the-art techniques, and like any powerful techniques, they come with their own constraints and procedural requirements. This guideline was created to address both ethical and safety issues with some of these techniques (Institute as well as from other technique developers).

Practitioners obligated to use this code of ethics are listed in the PeakStates website under "Find Trained Therapists".

1. Client Suitability
   a) Establish a client's ability to utilize and healthfully integrate trauma healing, as far as is possible.
   b) Not discriminate on the basis of race, ethnicity, gender, religion, sexual orientation, age or appearance.

2. Contract with Clients
   a) Establish clear contracts with clients regarding the number and duration of sessions and financial terms.
   b) Establish clear boundaries and discuss the possible employment of touch.
   c) Practice my skills primarily for the benefit of the client, rather than solely for financial gain.
   d) Maintain confidentiality of client information and security of records of client session content.

3. Practitioner Competence
   a) Practice within my area of professional competence, training and expertise, make this clear to my prospective clients, and not make claims for my service that cannot be substantiated.
   b) Continue to develop personally, practicing the technique that I offer to others while nourishing passion and reverence for my calling, and keeping a healthy balance in my work and self care.
   c) Seek supervision and consultation when appropriate.

   "If psychological, medical, legal, or other relevant issues are presented by the client that are outside the scope of practice of the Peak States Therapist, the therapist will provide a referral to the relevant provider or direct the client to the appropriate resources."

4. Practitioner/Client Relationship
   a) Establish and maintain healthy, appropriate and professional boundaries, respecting the rights and dignity of those I serve.
   b) Refrain from using my influence to exploit or inappropriately exercise power over my clients.
   c) Refrain from using my practice to promote my personal religious beliefs.
   d) Refrain from all forms of sexual behavior or harassment with clients even when client initiates or invites such behavior.

e) Provide clients with information about community networking, educational resources and holistic lifestyle with their consent and within my scope of knowledge.
f) Refer clients to appropriate resources when they present issues beyond my scope of training.

5. Practitioner Interrelationships
   a) Maintain and nurture healthy relationships with other practitioners.
   b) Give constructive feedback to other practitioners who I believe have failed to follow one or more of the ethical principles. If this does not sufficiently resolve the issue, seek consultation with the most appropriate professional and/or civil authorities within my local region for the protection of the clients involved.

6. Charge for Results

Therapists certified by the Institute use a 'pay for results' fee structure in all their psychotherapy work (whether they use Institute techniques or not). This means that at the beginning of treatment, the client and the therapist first agree on what they intend to accomplish. If the goal is achieved, the client is charged the previously agreed upon amount - if not, there is no fee. In some cases, the Institute pre-sets what the result must be: the addiction technique must fully eliminate cravings, the voices that schizophrenics hear must be completely gone, targeted peak states must have the listed characteristics, and so on. Note that in some cases the 'pay for results' fee system isn't applicable, such as in training situations.

7. Only Use Techniques While in Communication with the Client, and with their Consent

"I agree to only use techniques that heal clients at a distance (surrogate EFT, aWHH, etc.) with the clients' or guardians informed consent and only when I am actually able to communicate with the clients."

At this time, we permit the use of Distant Personality Release (DPR) without these restrictions, due to its usefulness and demonstrated minimal issues. However, if possible, we still strongly suggest that it still be used only with the other person present, and with their permission, for both the ethical and safety reasons.

Key Points

- Many trauma therapists need additional training in suicide prevention, mental illness, and spiritual emergencies for client safety.
- There are risks when healing trauma with any technique. Albeit uncommon, these include uncovering more severe trauma issues or subcellular cases, decompensation, cascading problems, and trauma flooding.

- Informed consent forms cover the risks of psychotherapy and are legally required in many countries. Institute certified therapists are required to use them with all clients.
- Therapists need to watch out for prescription drugs causing psychological problems in their clients.
- The Institute's experiential training in subcellular psychobiology is not suitable for students with suicidal or mental illness problems; and requires therapists take safety precautions for a time after training.
- Subcellular psychobiology adds new ethical problems for therapists. Adequate training for safety, problems involving parasite interactions, remote healing issues, and inappropriate disclosure of experimental work are just a few of them.
- Networking with other therapists who specialize in problems you are not qualified (or interested) in working with is both useful and in your client's best interests.

Suggested Reading

- *Therapeutic and Legal Issues for Therapists Who Have Survived a Client Suicide*, Kayla Weiner ed. (2005).
- *Surviving Schizophrenia, 6th edition* by E. Fuller Torrey MD (2013).

Online resources on suicide
- 211 Big Bend suicide hotline at www.211bigbend.org. (USA)
- Stop a Suicide Today at www.stopasuicide.org
- National Alliance on Mental Illness at www.nami.org.
- Metanoia at www.metanoia.org
- HelpGuide at www.helpguide.org
- Centre for Suicide Prevention at www.suicideinfo.ca

Online resources on psychopathology
- National Alliance on Mental Illness at www.nami.org.
- HelpGuide at www.helpguide.org

Online resources on professional ethics in psychotherapy
- "What Should I Do? – Ethical Risks, Making Decisions, and Taking Action". An online course at www.continuingedcourses.net.

Online resources on spiritual emergency
- "DSM-IV Religious and Spiritual Problems" and "Ethical Issues in Spiritual Assessment" by Dr. David Lukoff at www.spiritualcompentency.com.

Section 3

Subcellular Diseases and Disorders

Chapter 7

The Four Biologically Distinct Trauma Types

The *usual* cause of most clients' problem is one of the three trauma types: biographical, associational or generational (a fourth type exists, what we call 'core trauma', but clients seldom come to a therapist for this problem). The DSM diagnostic category 'post traumatic stress disorder' (PTSD) is generally the biographical trauma type. Therapists can help many, and probably most client problems by healing only sensations directly due to trauma while ignoring any subcellular cases. A competent therapist is skilled in several trauma-healing approaches; some clients or problems respond better to one approach over another. (Incidentally, this understanding that most client problems are directly due to trauma is a relatively new development in the field of psychotherapy – most therapists still believe that trauma is a rare problem involving severe PTSD-type experiences.)

In practical terms, each trauma type is experienced quite differently. Hence, the therapist can usually target just the type of trauma, choose a technique to deal with it and usually move fairly rapidly through the healing process. Yet often we find that two or more of the trauma types are involved. In this case, the rule of thumb is to start with the body associations – this keeps the body from trying to recreate the client's symptoms by any means it can. Then move on to the generational traumas, as this is the type that is involved with the structure of the cell itself, and causes the feeling that there is something fundamentally wrong with the person (a feeling is very 'personal'). Then lastly, heal biographical trauma – these cause inappropriate, stuck feelings and fixed beliefs.

In terms of treatment, the therapist focuses their technique on the presenting symptom once the trauma type is determined. (Treatment success is measured in clear, unambiguous terms – the symptom vanishes, cannot be evoked again, and is succeeded by a feeling of peace, calmness, and bodily lightness.) Hence, we sometimes refer to the different trauma types as being 'simple' trauma because the feeling in the present is the same in the past trauma. However, although trauma healing may be simple in a procedural sense, it can also be overwhelmingly painful and therapeutic skill is sometimes needed to get the client to face the pain for healing.

From a subcellular biology view, the vulnerability to acquiring a trauma is due to pre-existing biological damage found in the earliest, primordial germ cell stage of development. Trauma is *not* directly due to outer circumstances, such as injury, abuse, severity or type of a traumatic event in the client's life. This is why several people can go through exactly the same experience, yet be affected differently – some with severe PTSD, some with a mildly painful memory, and some without any trauma at all. The underlying biological problem is in the histone that covers a person's genes. In essence, when a person needs to react to some event, be it with an emotion or action, their cells express the appropriate gene to make a relevant protein. Because of damage in the histone coating of that particular gene, the process gets stuck and the protein does not get made. In psychological terms, we experience this as a traumatic event that stays with us.

There are three different kinds of traumas because there are histone problems in three different groups of genes. These groups correspond to their usage by the cell – some of the genes are specifically used by ribosomes in the cytoplasm (biographical trauma), some by ribosomes in the endoplasmic reticulum (associational trauma), and some by non-ribosomal structures in the cytoplasm (generational trauma).

Suggested Reading

- *The Basic Whole-Hearted Healing™ Manual* 3rd edition (2004) by Dr. Grant McFetridge and Dr. Mary Pellicer. The Institute's regression technique for trauma and research.
- *Peak States of Consciousness*, Volumes 2 (2008) and 3 (unpublished) by Dr. Grant McFetridge et al. Gives a detailed discussion on the subcellular basis of trauma.
- *Trauma-informed: The Trauma Toolkit* 2nd Edition (2013) by the Klinic Community Health Centre - For service providers working with traumatized clients, including sections on abuse and First Nations issues. Free online.
- *The Whole-Hearted Healing™ Workbook* (2013) by Paula Courteau. Gives updated information on the Whole-Hearted Healing regression technique for trauma.

Biographical Trauma: "Stuck beliefs, triggered feelings"

Biographical trauma is the type that laypeople and most therapists consider when they think of trauma or PTSD. It is formed from a frozen moment of time, with an out-of-body image, emotion, sensation and belief or decision. Biologically, it occurs because at the moment of trauma a protein is needed, but the mRNA string that is copying the gene gets stuck to the gene's covering histone. This results in an mRNA string that extends out of the nucleus, with ribosomes attached along its length. These ribosomes contain the trauma information. (More precisely, crystalline fungal material embedded in these stuck ribosomes allows them to act as 'gateways' ' to trauma moments in the past.) The genes that can cause biographical trauma are all from the prokaryotic cell that will form the 'heart' triune brain later on in development.

Since about 1995, powerful therapies that can heal this type of trauma have just become available. Each exploits a different biological mechanism to heal. It turns out that many people's problems are due to this type of trauma. However, although the decisions formed in those moments inappropriately guide later behavior, stuck emotions from this type of trauma don't feel particularly personal.

As an aside, a subcategory of 'positive trauma' is included as a subcellular case in a later chapter. Although it is not biologically different than the usual, painful kind of trauma, it is covered separately because most therapists don't realize this problem exists. Additionally, these positive traumas can also be of any type: generational, associational, or biographical, although the biographical are usually the most common in clients, with associational next in frequency.

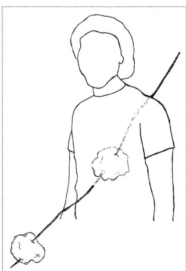

Figure 7.1: (a) Trauma experienced as an area in the body.
The ribosome gateway structure is superimposed on the body image.

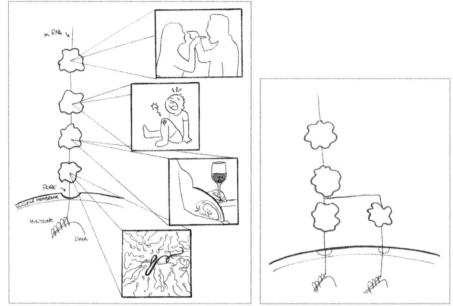

Figure 7.1: (b) A biographical trauma string seen as a stuck mRNA in the cytoplasm with attached trauma ribosomes. (c) A "multiple root" trauma string (an mRNA string attached to several stuck genes).

Symptom Keywords
- Physical and/or emotional discomfort: I feel …
- Fixed or dogmatic beliefs: I believe … this is the way it is.

Diagnosing Questions
- How does it feel?
- Where is the feeling?

Differential Diagnosis
- Generational trauma: the emotions and sensations can be virtually anything. However, if the problem feels 'personal', then the trauma is generational or a biographical with a generational trauma of a similar feeling.
- Copy: Test empirically by healing. If tapping changes symptoms, you have a biographical trauma. Copy also has a personality with the feeling, and is partly outside the body.
- Core (spinal) trauma: A core trauma has no feeling with the belief; a trauma-driven belief does.
- Other subcellular cases: watch for subcellular case symptoms to differentiate them from a biographical trauma.

Treatment

- Any trauma healing technique, e.g. WHH, EMDR, TIR, meridian therapies like EFT, etc.

Typical Mistake in Technique

- When using tapping, if change hasn't happened after 2 or 3 minutes, stop. This means that there is psychological reversal or the problem is actually a subcellular case.
- Not healing any relevant generational traumas first to reduce resistance to the feelings.
- When using regression, not going to the first trauma event; being out of body while trying to heal; not recognizing multiple roots.

Symptom Frequency & Severity

- Very common; this is in over 70% of client problems. Severity ranges from minor to extreme.
- There are thousands of trauma strings in a typical person.
- The Inner Peace state minimizes trauma access and triggering.

Underlying Cause

- Damaged histone around a heart p-organelle gene.

Risks

- The usual for trauma psychotherapy. Extreme emotions and sensations can be triggered.
- In unusual cases, healing can trigger awareness of a more severe underlying problem.
- In unusual cases, 'trauma flooding' (triggering of issues one after another over long periods of time) can occur.

ICD-10 Codes

- F43, F45, F48.1, F51, F52, F62, F93, F94, R45
- Many others more indirectly.

Body Associations: "Irrational motivations and addictions"

This type of trauma caused Pavlov's dogs to salivate when a bell was rung. It causes one or more sensations or emotions to become coupled together, totally without any logical reason. This becomes the basis of a lot of different types of very strange emotional problems, behaviors, and illnesses. The subcellular mechanism is similar to that of biographical trauma. Genes that were from the prokaryotic cell that later becomes the endoplasmic reticulum (ER) are the basis of the problem. When the ER needs a protein made, an mRNA string is made as a copy of the gene, and released out through the ER. Unfortunately, when the gene's histone covering is damaged, the string gets stuck, and a ribosome then anchors into it on the surface of the membrane. (This is the origin of 'rough ER'.) The association feeling or emotion is inside the stuck ribosome on the surface of the ER. This is bad enough, but it then connects to other ribosomes via connecting mRNA strings. These interconnections form the basis for (the often bizarre and illogical) body associations. The sensations and emotions in the associations can be positive or negative.

    Body associations drive the body brain to act in very odd ways that could make one believe that their body is completely insane. Unfortunately the body does not have judgment (if it is disconnected from the mind brain) so it uses these associations to guide its behavior. This trauma type has a huge impact in ones life – and must be healed to keep the body from trying to act in ways that are harmful for the person.

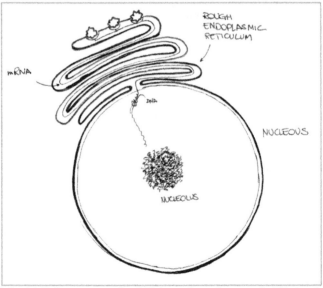

Figure 7.2: (a) Ribosome and mRNA stuck in the rough ER (endoplasmic reticulum).

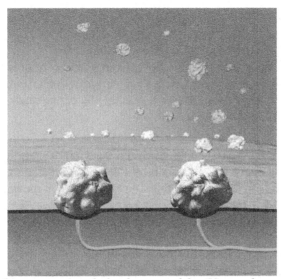

Figure 7.2: (b) A more detailed side view of the ER membrane with mRNA shown.

A key concept involving body associations is that of 'sensate substitutes'. In prenatal trauma, during injury the sensations of the fetal environment (for example, the emotional tone of the surrounding mother) can become associated with the fetus's efforts to survive. After birth, the body will try to find a substitute that feels similar, either inside the primary cell, in the outer world or both. (In this example, the adult becomes sexually attracted to someone who often has the same emotional tone that the mother did.) This principle is also the basis for most addictions. This concept can also be extended to body symptoms – if the body has associated survival with a symptom (for example, deafness) it will find new ways to replace the symptom no matter what you heal – until you eliminate the symptom/survival association, that is.

Symptom Keywords

- Addiction, withdrawal.
- Allergy.
- It doesn't make any sense. Illogical associations.
- Positive associations.
- Sexual feelings.
- I don't get better; trying to heal makes it worse.

Diagnosing Questions

- Is this a repeating pattern in your life?

Differential Diagnosis

- Tribal block: resistance vs. drive (I want to do something but can't versus I don't want to do something but must)
- Positive trauma: test empirically by biographical trauma healing.
- Time loops: does the problem keep coming back after healing the cause? Check for time loops causing exactly the same cause to return, not a new cause with the same symptoms.

Treatment

- Body Association Technique: One or two hands variation. If there is no feeling in the hand, then it is not a body association. A less reliable approach is to send love and joy down the tube in the hand into the body to dissolve the gene histone damage.
- Meridian techniques like EFT will sometimes heal body associations, but this may or may not work in any given client or problem. A technique that explicitly targets this problem (like the Body Association Technique) is usually more useful.

Typical Mistake in Technique

- In the loving version of the technique, a common mistake is to send love into the ribosome (crumpled bag) instead of into the tube in the palm under the ribosome.
- In the tapping version of the technique, a common mistake is not to check the left and right hands separately; or to forget that there can be many associational traumas with the targeted feeling; or do visualizations rather than feel the experience.

Symptom Frequency & Severity

- Very common.
- Potentially very disruptive.

Underlying Cause

- Damaged histone around a body p-organelle gene.

Risks

- The usual for trauma psychotherapy.
- Might lose interest in a person, job or activity that had an association to it.
- In the case of sexual addiction, the client might become upset that their sex drive has changed.

ICD-10 Codes

- F48.1, F63, F93

Generational Trauma: "I am fundamentally, painfully flawed"

Generational traumas are now called 'epigenetic damage' in biology texts. What they don't realize is how these problems can be accessed and healed using what appear to be psychological-like techniques – although are really interventions into the primary cell itself. This type of trauma is caused by the same mechanism that the other trauma types have: a gene (from the prokaryotic cell that later becomes the perineum triune brain) has a damaged histone coating. When the perineum or the third-eye organelle (they are complementary organelles from the egg and sperm respectively) needs a protein, an mRNA copy is made. In the case of trauma, the mRNA gets stuck to the histone. The mRNA string extends outside the nuclear membrane into the cytoplasm and structures that look like pearls attach along its length. These 'pearls' also contain traumatic information; in this case, the image and trauma sensations involving the ancestors of the client that also had the same generational problem. Note that generational traumas are not 'collective' traumas, where large groups of humans through history share a common sensation – instead, they are a common feeling from a series of ancestors.

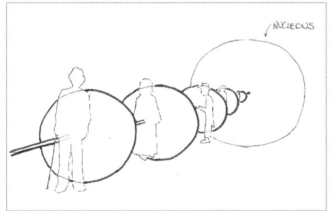

Figure 7.3: (a) The spherical structures on the mRNA contain gateways into generational trauma moments in the past.

Often symptoms in the client are easily tracked to a generational string because the presenting symptom feels the same in the ancestral trauma. Psychologically, generational traumas give painful feelings that feel very personal, as if the person was intrinsically defective. Putting attention on the grandparents' presence in or near the body can easily access this trauma type. From here, the generational trauma string can easily be accessed for healing. Interestingly, these 'grandparents' are actually a class 3 amebic parasite, which is why one can still access their grandparents even when one has never met them.

However, many generational traumas have an indirect effect and there won't be an ancestor who has the presenting symptom. Generational trauma causes defects in the way the primary cell is built. They create 'structural problems' in the primary cell – the damage they cause gives the client feelings and sensations that are different than the feeling of the trauma itself. By analogy, if the roof of your house has a hole in it due to a mistake in the house plans (the generational trauma), your upset about the soggy, moldy mess your furniture becomes after a rain (the symptom) is not the same as your original feeling about the house plan error.

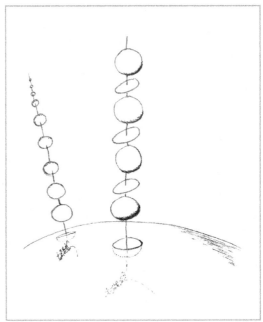

*Figure 7.3: (b) Stuck mRNA strings coming out of the nucleus.
Strings with discs attach to 3rd eye brain genes;
strings without discs attach to perineum brain genes.*

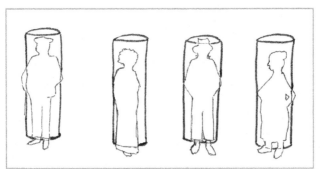

*Figure 7.3: (c) The presences of the four grandparents can be felt outside the
body. These are actually cylindrical structures that are attached to a bacterium
through small tubes.*

Symptom Keywords

- Something's wrong with me; who I am is defective; I'm defective at my core.
- The issue feels very personal; it's about who I am; I've always had this.
- Other family members or ancestors have the same problem.

Diagnosing Questions

- Does it feel personal?
- Is it in your genetically-related extended family (siblings, grandparents, cousins)?

Differential Diagnosis

- Biographical trauma: it is not personal.
- Collective trauma: the client feels the group suffering of people in the past, such as concentration camp survivors, incest survivors, etc. By contrast, generational traumas are individual ancestors who had the same traumatic feelings.
- Copies: does the feeling have a personality of someone else? Is it partially out of your body?
- Column of self: A void in the column causes feelings of dread or annihilation, with rigidly held roles or self-identities as a way to block these feelings. Only the loss of the role(s) triggers these feelings.
- Past life: you can recognize yourself in a past life, but in generational trauma your ancestor(s) don't feel like you.

Treatment

- Generational trauma technique.

Typical Mistake in Technique

- Forget to sense the grandparents' ancestors during the healing process.
- Hanging onto the image of the ancestor when it wants to dissolve.
- Forgot to check all 4 grandparents for similar problems.

Symptom Frequency & Severity

- Very common

Underlying Cause

- Damaged histone around a perineum or third eye p-organelle gene.

Risks

- The usual for trauma psychotherapy.
- Subsurface genes can exist and be activated later (see 'Rule of Three').

ICD-10 Codes

- F43, F44, F48.1, R45

Core (Spinal) Trauma: "This is just the way the world is"

We noticed a number of years ago that there were traumatic sensations and feelings located in the vertebrae of the spine. It turns out that these spinal 'core traumas' as we call them cause a person to have beliefs that define the person's world. These core traumas, although they cause immense problems for people, are seldom worked on in clients because they simply can't feel, see or notice the core belief without unusually difficult efforts. Occasionally a therapist will have to heal one to solve a client's problem; the often emotionally painful results of a core trauma in one's life are much easier to notice than the belief itself. Finding a core trauma belief is not easy with current techniques, but one can be proactive and simply work down the spine, stimulating core traumas by pressure and awareness, healing as one goes.

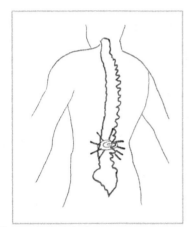

Figure 7.4: (a) A core trauma as experienced is an area of pain in the vertebra.
(b) The corresponding chain connecting the ring to the merkaba
(also a fungal structure) in the nuclear core.

Core traumas don't affect spine alignment. Nor do core traumas cause back pain. To feel pain from a core trauma, you have to put your CoA inside the vertebra.

Biologically, core traumas can be seen as interconnected stuck traumas inside the nucleus. The vertebrae sensations correspond to damage in links in the fungal 'chain' that connects the ring to the merkaba in the nuclear core.

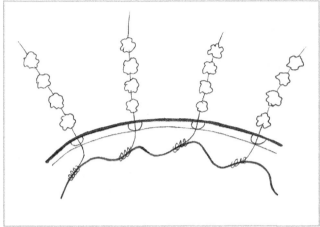

Figure 7.4: (c) A core trauma as seen in the primary cell,
as a chain of connected genes with associated mRNA trauma strings.

Symptom Keywords

- This is just the way it is; this is how it is; I can't do anything about this.
- It is just true; it is just obvious.
- I can't seem to heal this issue.

Diagnosing Questions

- "What would happen if this wasn't true?"
- "Do you have this problem in many aspects of your life (things like I am not good enough, or I am bad)?"

Differential Diagnosis

- Biographical trauma beliefs: unlike biographical trauma, there is no underlying emotional feeling to the core trauma belief. Thus, the core trauma belief is far harder to notice than biographical trauma beliefs.

Treatment

- Core (spine) trauma technique.

Typical Mistake in Technique

- Wasting time with client rationalizations. Move to spine as soon as possible.

Symptom Frequency & Severity

- Core traumas are in virtually everyone, but are very hard to notice. Some people have many core traumas.
- Clients seldom come into therapy for this problem, as these traumas are very hard to be aware of.

Underlying Cause

- Damage to the fungal chain structure in the nuclear core.

Risks

- The usual for trauma psychotherapy.

ICD-10 Codes

- Not yet determined.

Chapter 8

Subcellular Cases – Most Common

Most typical client issues are directly due to trauma, and thus treatment is straightforward, albeit sometimes painful or difficult. However, about 20-30% of the time, the physical or emotional symptoms are a direct experience of present-time primary cell defects, injury or parasite interactions – not a feeling from past trauma. We call these primary cell issues 'subcellular cases'. Diagnostically, if trauma healing does *not* eliminate a symptom, it means you have a subcellular case on your hands.

However, many of the subcellular cases (covered in this and subsequent chapters) are *indirectly* due to trauma. Thus, mastery of various trauma-healing techniques is still necessary for healing many of the subcellular case problems. Additionally, therapists sometimes find that healing a presenting trauma can end up uncovering a subcellular case problem – one that the client may feel is far worse than the original symptom.

In our training classes, the therapist is expected to memorize each of the subcellular cases (and their treatment technique) so that they can do efficient, on-the-fly diagnosis on clients. This manual is intended both as a study aid, and as a desk reference for the various subcellular cases and their subtleties when working with clients. It also has visual images of the subcellular problems to aid in remembering and separating different diagnostic possibilities. Hence, once the type of cellular damage is understood, the therapist can usually spot the feelings and sensations that arise from a given subcellular case's injury or dysfunction. This is similar to medical training where the doctor is expected to diagnose based on their knowledge of various diseases and conditions.

Unfortunately for the casual reader, it is often difficult or impossible to start from a symptom and diagnose using the names of the subcellular cases. In fact, many of our subcellular case names identify the subcellular problem, not the psychological symptom. In addition, since there is a lot of overlap in symptoms, differential diagnosis is often needed. We've found empirically that it is far better to diagnose from an understanding of the nature of the subcellular problems and their resulting psychological manifestation. Chapter 12 also covers a variety of common client issues and their possible causes; some of these can be rather tricky.

Suggested Reading

- For detailed instructions on healing subcellular cases, see *The Basic Whole-Hearted Healing™ Manual* and *The Whole-Hearted Healing™ Workbook*.
- For a detailed discussion on subcellular problems and their causes, *see Peak States of Consciousness*, Volume 3.

Copy: "My feeling is from someone else"

Copies are just that – a copy of someone else's symptoms but retained in one's own body. This problem is experienced in regression as one's heart leaving the body and going into the heart area of another person during the trauma moment. At the subcellular level, a copy looks like a balloon attached to a ribosome in a trauma string. This balloon contains the sensation and the feeling of the personality of the person who was copied. In actuality, the physical copy structures are part of a larger hot-dog shaped bacterial organism in the cytoplasm of the primary cell.

This is a very important subcellular case because it is *the most common reason* why a properly conducted meridian or other trauma therapy has no effect – the feeling is not from a trauma. Copies can carry any possible feeling; and can show up in any client issue, such as addictions, physical problems, etc. However, unlike trauma, a copy has no stuck belief or decision associated with it – it is just an emotion, sensation or a combination of the two.

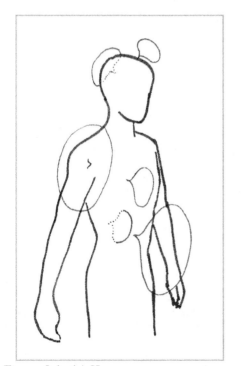 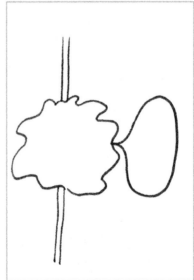

Figure 8.1: (a) How a person experiences copies, as partly in and partly out of their body. (b) A copy looks like a balloon attached to a ribosome biographical trauma.

Figure 8.1: (c) A primary cell image of two copies (a bacterial organism) attached to ribosomes on an mRNA trauma string in the cytoplasm. Note the tubes running to the body (not shown) of the parasite.

Symptom Keywords

- I can't let it go. Tapping does not work.
- "I feel like my ____ [mom, dad, friend]".
- This emotion has personality of someone else, and is half sticking out of your body.
- Can be any feeling from emotionally positive to physical pain.

Diagnosing Questions

- Does the feeling seem to be inside and outside the body, as if in a balloon?
- Does the feeling have someone else's personality (especially if you put your awareness inside the copy structure)?

Differential Diagnosis

- Biographical trauma: copies have no belief or decision; tapping does not work on copies; a copy has the feeling of someone else's personality; the feeling of the copy extends outside the body.
- Generational trauma: copies do not feel personal. They just have a feeling in them.
- Crown brain structure: A structure has a geometric shape, kinesthetically rigid, often causes pain, is almost always all inside the body, and has no feeling of a personality.
- Curse: it has the specific sensation of a nail or arrowhead in the body, along with the feeling of someone else's personality. A curse also has a phrase radiating from it – a copy does not.
- Cord: the feeling is in someone else outside the client's body.

Treatment

- Simplest: send love to the junction between the ribosome and the copy, as if sending solvent to the nozzle of a balloon.
- Harder: regress to moment of trauma and feel your own emotion instead of the other person's. (Eliminating the trauma string is not necessary.)
- Hardest but with the most global effect: eliminate the bacterial copy organisms (there can be several of them). This is a Peak States certified process.

Typical Mistake in Technique

- The client tries to love/feel compassion for the copy [mom, dad, friend] instead of using love like a solvent at the junction between the copy and the ribosome.
- Copies from parents are usually difficult to notice because remnants of the sperm/egg consciousness (which feels like young versions of the parents) are still present in most people. Clients have to be specifically directed to check for this possibility.

Symptom Frequency & Severity

- Very common, especially in therapists and other types of healers (who tend to be empathic).
- Copies remain unless deliberately healed.
- They can have any range of intensity or content.

Underlying Cause

- Copies are part of a larger bacterial parasite.
- They occur when the person sends their 'heart' into the heart of the other person. (This can be for a variety of reasons, such as wanting to help, being lonely, etc.)
- Copies sometimes cover a person (as if surrounded by airbags), because they give the client a feeling of safety or protection.

Risks

- The usual for trauma psychotherapy.
- Some people use copies as a shield, so feelings of being open and vulnerable might be triggered.

ICD-10 Codes

- F45, F93
- Copies can imitate many other codes.

Cords: "I can sense another person's personality or feeling"

The word 'cord' comes from the psychic tradition popularized by the Berkeley Psychic Institute, partly because they can be 'seen' as tubes that connect two people. From an experiential standpoint, one feels another person's emotion at a distance, a feeling usually described as their 'personality'. These feelings can be positive or negative. Cords 'connect' between two people's complementary traumas. There is also a 'trauma phrase' being sent to the other person from each trauma, as if the cord was a telephone made out of tubing. A 'borg' fungus causes this problem.

     This problem often shows up in couples counseling, when one partner does not like the emotional tone they sense in the other partner. Cords can also stimulate behaviors and experiences in the other person by stimulating a trauma in them; for example, inhibit sexual feelings, cause a person to act stupid or clumsy, etc. Treatment can be on a cord-by-cord basis, or removed globally by creating immunity to the fungus.

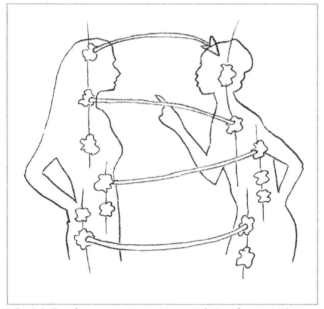

Figure 8.2: (a) Cords connecting two people's ribosome (experiential).

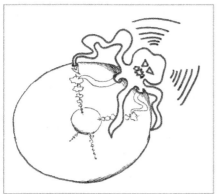

Figure 8.2: (b) Borg fungus connecting to ribosomes in a person's primary cell. (c) Borg fungus in two different people connecting like mobile phones.

Symptom Keywords

- That person feels _____ [emotion or personality tone] to me.
- I act differently when the person's there.
- Issues with my spouse.
- Usually different people feel differently.
- I can't stop thinking about the person after we had an interaction.

Diagnosing Questions

- What does the other person's emotion or personality feel like to you?
- Cords are directional. Some people can feel a tugging sensation when turning around.

Differential Diagnosis

- Projection: a person who is projecting can flip roles (i.e., abuser and abused); one usually projects the same feeling onto several people; and objects can be projected onto. Cords cannot have these qualities. Can't cord with objects, only with people.
- Curses: they are structures attached to the end of a free-floating cord. Curses feel physically painful. Cords do not cause physical pain.
- S-Hole: another person with an s-hole can feel like they are sucking energy from the client; or they can use the feeling of "love" as bait to allow the draining. Cords allow one to sense another's traumatic emotional feeling, which can be anything.
- E-Cord/ E-Hole: the e-cord emotion in the other person has an underlying evil feeling to it (but this is not fully conclusive as this can also occur, rarely, with cords); the location and feeling in the other person is the same as in the client – this is conclusive.

Treatment

- Distant Personality Release (DPR). Note: DPR works on e-cords also. This is the simplest but only works on one cord at a time.

- Silent Mind Technique (SMT). This is a much harder process, but permanently eliminates this problem.
- Heal the trauma being activated at your end. It can be hard to identify the trauma.

Typical Mistake in Technique

- DPR: in step 2, the feeling of love is not unconditional.

Symptom Frequency & Severity

- Very common. Much more common than projection.
- Cords directly stimulate trauma, with a large range of severity/strength.

Underlying Cause

- A cord is a tentacle of a borg fungus that connects to trauma ribosomes in the primary cell. If two people interact who have complementary traumas, their fungi then communicate the emotions and trauma phrases as if the tentacle were some kind of old-fashioned speaking tube. The people involved may or may not want to have a connection in the present; the unconscious drive is to recreate the original trauma moment's multi-person interaction.

Risks

- The usual for trauma psychotherapy.

ICD-10 Codes

- F52

Ribosomal Voices (Obsessive Thoughts, Schizophrenia): "I can't shut up my mind"

This primary cell problem is the dominant cause of ordinary, everyday mind chatter in people. This problem is actually a spectrum disorder; some people have mild symptoms ("thoughts", "mind chatter", "busy mind"), some more severe ("obsessive thoughts"), and some extreme ("hearing voices", channeling, schizophrenia). This problem is the result of an indirect effect of the 'borg' fungus. The fungus can inject a crystalline material into particular ribosomes that are imbedded in the endoplasmic reticulum; these ribosomes then contain entire personalities, as if there were real people trapped in fixed locations in or outside the client's body. The client 'hears' these 'people', giving rise to the experience of thoughts in the mind. The emotional tone of each ribosomal voice is fixed but varies from ribosome to ribosome; they can be negative or positive. A typical person has around 15 or so of these ribosomal voices. Unfortunately, virtually everyone is infected with this parasite – hence, society considers having 'thoughts' to be normal. Most people assume that these thoughts are their own; yet when either these ribosomes or the fungus are eliminated, the client's mind becomes silent, without background thoughts. We call this the 'silent mind' state.

The particular body association ribosomes that can have 'voices' are formed during *in utero* survival trauma. The association links survival with the mother's emotional tone during the event. These associations also cause other odd problems in almost everyone: they are the dominant cause of sexual attractions; and create an unconscious drive to manipulate others so they always have a particular emotional state. For example, this mechanism can trigger a child's temper tantrum as the child desperately tries to re-establish the target feeling (positive or negative) in the parent.

Figure 8.3: (a) Thoughts (or 'voices') experienced in fixed locations in space around the body.

Specialized training is required if the therapist works with psycho-actively medicated clients or clients who are unstable emotionally or mentally. For more detailed information, see our book *Silence the Voices*. Similar 'hearing voices' problems can be caused by other disease mechanisms, but they are far less common.

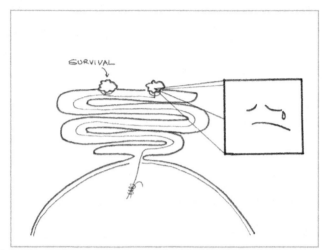

Figure 8.3: (b) A ribosomal voice imbedded in the endoplasmic reticulum.

Symptom Keywords

- "I have ____ [anxious] thoughts"; obsessive thoughts; mind chatter; my mind is racing; I have terrible thoughts.
- Hearing voices; schizophrenia.
- Channeling; demonic possession.
- Obsession, sex addiction, sexual attraction to people.

Diagnosing Questions

- Is your feeling actually from a thought?
- Are you sexually attracted to someone you don't really like?
- Do you have an obsessive thought?
- Does this thought have someone else's voice tone?
- Is the thought located in a fixed location outside your body?
- Does the voice look like a grey or dark cloud outside the body?

Differential Diagnosis

- Sound loops: they are just recorded audio without any emotional feeling.
- S-hole: the obsession is focused on getting love/attention.
- Trauma: Thoughts cause the feeling, not feeling causing the thoughts.
- Class 3 amebic parasite: A simple, repeating obsessive thought or phrase, but duplicated in different spots, and usually inside the body.

- Class 1 bug-like parasite: the voices are not in fixed locations, and they feel more like telepathy.

Treatment

- For an individual voice: use the Body Association Technique targeted on the emotional tone of the voice.
- For global healing: use Silent Mind Technique (SMT) to become immune and so eliminate the fungus.

Typical Mistake in Technique

- Unaware that the client problem is caused by a thought, not by a feeling.
- In serious schizophrenia, the underlying motivation for having voices is loneliness. If you heal one voice, the client will get more voices to compensate. These people need the full Silent Mind Technique process.

Symptom Frequency & Severity

- Almost everybody has this problem, it is only a question of suppression.
- A person in the Beauty Way state has no voices (i.e., no background thoughts).

Underlying Cause

- Caused by a combination of the 'borg' fungus and a particular type of life-threatening prenatal trauma that causes the compulsion to be surrounded by particular emotional tones (sensate substitutes).

Risks

- More than usual for trauma psychotherapy. Global healing (SMT) can cause adjustment problems with partners and children, because the person may now feel more 'distant' and 'unloving' to intimate others. They may need treatment for their feelings; in some cases, they will also require SMT.
- Healing this can trigger extreme loneliness and attempts to compensate for the missing voices.
- Therapists require specialized training to treat unstable or medicated clients; these clients need monitoring during and after treatment, and medical supervision for medication effects and changes.

ICD-10 Codes

- F20, F44.3, R44

Soul Loss: "I miss someone (or some place)"

Our use of the word 'soul loss' comes from the shamanic tradition as popularized by Sandra Ingerman (*Soul Retrieval*) and Michael Harner (*The Way of the Shaman*). It describes the sensation of having a missing piece of consciousness. In regression, an image of oneself moves away from our body when this happens. In the primary cell, this problem can be seen as an absence of cytoplasm around the trauma string containing the moment when the soul loss occurred; or at a more fundamental level, as missing material in the structure that causes the body image. In fact, this problem can be 'seen' in the spaciousness state: a volume of the body is just missing, as if a scoop has been taken out of the flesh.

An awareness of the problem frequently gets triggered when relationships end. The sadness, loneliness or loss is *not* due to triggered trauma or because the partner is absent; instead, these feelings are from putting attention on the missing piece in the primary cell. These feelings are sometimes called 'depression' by clients.

In some extreme cases where there is so much soul loss that most of the body image is gone, the client may say they feel 'emotionally numb' or 'can't feel'. The lack of the usual 'loss' feelings can make this case hard to recognize.

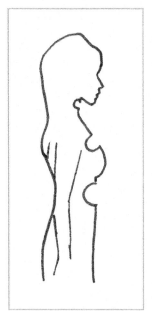 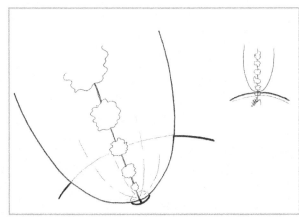

Figure 8.4: (a) Soul loss feels and looks like missing chunks of the body. (b) Soul loss as seen as an empty area along the corresponding biographical trauma string. Left is the cytoplasm view – the right is a cutaway view through the nucleus.

Figure 8.4: (c) A 3D drawing of the primary cell trauma string that has soul loss associated with it.

Symptom Keywords

- Longing, loss, loneliness, missing someone or someplace, sadness.
- Obsession.

Diagnosing Questions

- Do you miss or long for someone specifically, or a place?
- Does it feel like a region of your flesh is missing?
- Do you want something and never get it?

Differential Diagnosis

- Abyss: the client feels to 'move forward in life' is to be annihilated. In soul loss, the client wants to move, act or change the past ("if only…") to feel better.
- Copies: a copy has someone else's personality in it; they feel partly outside of the body (unlike soul loss which is an absence of a 'piece' of body). Tapping and trauma healing techniques don't work on soul loss symptoms or on copies.
- S-hole: they have body locations along the front midline. The client will 'suck' on anyone they can, while the soul loss issue is specific to a person or place.
- Hole: the hole feels distinctly deficient and bottomless, usually with anxiety and attempts to fill it with sensations; while soul loss is only about loss, sadness, and getting something back.
- Biographical or generational trauma: a trauma will heal with tapping or regression; soul loss won't.

- Cords: the client can feel someone else's personality with a cord; with soul loss, there is only the loss feeling.

Treatment

- Generational trauma technique (easier): heal the feeling of the soul loss directly.
- Regression technique (harder): heal the trauma moment of the soul loss – the trauma emotion can be anything except loss. After healing, sing the first tune that pops into mind until symptoms of loss are fully gone.

Typical Mistake in Technique

- Mistakenly assuming the soul loss feeling is the same as the feeling one had when the soul loss occurred.
- Not singing long or loud enough to fully eliminate the feeling of loss during the session.

Symptom Frequency & Severity

- Very common, although usually suppressed.
- Not continuously a problem for most, because they find strategies to avoid the feeling.

Underlying Cause

- Damage to the body image structure by a class 1 bug-like parasite. Usually triggered by refusing to feel/experience a situation to the point of rejecting the pain/emotion.

Risks

- The usual for trauma psychotherapy.

ICD-10 Codes

- F32, F33, F34

Sucking Hole (S-Hole): "I have to be the center of attention"

This problem is due to generational traumas that cause very early developmental event damage. During a fundamental detachment moment, feeding tubes to the fungal 'column of self' don't detach correctly. This leaves holes in the front axis of the body that never heal; the client feels it as a constantly sucking hole in the body that they feel they have to keep trying to fill. This event also damages the network of tubes that make up the past life oversoul network. Clients typically either try to live with the terrible feeling of endless need in their body; find other people who feel 'loving', so they can 'feed' on their energy via a class 3 bacterial parasite in the s-hole (the loving person also has the s-hole problem); or cover the s-hole with a class 1 bug parasite which links to another person who they can 'feed' from. This problem is the root cause for most people's need for constant attention and endless need to hear that they are special and unique.

This problem is *very* common among the psychotherapy client population. These people tend to have 'tried everything' and nothing has worked; they usually blame the therapist for failing. Some are aware of the problem; others come in if their coping strategies fail. People with this problem often cause organizational and training drama: they will try to disrupt the organization so they can become the leader or center of attention.

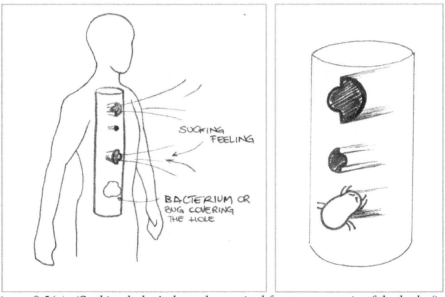

Figure 8.5(a): 'Sucking holes' along the vertical front center axis of the body (in the 'column of self'). (b) A close-up of the column. Note the left and right sides of the hole is different. The bottom hole is covered by a parasite that 'feeds' the sucking hole.

Symptom Keywords

- Crave attention/love, addicted to love, want love, take things personally, needy, insatiable, desperation, anxious if alone, feel deeply flawed, it's their fault my needs not met, energy vampire, sucking my energy.
- Healing does not work, nothing works on me, I never feel better, I can't heal.
- Need for recognition; I betray people that trust me; I disrupt the organization I'm in.
- Strange irrational (uncontrollable) behavior: I do crazy things to get what I need (love, attention) in the moment; I reject people that don't love me all the time.
- Borderline personality disorder: excessive worrying, self-importance, self-centeredness.

Diagnosing Questions

- Do you have a sucking sensation at places along your central axis of body assuming symptoms are present? Is there a gaping hole that sucks?

Differential Diagnosis

- Hole: a hole has no sucking sensation.
- Generational trauma: you can't tap s-holes away; generational traumas cause one to avoid human interactions, while S-hole clients need interaction.
- Soul loss: the feeling of loss or need is specific to just one person.
- Core trauma: they both cause problems in many situations, but core traumas have no emotional content or body sensations.

Treatment

- This is currently a licensed Peak States certified therapist technique.

Typical Mistake in Technique

- An s-hole that is covered by a parasite is not felt by the client, so is not found and healed. The trick is to feel 'underneath' the parasite at the surface of the skin to find the empty s-hole.

Symptom Frequency & Severity

- Very common in clients (~70%).
- These people are often found in dysfunctional organizations; they also generally find work where they can be the center of attention (e.g., actors, teachers, politicians, managers, spiritual teachers or gurus, etc.)

Underlying Cause

- Damage to areas in the vertical midline of the body, where tubes ripped out of the 'column of self 'structure at its origin, leaving holes.

Risks

- The usual for trauma psychotherapy.

ICD-10 Codes

- F24, F60.3, F60.4, F94.2

Tribal Block: "I do what my family and culture expect"

The tribal block is one of the most serious problems humanity has. It is caused by a fungal organism (we call it the 'borg' fungus) that can influence, and in some people completely control people's actions. Our species has adapted to this problem – it is what causes different cultures around the world. This is what gives a person the 'rules' of a culture.

  The fungus pushes people to obey restrictions, be they cultural or from one's family group. High-functioning clients particularly notice this influence, when they want to move forward in new ways in their life, and can feel that they are somehow being blocked. It also shows up in people who are trying to either be or are becoming bi-cultural.

Figure 8.6: (a) The borg fungus acts like a group of people telling the client what to do.

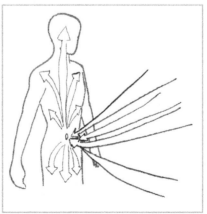

(b) The borg fungus controlling the client by sending emotions into their navel.

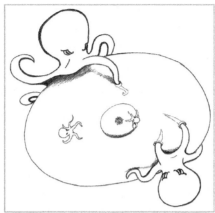

Figure 8.6: (c) The borg fungus, which looks similar to an octopus, penetrating the primary cell membrane. They have a range of sizes and live both inside and outside the cell.

Symptom Keywords

- Feel strong resistance, or feel heavy (like carrying a backpack) when want to change for the better (e.g.: I want to change/ grow/ feel better/ be happier/ be more positive, but can't.)
- Giving in to the tribal block makes the person unenthusiastic or emotionally flat about their past desire.
- Causes multi-cultural issues (location, culture, conflicts).
- Any phrase that has the word 'burden' in it, such as "I carry a burden on my shoulders".

Diagnosing Questions

- Tribal block issues are the most likely cause of a high-functioning client's problem.
- Do you feel like you can't move forward in your life? Does it make you feel heavy?
- Are you trying to make a positive change in your life?
- Did you start a new project but find it very hard to continue?
- Is the problem to do with your old or your new culture? Did you recently move to a new country/ culture?
- When you think about the issue, can you feel emotions coming at you from outside the navel?

Differential Diagnosis

- Abyss: to 'move forward in life' brings up feelings of annihilation; the tribal block makes a person feel heavy or feel like people are blocking or resisting their desires. The abyss experience is far less common.
- Biographical trauma: unlike trauma, the tribal block feelings are externally imposed in the present; people who resist the tribal block

influence feel heavy, while resisting traumas strengthens their emotional symptoms; you can have many traumas around an issue; the tribal block's pressure goes completely away if you stop wanting to change.

- Generational trauma: a generational trauma makes you feel personally flawed while the tribal block does not.
- Body association: if the feeling can be found in the hand, it is a body association.
- Flattened emotions: the range of all feeling is reduced. Tribal block can make the person heavy if they resist it; and emotionally flat and calm if they don't, but only around the particular issue.

Treatment

- For a specific issue, use the Tribal Block Technique.
- For a global solution, use the Silent Mind Technique (SMT) to eliminate the borg fungus.
- When this is healed the heaviness lifts, leaving a feeling of lightness; and the feeling of an obstruction to moving forward is gone.

Typical Mistake in Technique

- Not focusing on the emotion coming in the navel, but instead your response to it.
- Blanking out the emotion coming at you. (The visuals are not important, but can be useful as a guide to the presence of emotions.)
- The client moves from issue to issue without realizing it, so that the session never ends.
- Sending the CoA out the navel can cause serious problems (dehumanization, etc.) in some people.

Symptom Frequency & Severity

- Almost everyone has this problem; only a few people try to resist and so notice symptoms.
- Causes cultural group conflicts.

Underlying Cause

- A species of fungal infection affecting the primary cell.
- A more serious form of the infection occurs when the client's awareness surrenders itself into the borg fungus, and gives up self to feel power/powerful.

Risks

- The usual for trauma psychotherapy.
- Extreme emotional reactions to feelings coming into the navel during treatment.
- Nausea and other unpleasant physical sensations during treatment.

ICD-10 Codes

- F43.2

Chapter 9

Subcellular Cases – Less Common

Although these subcellular cases exist in most people, clients don't usually come in for these problems because most people have unconscious, compensating strategies that adequately block their awareness of them. Thus, the therapist should keep these problems in the back of their mind, but not try and see them in every client who walks through the door. Some of these cases are pretty unusual – people who have them have often been searching a long time for healing on their particular problem. They often mistakenly explain their symptom with conventional ideas (for their social group): "it is a medical problem", "aliens did it to me", "it is an imbalance in my chi", and so on.

Bacterial Parasite Problems (Class 3): "I feel toxic, tired and numb"

In this subcellular case description we will cover the more general bacterial symptoms. (Other bacterial cases in this handbook are from specific species: they cause the phenomena of copies, sound loops, e-holes, trauma bypasses, and the presence of grandparents near the body.) We suggest that therapists learn the general bacterial subcellular case by visualizing a bacterial cell inside the primary cell, and then thinking about the problems it can cause rather than just trying to memorize a list of symptoms.

Virtually everyone has some degree of bacterial parasite problems in the primary cell. For most people there are no obvious symptoms, as they have learned to avoid any activities that stimulate bacterial responses. However, in some cases the client has either had something trigger this problem, or it was already a chronic issue.

Although most bacteria are rather usually soft, balloon-like and transparent, some have a more solid surface, like that of a slug or worm; and some have filaments they can insert into the client's primary cell structures. If the client is sensing a bacterium or a region with bacteria in it (they can be experienced inside or outside the body), the primary symptom is usually toxicity. (Note that the sensation from bacteria is toxicity or poisoning, in contrast to the sensation from fungus of nausea). Other symptoms can include fear, sensations of evil, or sensations of boundaries or blockages. There can also be sensations of pressure that can range from mild to extreme pain due to a bacterium pushing against a cellular membrane. Clients who have put their CoA inside, or partly inside a bacterial cell usually come in with problems involving tiredness and physical and emotional numbness, although from the clinicians viewpoint they usually also exhibit paranoia and/or unusual levels of negativity .

There is another set of disturbing bacterial parasite problems involving interpersonal issues. Some people, usually as an unconscious defensive reaction, project their awareness into one of the client's bacterial cells in order to 'attach' themselves to the client. This gives the sensation to the client that the other person is uncomfortably 'in my space', with the sensation being attacked or threatened (due to filaments inserted into the client's 'body'). This causes reactions that range from anxiety/fear to annoyance/anger. Another strange interpersonal bacterial parasite problem: in most people there are large clusters of transparent bacteria at the inner cell membrane. Some people have a negative emotional imprint in these organisms (giving them a darker color), and this can be sensed by others as if there were a negative 'aura' extending out quite a distance around the person. Worse, if someone extends their CoA towards this person, they may accidentally duplicate the sensation into their own cytoplasm bacteria. This mechanism is similar to the copies case, but more generalized and not just during moments of trauma.

Yet another, fortunately less common bacterial problem can exist. Some people have bacterial cells that contain the awareness of extremely evil-feeling ancestors. They are not ancestors from a generational string trauma moment, but rather living and active in the present inside the primary cell in the present. Worse, in some people these bacterial cells can temporarily 'take over' the client. Since this problem started prenatally, the client experiences the switch to a negative state as normal. In a milder version, an emotionally negative bacterium can 'push' into the client's body, stimulating a series of very negative feelings and thoughts (even in clients who no longer have fungal ribosomal voices). Incidentally, there is a direct correlation between a person's negativity (or inner evil), the magnitude of the bacterial infection in their primary cell, and their need to survive at any cost.

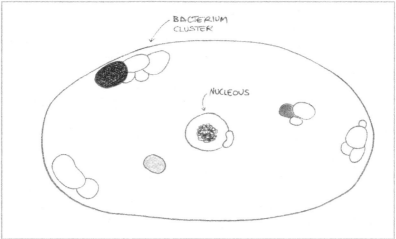

Figure 9.1: Bacterial parasites in the cytoplasm of the primary cell. There are bacterial clusters commonly found at the interior surface of the cell membrane.

Symptom Keywords

- I can't feel anything.
- Blob, ancient, gooey, gelatinous.
- Poison, toxic, tired, exhausted, numb, flue.
- Evil, negative, eats good feelings.

Diagnosing Questions

- Does it feel like you are being hurt in the present in that location?
- Does the sensation feel like it comes from a blob pushing on you?
- Are you feeling like you want to reject or push someone away, as if they had stuck filaments into your body?
- Do you sense a gelatinous mass, or something that feels toxic?
- Can you briefly move your awareness out of the numb feeling?
- Does the problem feel like it has a life of its own, or feels like someone else?

Differential Diagnosis

- Trauma memory: with both, symptoms can come and go; but the bacterium sensation is in the present, not the past; focusing on the symptom in the present can make it worse.
- Blanket curse: DPR works on this; the blanket curse has the sense of someone else's personality; the blanket curse makes one feel tired under it. The bacterium is usually without personality and DPR won't affect it. Use the different treatments as a test.
- Crown brain structure: a structure doesn't move around; the structure feels mechanical, not soft and organic.
- Borg toxic 'spray': activated by another person who hates you, or who doesn't want you to see the truth; the spray feels acidic, and makes you tired if continued long enough. All fungus and fungal sprays makes a person feel nauseated; by contrast, the bacterium emits toxins that make you feel poisoned.
- Class 1 bug: the bug is hard and can rip, tear, or burn the client. Bacteria generally stay near the same location, and don't tear or rip, and have a softer exterior. Both can send extensions into the person, but the bug's is solid, like a hard tube, while the bacterium's is more like softer filaments.
- Chakra: the chakra fungal organism can respond to attention by stimulating the sensation of (often painful) pressure in any or all of the classical chakra locations (forehead, heart, etc). Bacterium pressure locations are located in any place in the body, although the upper forehead is very common.
- Copy: a copy can give nearly any feeling or sensation, but it has the personality of the person copied and is partly outside the body.

Treatment

- Start by eliminating any body associations on the sensations of the bacterium's body, and any emotional content.
- Eliminate generational traumas on those physical bacterium sensations (not on emotional content).
- Regress to the moment when the bacterium was acquired, and heal the event trauma (especially the generational) until it does not enter the organism. (Caution – this can also involve bug damage).
- For a bacterium causing emotional numbness, use a modified version of the Courteau Projection Technique on the feeling of 'comfort'. This triggers the traumas that caused the client to pull the bacterium to them. Focus on the negative reactions to the projection and heal those. This causes the bacterium to dissolve and restores the ability to feel.

Typical Mistake in Technique

- Trying to heal the symptoms the bacterium causes, rather than the sense of the bacterium's body itself.

Underlying Cause

- The symptoms are caused by parasitic bacteria in the primary cell. They can cause feelings of pressure, sensations of being inside a glass box, or emit toxins that cause nausea.

Symptom Frequency & Severity

- Roughly 1% to 10% of clients have symptoms (triggered by psychotherapy, spiritual practices, or life circumstances) that range from mild to excruciatingly painful and completely debilitating.
- Symptom duration can be short, intermittent or long term.

Risks

- Can vary from none to life-threatening. Should only be worked on by trained professionals.

DANGER

This subcellular case is potentially dangerous and even life-threatening to the client if the problem is severe. Problems can include severe numbness, toxicity, electric shock, and heart failure. Only therapists with training and backup should attempt to work with this case.

DANGER

Do not attempt to kill primary cell parasites, nor allow your client to experiment in doing so. If successful, the body will compensate by getting more parasites, making the symptoms worse or more dangerous.

ICD-10 Codes

- Not yet determined.

✓ Bug-like Parasite Problems (Class 1): "I have a burning, ripping, or stabbing sensation"

We had seen these problems of pain in our students, clients, and in clients who had uses other therapies. Symptoms can be brief, sometimes intermittent, and sometimes continuous for years. This problem is caused by class 1 parasites (that look like bugs) in the primary cell. We tell our therapists *not* to explain this issue to clients because it can stimulate the problem if the client focuses on it. In extreme cases, this can be life threatening. This problem is extremely dangerous to research – only use the techniques that we've specified are safe to use. We've had clients who try to kill these bug-like parasites through will, and because they don't understand that their primary cell is in equilibrium with the problem, they can make things far worse as the organisms increase in number to compensate, and respond aggressively.

Figure 9.2: (a) Bug secreting a caustic, burning substance onto the membrane.

Figure 9.2: (b) Bug ripping the membrane.

Figure 9.2: (c) Bug burrowing into the membrane.
(d) Bug walking on and penetrating the membrane.

Symptom Keywords

- Burning, ripping, stabbing, crawling, something is moving on my body.

Diagnosing Questions

- Does it feel like you are being hurt in the present in that location?
- Does the location of the pain move around?
- Does it feel like it has a life of its own?

Differential Diagnosis

- All other subcellular cases: the pain(s) doesn't move around, while bug-like parasite caused pains might.
- Trauma memory: with both, symptoms can come and go; but the bug sensation is in the present, (although sometimes activated by attempting to regress or heal in other ways); bug pain is more severe than a memory and has a different quality; focusing on the symptom in the present can make it worse.
- Curse: DPR doesn't work on bugs; generational healing does not work on curses, so use the different treatments as a test. The curse sensation is continuous, in contrast to bugs that can move or stop injuring the client.
- Crown brain structure: a structure doesn't move around; there is no feeling of a structure; there is no emotion in a structure; focus on the symptom doesn't change it.
- Copy: copy sensation is steady; a copy has a personality feeling; a copy is half-in half-out, like a balloon. The bug is either on, above, or in the surface of the body and causing pain there.
- Class 2 fungal borg toxic 'spray': it is caused by another person (who hates you, who doesn't want you to see the truth); the spray is caustic and makes you tired and irritable if continued long enough.

Treatment

- Identify the fixed emotion the bug is using as a 'disguise'; eliminate the corresponding body association; and then eliminate the generational string that feels exactly the same. Most bugs only use one emotion; very large bugs have up to three emotions.

Typical Mistake in Technique

- Don't explain the source of the problem to clients – this can evoke more serious symptoms or cause the client to start experimenting on the problem.
- Not doing the body associations first.
- Losing the sensation of the problem, so stopping before the healing is finished.
- Not having more skilled backup available in case of problems.

Underlying Cause

- Parasitic organisms in the primary cell that damage membranes or excrete acidic toxins cause the symptoms.

Symptom Frequency & Severity

- Roughly 1% to 10% of clients have symptoms (triggered by psychotherapy, spiritual practices, or life circumstances) that range from mild to excruciatingly painful and completely debilitating.
- Symptom duration can be short, intermittent or long term.

Risks

- Can vary from none to life-threatening. Should only be worked on by trained professionals.

DANGER

This subcellular case is potentially dangerous and even life-threatening to the client if the problem is severe. Only therapists with training and backup should attempt to work with this case.

DANGER

Do not attempt to kill primary cell parasites, nor allow your client to experiment in doing so. If successful, the body will compensate by getting more parasites, making the symptoms worse or more dangerous.

ICD-10 Codes

- F45, R20.2, R52

Column of Self – Void: "I feel terrible since I lost my role as _____"

In almost everyone, the triune brains have *self-identities*; they pretend to be someone or something – they act like five year olds pretending to be firemen. This isn't normally a serious problem, albeit a bit like having a child who won't take off his fireman hat. But, it becomes a major problem *if* the person also has a missing region (a 'void') in the center axis of what we call the 'column of self'. Becoming aware of the missing region causes the symptoms – people with this void feel like they will be annihilated if they move their CoA fully into their body along the central axis. These people normally keep their 'center of awareness' (CoA) away from their core by staying in a triune brain awareness; the client thus becomes identified with its 'pretend' identity. When outer circumstances remove their role in life, their CoA involuntarily moves towards their core, and feelings of dread and annihilation arise.

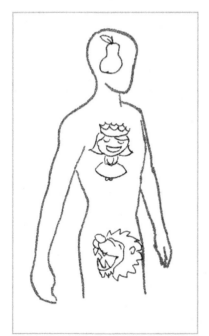 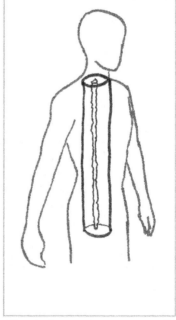

Figure 9.3: (a) The triune brains pretending to be someone or something. (b) 'Column of self' (fungal) structure superimposed on body image. This one is shown with damage of a void in the center axis that can cause symptoms of dread when a client tries to feel their center.

Typically, clients do not feel symptoms as long as they hang onto their role (although this can also cause problems due to their desperation around keeping it, or around needing a dysfunctional role). Instead, they show up for therapy after the role loss because they just are not able to cope. This problem can also be triggered by meditation or other spiritual practices that cause the client to move their CoA into the central region of their body. This is a good example of a serious emotional problem that is directly due to a structural damage in the primary cell. Thus, trauma-healing techniques won't work on the presenting symptoms.

The column of self is a very common class 2 fungal structure – people identify with it as if it were part of their own body. It is usually felt from the perineum to the throat.

Symptom Keywords

- "If I can't be a [role: doctor, mother, etc.], I'm a wreck." "I just can't cope with losing my job/ role." "Now that the children have left, I feel terrible all the time." "Since I was fired, I am so depressed that I can't function."
- "I'll do anything to be a [role: doctor, mother, etc.], otherwise I feel terrible dread, annihilated, killed, fear.

Diagnosing Questions

- Did you recently lose your job (or role in life)? (Note: the person sometimes has another identity as a backup.)
- If you gently move your awareness into the center axis of your body, how do you feel? Do you feel dread?

Differential Diagnosis

- Biographical trauma: trauma that creates a self-image ("I'm a nice guy; I'm a dominant male.) The emotional feeling driving this responds to trauma healing. Moving the CoA into the central column of the body will not cause feelings of dread or annihilation to suddenly appear.
- Generational trauma: the loss of the role could feel very personally painful, with feelings of being flawed or defective; but not cause sensations of dread or annihilation. Self-identities feel good by contrast.
- S-Hole: they can switch strategy easily in order to get 'fed' ("I'm willing to do anything to get your love.")
- Tribal block: trying to get a new role can trigger the tribal block, making a person feel heavy or resisted by circumstances and people; but does not cause extreme symptoms from the loss of their role.

Treatment

- This is currently a licensed Peak States certified therapist process.

Typical Mistake in Technique

- Misdiagnosis because the client avoids moving their awareness into their core.
- Over-emphasizing the benefits of healing when symptoms are not present.

Underlying Cause

- The need for a self-identity is a way to avoid feeling the symptoms of a void in the 'column of self'.

Symptom Frequency & Severity

- Almost everyone has triune brains with self-identities. This is usually not a problem.
- About a third of the population have a significant degree of this problem, but suppress reasonably well (it is more common in the client population.) The degree of damage to the structure also varies considerably. Clients rarely come in unless their roles in life are blocked or lost.

Risks

- The usual for trauma psychotherapy.

ICD-10 Codes

- F43.2

Crown Brain Structure: "I have a chronic pain there"

This interesting subcellular case clearly demonstrates the physical and emotional consequences of inappropriate 'helpfulness' by the crown triune brain. Its task is to maintain the primary cell membrane integrity and shape; but it can inappropriately create structures inside the cell. These structures feel like they are inside the body, or anchor different parts of the body together. They generally cause pain or other sensations. These structures are often created during moments of physical injury to the body. These structures 'look' and feel mechanical, not organic. In our experience, people who believe they have 'alien implants' in their body are actually describing these structures.

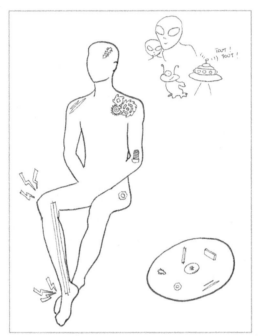

Figure 9.4: Crown brain structure giving the sensation of a geometric, manufactured structure in the body. Upper right: sometimes called 'alien implants' by clients. Lower right: structures are actually inside the cell.

Symptom Keywords

- Pain; pain when I move; the pain comes and goes; the sensation is chronic and in the same location.
- I 'see' (or feel) a mechanical, angular or geometric structure in my body.
- Alien implant.
- Traumatic injury that still has pain or stiffness.

Diagnosing Questions

- Do you see (or feel) some kind of rigid, geometrically shaped structure in your body?
- Is there something enclosing (or connecting) two parts of your body together?
- Is there chronic pain in a fixed location in your body?
- Did you have a traumatic injury that isn't healing and still has pain or stiffness?

Differential Diagnosis

- Curse: the curse structure has personality in it, and the pain feels like from a nail or spearhead.
- Copies: a copy has personality in it; located partly inside and partly outside the body, and shaped like a balloon.
- Biographical trauma: the trauma shape is irregular or in the whole body. Tapping doesn't work on a crown structure. A crown structure just hurts; there is no corresponding belief as with a trauma.
- Time loop: a time loop is shaped and feels like an eggshell and encloses a number of traumas; in regression, one finds oneself caught in a 'loop' of repeating time.

Treatment

- Temporary: gratitude to the crown brain for creating the structure (can also be used for diagnosis).
- Permanent: regress to the creating trauma, and heal the need for the structure.

Typical Mistake in Technique

- Not verifying that the structure is permanently gone.

Underlying Cause

- The crown brain creates and maintains the structural support shaping the primary cell outer membrane. It mistakenly tries to repair or support a broken part of the physical body by building a structure inside the cell.

Symptom Frequency & Severity

- Most people have these structures, but in locations that seldom cause difficulties or pain.
- Most psychotherapy clients don't come in for this problem.

Risks

- The usual for trauma psychotherapy.

ICD-10 Codes

- R52.

✓ Curse: "That person really hates me"

Surprisingly, the fairy-tale idea that someone can 'curse' another actually has a basis in subcellular biology – they occur when someone wants to harm or inhibit another and unknowingly trigger the borg fungus to do it. The fungus in the victim extrudes a sharp-edged, black, obsidian-like object (the physical container of the 'curse') at the end of a tentacle in the cytoplasm. This will often cause a physical pain (but not always, as the sensation can be repressed), like a nail, knife or arrowhead is imbedded in the body in the area that corresponds to the location of the curse in the cytoplasm. If one's CoA is moved into the curse object, one can feel the 'attacking' person's personality in it, along with a phrase that repeats over and over. Many people unconsciously attempt to obey the curse phrase, and so create various problems in themselves. Like a cord, it 'connects' to a trauma in the attacking person. Unlike a cord, the client can be harmed without any conscious or unconscious participation.

Although this problem is common, the symptoms of a 'curse' are either mild or temporary enough that treatment isn't needed; however, in some cases, a curse causes very serious, long-term physical and emotional symptoms. These symptoms can cause the client to seek medical attention for the physical or mental problems they have induced. A single curse can be removed relatively quickly. However, the best long-term strategy is to have immunity to the borg fungus, as this permanently eliminates this problem.

We also identify a second type of curse: it feels like a blanket that covers part (or all) of the body, and causes extreme tiredness in that area. The symptom is due to a covering on part of the nuclear membrane. It also has the personality of the 'attacking' person in it, and is tied to the borg through a tentacle.

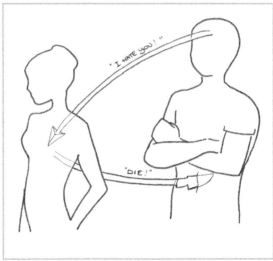

Figure 9.5: (a) An obsidian arrowhead-like curse between two people.

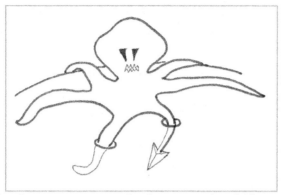

Figure 9.5: (b) A borg inserting an obsidian, arrowhead-like structure into the cytoplasm.

Symptom Keywords

- Arrow type: stabbing pain; can't find the cause of a mental or physical problem; feel disabled; I feel their anger, hatred, or repression towards me.
- Blanket type: part or all of the body feels tired, heavy, wrapped in a blanket, covered, exhausted.

Diagnosing Questions

- Was someone very angry with you when the problem first started?
- Does it feel like a nail or arrowhead is in your body?
- Are you tired only in some areas of your body?

Differential Diagnosis

- Tribal block: it makes you feel heavy; the blanket curse makes you feel tired in the areas it covers.
- Copies: although copies can cause pain, they don't cause the feeling of a nail in the body.
- Crown brain structure: you can have pain from a structure, but it has no personality to it.
- Blocked nuclear pores: level of tiredness varies, and it is a full body experience; while a blanket curse makes you tired all the time in areas of the body.

Treatment

- One curse: use Distant Personality Release (DPR).
- All curses, and to make one immune to the problem: use the Silent Mind Technique (SMT).

Typical Mistake in Technique

- DPR: not being able to fully feel unconditional love for the negative feeling in the 'attacking' person.

Underlying Cause

- Caused by a person who wants to harm, block or inhibit you and does so via the borg fungus.

Symptom Frequency & Severity

- Common in people. Rarely severe or long-term; but if it is, it requires treatment.

Risks

- The usual for trauma psychotherapy.
- Some 'attackers' send many curses – SMT would be a better choice in this case.

ICD-10 Codes

- F45.4, F45.9

Dilemmas: "Which should I choose?"

This problem occurs for most people at one time or another. Only rarely is it severe enough that clients want to pay for treatment. The sensation is quite distinct: the person feels pulled in one direction, then in another, back and forth. No decision can be made without being pulled back to the other choice(s). This problem is due to an unusual configuration of several stuck biographical trauma strings in the primary cell. In this subcellular case, two (or more) strings all join inside a given ribosome.

Figure 9.6: (a) A dilemma has the sensation of being pulled in two directions at once.

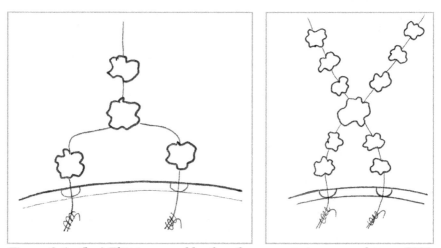

Figure 9.6: (b,c) This is caused by the ribosomes trying to read two mRNA strings in different directions at the same time.

Symptom Keywords

- Dilemmas; can't decide or make up my mind; two opposing thoughts or views are true.
- Being pulled in different directions (by an issue or decision).

Diagnosing Questions

- Does it feel physically like you are being pulled in different directions?

Differential Diagnosis

- Tribal block: The tribal block also has a polarity, but it is between your desired objective (with a heavy feeling in the body) versus not doing it (which feels far easier).
- Guarding trauma: there is no pull between polarities.
- Projection: although roles can flip in a projection, the person is not pulled back and forth continuously.
- Mind brain shutdown: the dilemma is only on a specific issue; the shutdown inhibits all judgments.

Treatment

- Heal each part of the dilemma separately using any trauma healing technique.

Typical Mistake in Technique

- Getting distracted by the other choice and not getting the healing finished on the leg of the dilemma.

Underlying Cause

- An unusual configuration of biographical trauma strings.

Symptom Frequency & Severity

- This is a common problem, but clients rarely come to a therapist for it.

Risks

- The usual for trauma psychotherapy.

ICD-10 Codes

- Not yet determined.

Hole (Emptiness): "I am anxious in this spot"

Holes are experienced as bottomless holes in the body that feel horribly empty and deficient. They typically 'look' black inside, with raised, hard rims around an opening in the skin (although they can also be completely enclosed inside the body). Partially healed holes are grey inside, and don't feel bottomless. Holes are almost always blocked from awareness by various trauma-driven strategies that mask the hole sensation (such as muscular contraction or emotions at the area of the hole). Thus, holes can be accidentally exposed by trauma healing processes, or by meditation that increases awareness in a person. Holes are caused by physical injury to the body; large holes are almost always formed during pre- or perinatal damage. In the primary cell, trauma strings that include moments where a hole formed have stuck genes that feel dead.

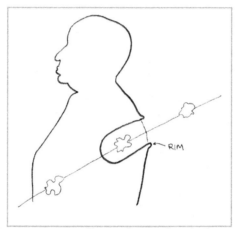

*Figure 9.7: Experientially is a bottomless hole in the body.
A biographical trauma is superimposed midway into the hole location.*

Symptom Keywords

- Anxiety (or fear); deficient emptiness; bottomless hole or dark empty spot in the body.
- Muscular tension.
- Feeling of not being present (here) in the world.
- Spiritual emergency (the client was doing meditation or related practices like yoga or tantra that caused the hole to come to awareness).
- Obsession (rare).

Diagnosing Questions

- Where is your anxiety in your body?
- Is there a physical distortion in your body (a depression or built up area)?

Differential Diagnosis

- Crown brain structure: they have no emotion, sensations or trauma images inside them.
- S-hole: they are always along the midline of the body front; they have a sucking feeling in them; they cause 'wanting attention' behaviors.
- Biographical trauma: the sensation of deficient emptiness is not found in traumas; tapping or other trauma techniques will heal it.
- Copies: check for personality in the copy; and if they are both inside and outside of body, as in a balloon.
- Ribosomal voices: the voice can be anxious. Holes have no voice.
- Column of self: annihilation is in the vertical core of body. This feels different than the deficiency of a hole.

Treatment

- Optionally, eliminate the feeling of deficient emptiness with generational healing. This makes the remaining hole sensations far easier to face.
- Choice 1: Go inside the hole to the midway point, and then heal the trauma image/moment there.
- Choice 2: Go inside the hole, and then accept the injury pain at the bottom layer. (The hole feels bottomless, but does in fact have a bottom that can be reached using some determination.)

Typical Mistake in Technique

- Client says nothing is happening, but they need to go deeper into hole or stay longer.
- There can be multiple, overlapping holes that need to be treated individually.
- Client only partially heals the hole (leaving it grey, or leaving a surface rim).

Underlying Cause

- Caused by severe physical injury to a particular spot in the body.

Symptom Frequency & Severity

- Common but suppressed, compensated by other means (muscular tension).

Risks

- The usual for trauma psychotherapy.

ICD-10 Codes

- This case may show in different F40-F48 codes, and others.

Past Lives: "There was an instant recognition"

To our surprise, past life traumas do exist. They are due to a damaged 'oversoul' network on the inside of the primary cell membrane. The past life network on the cell membrane is a fungal organism. If a node in the network leaks, this creates a structure in the cytoplasm that attaches to a stuck mRNA trauma string, giving the experience of a past life trauma. Hence, there are three obvious ways to heal this problem: treat the individual trauma; repair the damaged and leaking past life network; or eliminate the past life fungal organism.

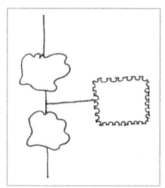

Figure 9.8: (a) A past life gateway structure attached to an mRNA trauma string.

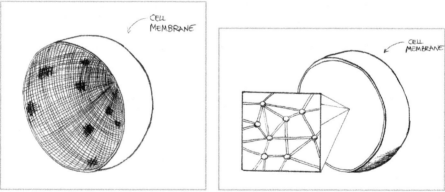

Figure 9.8: (b) The oversoul network on the inner surface of the cell membrane. (c) A close-up of nodes that correspond to individual past lives.

Symptom Keywords

• Past life; reincarnation; karma; spiritual emergency; conflict with religious belief; like I always knew that person.

Diagnosing Questions

- Does this problem or feeling trigger an image or sensation of people or places you don't recognize from your life?
- Does this problem involve people who it seems like you knew or somehow recognized from the first moment you met?

Differential Diagnosis

- Generational trauma: your ancestors are not you; you recognize yourself and other people in past life memories even if they have different bodies.
- Biographical trauma: a fake past life has grandiosity or similar types of delusional feelings driving it.
- Copy: the client senses the personality imbedded in a copy and confuses it with a past life. Copies are partly inside and outside the body, past lives are experienced via a gateway into the past.

Treatment

- Use WHH on the past life.
- Heal the damaged oversoul network using generational trauma – this is currently a licensed Peak States certified therapist process.
- Eliminate the fungal past life network.

Typical Mistake in Technique

- Judging the past life event, rather than accepting what was occurring (including death and injury).
- Moving to different events in the past life, rather than just healing the original past life trauma moment.

Underlying Cause

- Damaged oversoul network on the interior side of the primary cell membrane.

Symptom Frequency & Severity

- Not common; however, people with this problem often have many past life traumas.

Risks

- The usual for trauma psychotherapy.

ICD-10 Codes

- Not yet determined.

Peak State Bugs: "I abruptly lost my peak state and it never came back"

This tragic problem affects people with stable peak states, whether new or lifelong. During an emotionally charged encounter with someone, they suddenly lose their state, and worse, it never comes back. We called this problem 'veiled peak states' in Volume 2 of *Peak States of Consciousness*.

This problem can occur when someone notices that the client has a positive peak state (such as love, happiness, joy, and so on); this unconsciously triggers their feelings of lack and desperation about not having the state. To outside observers and to the client, that person becomes emotionally upset for no apparent reason, especially since the client is in a very positive mood. As the scenario plays out, the client's positive state is suddenly lost, and at that moment the other person usually abruptly becomes calm. The client never regains that particular positive feeling. Tragically, the loss occurs because the client attempted to help the other person by trying to share their positive state.

It turns out that the key to this problem is a bug-type parasite species that lives in both the person and the client's nuclear core. The emotionally distraught person extends their awareness through their parasite into the client's parasite (like using a waldo in a nuclear power plant) in an attempt to stop or acquire the other person's state. The parasite in the client then damages part of a torus structure in the client's nuclear core, causing the full or partial loss of the state. This damage in turn causes relevant gene expressions to become inhibited, interfering with the metabolic pathways that are experienced as the peak state. To the client, the remote controlled parasite inside their nuclear core 'feels' like the other person – their efforts to connect and share their state allows the parasite entry to their torus. In many cases, several classes of parasites are employed in this attempt to damage the client.

This problem is quite common, although may go unnoticed because of the emotional drama during the event. This is a species-wide problem that starts in childhood, which is one reason why peak states are so rare in the general adult population. Interestingly, some people have unconsciously worked out a strategy to avoid this problem – they feel 'distant' when people are in emotional upset at them, which blocks this parasitic mechanism. In traditional First Nations culture, great emphasis is placed on shamans deliberately concealing their peak states – among other reasons, this may be a cultural taboo to try and deal with this disease process. This problem also commonly occurs with spiritual teachers and healers – their ability to merge consciousnesses with the student/ client bypasses normal concealment strategies and may trigger either of them into harming the other via this parasite mechanism.

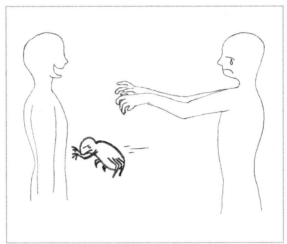

Figure 9.9:An experiential image of the peak state bug in action.
Although the parasite is actually inside the victim's primary cell,
it feels as if the bug is the other person in front of them.

Symptom Keywords
- I lost my feeling; can't love anymore; just don't feel like I used to; my life changed for the worse at that moment; depression.

Diagnosing Questions
- Did you permanently lose your positive feeling when you were with someone who was upset at you?

Differential Diagnosis
- Trauma: unstable states can be lost when relevant trauma is triggered. However, the state does eventually return. This is in contrast to permanently losing the state via the peak states bug mechanism.

Treatment
- Use the licensed Peak States certified process.

Typical Mistake in Technique
- This problem applies to most peak states. States in the Beauty Way class are not lost via this mechanism.

Underlying Cause
- The peak state bug selectively damages the torus in the nuclear core. This causes the peak state to be lost.

Symptom Frequency & Severity
- Almost everyone has this problem. This is a spectrum disorder – some people are more affected by it than others. It is also statistical in nature;

the problem depends on the right circumstances to trigger the attack and the vulnerability.

Risks

- More than usual with normal psychotherapy, as the client is often repeatedly exposed to the person who wants to harm them. This mechanism can cause extensive and potentially fatal damage to the primary cell.
- The therapist who is trying to help may also has this issue and unconsciously wants to harm the client because the client has peak states.

ICD-10 Codes

- No specific code for this case.

Positive Trauma: "I don't want to give up a positive feeling!"

In this case, the client has a behavior that is driven by a positive-feeling trauma, not a painful or negative one. Clients generally don't recognize this type of trauma as a problem, so don't come in for treatment; and therapists usually ignore or overlook this type of trauma as they are generally focused on the pain and suffering of their client. Worse, positive traumas are sometimes mistakenly assumed to be a good outcome of therapy. Unfortunately, since positive traumas also have beliefs or decisions coupled to them, they still cause people to act in dysfunctional or fixed ways. As the correct outcome of healed trauma is a feeling of calm, peacefulness and lightness (CPL), all positive-feeling outcomes without CPL should be treated as trauma; a genuine peak state feeling won't be removed with trauma healing. Positive traumas, be they generational, associational, or biographical, have exactly the same underlying biological structure as the negative-feeling variety, and are healed using the same techniques.

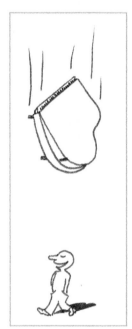

Figure 9.10: A positive feeling trauma is held in place by a negative feeling hidden under it. For example, in the illustration, the happy fellow is about to be traumatized when the piano lands on him, coupling a happy feeling over a feeling of pain.

There are two different kinds of 'positive' content: a negative feeling that is perceived as positive during the trauma moment, as in "I enjoy beating up people"; or an intrinsically positive feeling that has a negative feeling hidden 'under' it, as in "I was whistling happily just as the piano fell on me". Another variation on this problem is when a positive peak state has trauma associated with it, as in "I feel overwhelmed when I feel happiness."

Symptom Keywords
- It feels good! Positive emotional (addictive) habits.

Diagnosing Questions
- Do you have problems in your life when you have the nice feeling?
- Is there a sense that under this nice feeling is something else driving it?

Differential Diagnosis
- Body association: an association has no logical connection (e.g.: overeating); you can test by checking for associational ribosomes; there is no fixed belief or conclusion about life.
- Peak experience: the positive feeling is continuous with no sense of an underlying trauma; it does not cause stuck behavior during the experience (but can cause behavior to try and get the experience back again).
- Copy: it has a feeling of someone's personality; is half-in and half-outside the body; and has a balloon shape.

Treatment
- Any trauma healing technique (EFT, WHH, TIR, etc.)

Typical Mistake in Technique
- Assuming the positive feeling during treatment is a good outcome.
- Not recognizing that the positive feeling is due to a trauma.

Underlying Cause
- A positive feeling was simultaneous with a negative traumatic experience.
- Mistaking a negative feeling as a positive one.

Symptom Frequency & Severity
- Common but usually ignored or considered desirable.

Risks
- The usual for trauma psychotherapy.
- Some clients may not be happy giving up the positive feeling unless it is clear to them that it is driving their behavior in problem-creating ways.

ICD-10 Codes
- Not yet determined.

Projection: "They (or it) have a bad feeling"

Projections are just that – we sense in others (or in objects) feelings that we've split away from ourselves. Interestingly, no matter how much we don't like the feeling in the other, we also feel and behave that way on occasion. Thus, we switch roles (polarities) in different circumstances, but don't realize that what was so unpleasant in others we do ourselves upon occasion and it feels okay. The underlying mechanism is due to the CoA of the person switching awareness between conflicting and rejecting triune brains that were traumatized around a blocked brain fusion attempt. Interestingly, the brain shutdown subcellular case is an extreme example of this projection problem.

Examples of projection: in a relationship, you feel hurt when dumped by someone, but feel fine dumping someone else. Another example: I'm the enabler with one person, and mean with another person. A series of intimate relationships with the same issue can also be projection (although it can also be due to body associations).

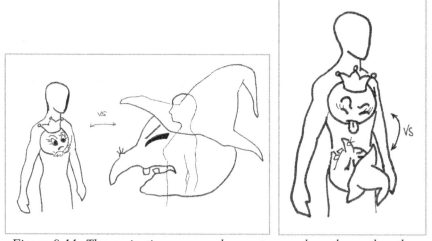

Figure 9.11: The projecting person plays out one role and sees the other elsewhere. Internally, two triune brains have these roles.

Symptom Keywords

- Have issue with other people's behavior. They have it! They feel like _____.
- Many people are like _____.
- An object is radiating a _____ feeling.
- I feel in them...

Diagnosing Questions

- Do you feel [this problem] in several people? Or in an object?

- Have you also acted or felt like that at some times in your life?

Differential Diagnosis

- Cords: they don't cause one to flip roles; you rarely have the same cord with several people; you can cord only with people, not objects; DPR doesn't work for projections.
- Biographical trauma: tapping does not work on projections; traumas have stuck beliefs; traumas don't cause other people or objects to radiate the unpleasant feeling.
- Tribal block: usually involves the family group or people with a personal connection; projection is on random people.
- Body association: the addiction to the feeling in the other person also usually causes sexual attraction.
- Dilemma: the dilemma pulls a person between two courses of action; the projection causes them to alternate behaviors and feelings.

Treatment

- Courteau Projection Technique.

Typical Mistake in Technique

- Forgetting to select several people to find their common traits.
- If the client can't feel the projected characteristic in the external blob, then it is not a projection.
- Incomplete healing of the projection is easy to miss. The entire body has to have sensations and be involved in the process. Be sure to check the presenting issue again when you think you are finished.

Underlying Cause

- An emotional conflict between two triune brains (about resistance to merging, although this is not evident to the person who is projecting). Thus it can be experienced as between male and female sides, upper and lower parts of the body, etc.

Symptom Frequency & Severity

- Common, but not as common as cording. For the most part, these people do not come in for therapy because the projection seems to be real.
- Projections can be strong or mild.

Risks

- The usual for trauma psychotherapy.

ICD-10 Codes

- Not yet determined.

Sound Loops: "I can't get that song out of my head"

We usually notice these when we can't get rid of an advertising jingle or song out of our heads. These small donut-shaped structures on the surface of the nucleus each contain a short recording of something heard by the person that plays itself over and over. These structures are part of a large bacterial parasite inside the nucleus – the sound loops are attached to the bacterium where it has extended itself through the nuclear pores. (Note: we currently believe it is a bacterial species, but it may actually be an ameba.) Interestingly, the mind brain can select and 'replay' any of these sound loops into the awareness of the person. The mind brain can use this ability to manipulate the person or the other triune brains; it usually does this playback as a way to try and be helpful.

This problem exists in almost everyone, but some people have it so badly that it is a problem requiring help.

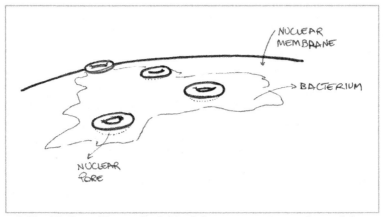

Figure 9.12: (a) Sound loops look like lifesavers on the surface of the nuclear membrane.

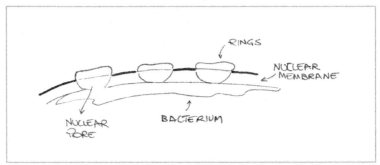

Figure 9.12: (b) They are part of a much larger bacterial organism that exists partly inside and partly outside of the nucleus.

Symptom Keywords

- Can't get rid of the music in my head. Can't focus. Too many thoughts in my mind.

Diagnosing Questions

- Does the music (or thoughts) in your head sound like repeating recordings?
- Are different songs or thoughts triggered by different situations in your life?

Differential Diagnosis

- Ribosomal voices: mind chatter sounds like it is from a person. The sound loop is a tape recording of something once heard.

Treatment

- Use the licensed Peak States certified therapist process to eliminate these bacterial organisms.

Typical Mistake in Technique

- There can be more than one bacterium causing the sound loops.

Underlying Cause

- They are part of a bacterial parasite that lives in the nucleus and extends itself out into the cytoplasm through nuclear pores.

Symptom Frequency & Severity

- Almost everyone has this problem. This is a spectrum disorder – some people are more affected by it than others.

Risks

- The usual for trauma psychotherapy.

ICD-10 Codes

- No specific code for this case.

Vortex: "I feel dizzy and nauseous"

This is the cause of the sensation of spinning that is common in most people when they drink alcohol to excess or get motion sickness. The cause is a mitochondrion in the cytoplasm that is damaged internally. It sucks in cytoplasm continuously, creating a spinning vortex of fluid, in an attempt to rinse out something causing it pain. The client becomes aware of this spinning fluid and feels the vertigo of being in the vortex.

Awareness of a vortex is sometimes triggered during trauma psychotherapy. There can also be dysfunctional associations, for example some people unconsciously access this nausea as a strategy to get attention (to block uncomfortable feelings like loneliness).

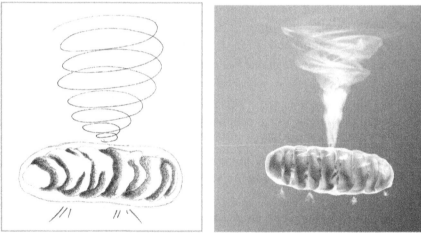

Figure 9.13: (a) A mitochondrion pulling in cytoplasm non-stop causes a vortex. This fluid is squirted out many small openings in its bottom. (b) A 3D view.

Symptom Keywords

- Spinning. Vertigo. Motion sickness. Nausea.
- Dizzy (must be spinning, not a back and forth sensation.)

Diagnosing Questions

- Does it feel like you are spinning in a vortex, like in a tornado?

Differential Diagnosis

- Class 2 fungus: A back and forth or random motion (without a spinning sensation) is caused by a fungal parasite moving primary cell structures in the nuclear core.
- Dizziness can also be caused by inner ear damage (calcium crystals, etc), although in our experience mechanical dysfunction of the inner ear is

rarely the cause of spinning symptoms. This biological inner ear problem is usually dependent on head position.

Treatment
- Use the Crosby Vortex Technique.

Typical Mistake in Technique
- The 'ringleader' or key object was not picked for healing; afterwards, there are still damaged 'items' inside the mitochondrion and the vortex is still present.
- Forgetting to 'feel' the discomfort in nearby mitochondria that were affected by the damaged one. This step is rarely needed.

Underlying Cause
- Caused by becoming aware of a mitochondrion that is sucking cytoplasm continuously into its body, forming a vortex in the fluid.

Symptom Frequency & Severity
- Almost everyone has many vortices, but one rarely comes into awareness.
- The spinning sensation can have different sizes, intensities and locations in and extending outside the body.

Risks
- The usual for trauma psychotherapy.

ICD-10 Codes
- H81, R42

Chapter 10

Subcellular Cases – Infrequent

The next group of subcellular cases is more unlikely to be the cause of a client's problem. Up to this point, we've been assuming that the general practice therapist is seeing random clients who can have the entire range of possible client issues. Hence, from that perspective the cases in this chapter are infrequently encountered, perhaps once in every 10 or 20 clients.

However, many people actually have many of these problems, but use various strategies to block awareness of them. They may use a sensate substitute to compensate inside the primary cell; rigidly limit their lives, choices, work or relationships to avoid triggering the issue; or choose external circumstances that help drown out the sensations. Thus, we see these people as clients either because their compensating strategy failed, or because the problem was latent but not active until something set it off. Common triggers are therapeutic processes, spiritual practices, or difficult relationships. In this case they need to identify the subcellular problem is and what triggered it into awareness. Both parts will likely need healing.

Some of these cases cause specific, unique problems that therapists can specialize in (for example, brain damage). As we've said elsewhere in this book, we highly recommend that therapists find the area they find compelling or fascinating and, at least part of the time, focus on working with and attracting clients with that issue.

Abyss: "I can't move forward or I will be annihilated"

The abyss is quite a distinct experience – you are standing on a stone ledge, looking down into a bottomless abyss. If you look up, there is another cliff on the other side of the abyss, and there is (or should be) a bright light there that you are trying to get to, but cannot. [Caution: Do *not* go into the abyss itself.] Most people have this abyss problem but are not aware of it. In some people, looking over the edge of a cliff or tall building can trigger the sensation of the abyss; you are afraid of falling yet want to at the same time. Others simply feel like they can't move forward in life. Yet others can see the abyss, and their descriptions reflect sensations of futility and loneliness.

The abyss experience occurs in a very early developmental event. Similar-feeling experiences occur at various later stages in development. This experience has a paternal and maternal component; generational healing is required.

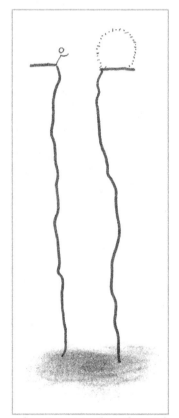

Figure 10.1: The person has to get to the other side where the light is, but cannot. This is usually experienced as a bottomless canyon with the person standing on a rock ledge at the top.

Symptom Keywords

- Loneliness; the abyss; standing on a big cliff near the ocean; I feel hopeless; I can't move forward in life.
- If I look up and see the light, I long for it. I really want to go there, but it is too far and impossible to reach.
- I am on the edge, if I move a bit forward, I feel fear looking down.
- I am at the bottom of despair and I can't get out.

Diagnosing Questions

- Does it feel like if you move forward you will fall into emptiness/ black nothingness?
- Is the issue loneliness/ despair/ complete isolation?
- Does it feel like there is no way out or forward from this despair?

Differential Diagnosis

- Soul loss: when they feel the missing sensation, they really want something to come back. With the abyss, there is a feeling of giving up.
- Tribal block: you feel heavy and a sense of resistance if you try and move forward, while the abyss feels like you will fall into nothingness and be destroyed if you do.

Treatment

- Generational healing on the experience of the abyss on both sides of the family until it fills; continue healing so the person merges with the light on the other side.

Typical Mistake in Technique

- There are two abyss events in development, one in each parent. Both need generational healing.

Underlying Cause

- A very early developmental event that went wrong.

Symptom Frequency & Severity

- Most people have this subcellular case problem, but suppress it.

ICD-10 Codes

- No specific code yet identified.

Archetypal Images (Internal): "There is a numinous godlike being inside me"

For most people, the triune brains have separate identities from each other, as if they were each a little kid. They often get into conflict and control issues, because each has a particular drive that they want to fulfill. When one of them 'sees' another, it can project – the most dramatic case being when one of the brains looks 'down' at the body brain and perceives it as an awesome godlike being. When this projection is negative, your client might say that there is a 'monster in the basement'. These internal perceptions are going on continuously – the client simply becomes aware of it when their CoA merges with the triune brain that perceives another triune brain.

This case is an internalized version of the projection phenomenon. This subcellular case is categorized as a spiritual emergency because of its numinous sensations.

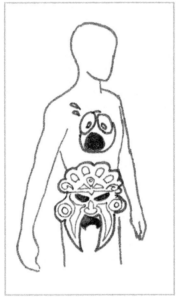

Figure 10.2: Occasionally clients experience a godlike being (ranging from monstrous to wondrous) in their belly. This is how other triune brains sometimes experience the body brain.

Symptom Keywords

- Deities, demons, an ancient god, monsters in the basement, numinous presence, overwhelming godlike being.

Diagnosing Questions

- Is this numinous presence or being you sense inside your body?

Differential Diagnosis

- Perception of a large parasite: parasites do not feel numinous.

Treatment

- The Courteau Projection Technique is the simplest approach; use the externally projected feeling for the process.
- Trauma healing around the resistance to merging of the relevant triune brains can be used instead, but it is harder to find the relevant traumas.
- This sometimes works: heal at birth before cervix opens; put client into birthing position. There is some risk of triggering suicidal feelings.

Typical Mistake in Technique

- Incomplete healing of the projection is easy to miss. The entire body has to have sensations and be involved in the process. Be sure to check the presenting issue again when you think you are finished.
- The projection can be positive or negative. Both should be healed.

Underlying Cause

- One triune brain perceives another triune brain, and the separation issue becomes translated into a perception of a numinous being.

Symptom Frequency & Severity

- It is very infrequent for people to experience this problem.
- It can feel very overwhelming and make one question one's own sanity.

Risks

- The usual for trauma psychotherapy.

ICD-10 Codes

- F22.0.

Asperger's Syndrome (mild autism): "I'm surrounded by a glass wall"

These clients have an inability to feel emotions or connect empathetically with other people. In more obvious cases this is diagnosed as Asperger's Syndrome, a mild form of autism. This specific problem is actually a spectrum disorder, with some high functioning people not even realizing that they have the problem, as it has always been there and they are used to it. The client sensation is that of a glass wall that surrounds their body, in a column shape, ranging from skin level to a few feet from their body.

This problem is caused by a bacterial cell that covers the fungal 'column of self', creating the sensation of being surrounded by a glass wall. It is treated by eliminating the covering bacterial organism(s).

Figure 10.3: The client's column of self is surrounded by a thick bacterial cell. To the client, it feels like they are stuck inside a glass tube that is also sealed at top and bottom.

Symptom Keywords
- Can't feel emotions; can't emotionally connect to others.
- I feel enclosed; I can't feel the empty space in the sky; I can't 'reach out' and touch the world.

Diagnosing Questions
- Do you feel like you are surrounded by a glass wall?
- Do you feel blocked from your emotions, and those of other people?

Differential Diagnosis

- Brain shutdown: there is no sense of being blocked or surrounded either internally or externally by a glass wall.
- Bubbles: This causes the person to become mentally and physically disabled to varying degrees. The Asperger's limits their ability to sense the world or connect emotionally but does not disable them.

Treatment

- This is currently a licensed Peak States certified therapist process.

Typical Mistake in Technique

- Missing areas of the 'glass wall'.

Underlying Cause

- A bacterial infection.

Symptom Frequency & Severity

- We estimate around 10% of the general client population have this problem to some extent. Adult clients rarely come for treatment, as they usually consider it 'normal' for themselves.
- This is a spectrum disorder, from mild to extreme: in the mild form, many well-functioning people have this problem and don't realize it until it is treated and goes away.

Risks

- The usual for trauma psychotherapy.

ICD-10 Codes

- F80, F94

Brain Damage (Prenatal or Traumatic Injury): "I simply can't do it"

We originally worked on prenatal brain damage because we thought it might be causing autism symptoms. (It turns out it wasn't; although in our experience some children are diagnosed with autism who only have brain damage.) We found that resilience to brain injury was something that varied from person to person; we developed a process that maximized this quality, so that past injuries quickly have little or no effect. (We haven't yet tested this process on many TBI (intracranial injury) clients, so we don't yet know if it will be effective in cases involving scarring or damage due to disease.)

Brain damage symptoms can range from extreme to subtle and can mistakenly appear to be due to simple trauma: for example, a client with a small area of prenatal brain damage had difficulty in remembering names. Surprisingly, we found that most ordinary people had some degree of brain damage in various areas of their brain. A client can notice this if they compare themselves to others. Cases of traumatic brain injury from an accident have a clear before-and-after condition, making treatment testing far easier.

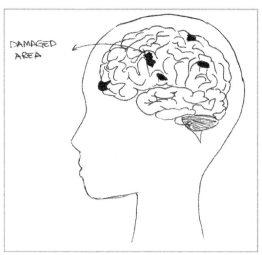

Figure 10.4: Areas of brain damage 'look' black. The brain material should 'look' transparent.

Symptom Keywords

- "I can't do something"; "I really can't do it"; "It does not work for me";
- Frustration about doing something; compensate; injury, lost a capacity; never been able to.
- Client has strategies to work around the disability in their life.

Diagnosing Questions

- Is this inability always there?

- Does this inability simply feel like something is missing in you?

Differential Diagnosis

- Brain shutdown: shutdown of the mind brain causes loss of the ability to make all judgments, positive or negative; brain damage involves partial or full loss of specific abilities, or more general learning disability.
- Trauma decisions: trauma causes suppression of ability driven by an emotional pain, versus an absence of ability from brain damage. With brain damage, there is no emotional content to the symptom other than the feelings about having the disability (no direct emotional charge). Tapping doesn't work on brain damage symptoms.
- Bubble: the bubble problem causes global inability and loss of ability to function versus specific inabilities with brain damage; you feel like you are in a bubble versus just your normal self; being in a bubble is painless versus traumatic brain injury, there will be other symptoms (like pain, incapacitated motor skills, etc.)
- Copy: a copy is like trauma that gives symptoms; brain damage causes an absence, or partial absence of some ability.

Treatment

- This is currently a licensed Peak States certified therapist process.

Typical Mistake in Technique

- Not fully healing the problem, because the client doesn't know what healthy feels as an endpoint.
- Not having someone who can 'see' brain damage double check the healing.

Underlying Cause

- Injury to the brain causing loss of specific function.

Symptom Frequency & Severity

- In accident trauma, there is a range of symptoms and intensity.
- Prenatal damage is common, but usually not severe.

Risks

- The usual for trauma psychotherapy.

ICD-10 Codes

- F07.8, F70-F79, F80, S06, I64.

Bubble: "I suddenly feel incapacitated"

This subcellular case occurs when a person suddenly but temporarily becomes to some degree mentally and physically incapacitated. This problem is obvious to observers, as the client suddenly becomes stupid and incompetent. This happens because a person temporarily moves their awareness into a small 'bubble' floating in the nuclear core. They do this because it provides a feeling of safety, a bit like a child hiding under the bed covers. Clients typically have a number of bubbles; the client can sometimes perceive them as floating around outside their body.

These bubbles have been ejected from their proper location in the 'pinecone' structure; they are damaged, and contain a class 1 bug-like parasite inside. Healing is in three parts: getting them out of the bubble; eliminating the client's need to go into bubbles, and then healing the particular bubble.

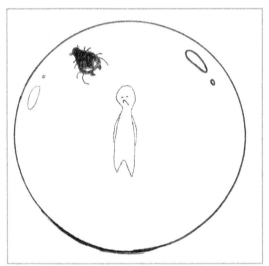

Figure 10.5: (a) The person's feels like they are partly or fully inside a bubble. It makes them feel safe, even though there is a bug inside with them.

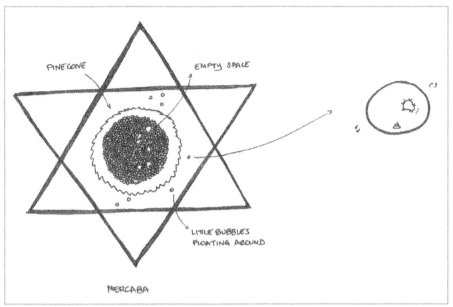

(b) The bubble is floating outside the pinecone; it should be inside the pinecone.

Symptom Keywords

- Incapacitated; disabled; stupid; unable; fuzzy; can't do normal activities (driving, math, etc.).
- Surrounded; bubble; feel like in a blanket.

Diagnosing Questions

- Do you feel like you are inside a round bubble? Do you feel encapsulated sometimes?
- If you expand yourself, does it feel like you become normal again?

Differential Diagnosis

- Autism: glass box, not necessarily stupid, not incapacitated.
- Biographical trauma: not feel inside a bubble.
- Mind brain shutdown: no self-attack, no bubble sensation.
- Soul stealing: it 'looks' like a cloud, not a bubble; feelings are scattered in space.

Treatment

- Have the client expand their awareness. Then heal the safety body associations. Then use a generational healing process on the bug-like parasite inside the bubble.

Typical Mistake in Technique

- Talking about bugs causes unnecessary alarm and can derail the healing process. It is far better to use non-threatening euphemisms when working on the bug-like parasite healing.

DANGER

Some people will search for parasites inside themselves once they realize they exist, and try to intervene at the primary cell level. This is potentially very dangerous: the parasites can react and harm the host; the body can cause parasite overgrowth to compensate; and can cause unnecessary fear and paranoia in the client.

Underlying Cause

- The client's CoA has partially or fully gone into a bubble that has been damaged and outside of its normal place in the nuclear core's pinecone structure.

Symptom Frequency & Severity

- Many people do this, but it is usually of short duration. The person can be fully or partially in the bubble; for example, their upper body is in the bubble but their legs are not.

Risks

- The usual for trauma psychotherapy.

ICD-10 Codes

- F43.2, F44.9, F70-79, F80

Cell Membrane Leakage: "I feel weak"

This rare problem causes a feeling of weakness in the client; in extreme cases, it can cause a person to go to a hospital. It results when membranes in the primary cell become porous and leak fluid across their boundary. The membrane can 'look' either too thin and has holes, or brittle and cracked. This problem is global: it occurs in all cell membranes, not just the cell or nuclear membranes. The origin is a defective parental membrane in the parental genesis cell stage when p-organelles are first being formed.

People with this problem have it as a pre-existing condition in our limited experience. However, we have seen the symptoms become far worse in some clients during trauma therapy or life events.

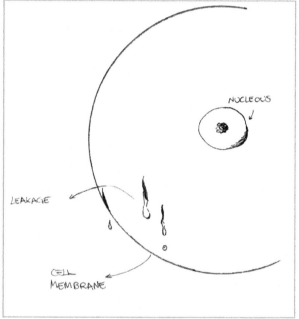

Figure 10.6: Any membrane in the cell can have the problem of leakage. Once triggered, in severe cases it can lead to hospitalization or death.

Symptom Keywords

- Nausea, weakness, drained, not enough energy to breathe, feels like I am bleeding; the problem is worse when trying to _____;

Diagnosing Questions

- What circumstances trigger your physical weakness?

Differential Diagnosis

- Blanket curse: it is usually in an area, but can be around the entire person. It makes a person feel tired, not weak.
- Class 1 bug injuries: a bug can rip through a membrane, and if the tear is large enough, the client has the sensation of bleeding to death as the cytoplasm pours out of the primary cell, and there is intense pain; but only in one place. Cell membrane leakage is everywhere and is usually not painful.
- Chronic fatigue: clients were well then acquired this problem; leakage symptoms are triggered by events but also are a lifelong problem.

Treatment

- This is currently a licensed Peak States certified therapist process, due to the possible safety risks involved.

Typical Mistake in Technique

- Not fully healing some areas of the Genesis cell membrane.

Underlying Cause

- Damage in the original cell membranes that the primordial germ cell is constructed from.

Symptom Frequency & Severity

- It is usually mild, but can be life threatening in some people in certain circumstances.

Risks

- Many people have some problem with their cell membrane integrity, but it is very uncommon to have significant leakage.
- Using therapies for other problems can trigger more severe symptoms.

ICD-10 Codes

- No specific code yet identified.

Chakra problem: "I feel painful pressure at my chakra"

There can be many severe physical and emotional problems associated with chakras. Chakras have a physical basis in the primary cell; they are parts of a single class 2 fungal organism found embedded in the nuclear membrane. Because they are alive, they will react to efforts to push or manipulate them – this can happen by accident when the client does an activity in their life that causes a corresponding activity in the primary cell. Examples: weight lifting that stresses the chakra areas; meditating with an intense focus on the third eye area, etc. Symptoms are usually pain or pressure in the locations of the body that correspond to chakra locations, singly or simultaneously at all locations.

Interestingly, the trigger to activate a chakra is motions and feelings that the mother had when she used her chakras; the fetus *in utero* learns how to use them by copying what she did at those moments.

Eliminating this fungal organism radically changes the pulses that are used to diagnose in Chinese medicine and eliminates the ability to use tapping techniques (but also eliminates the need for them – simply feeling a trauma now heals the entire trauma string.)

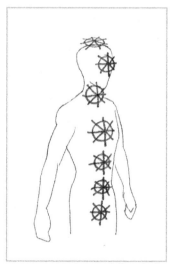

Figure 10.7a: Symbolic representations of the chakras in their approximate locations in the body. They are shown as sailing ship wheels due to their experiential nature.

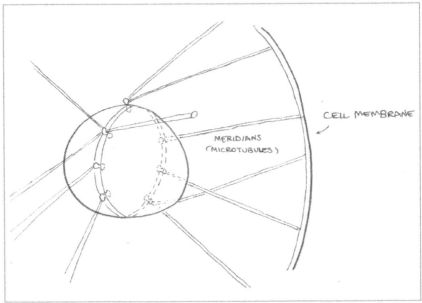

Figure 10.7: (b) The chakra (fungal) organism on the nuclear membrane along the left/right centerline with attached meridian tubes.

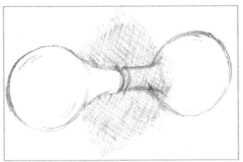

Figure 10.7: (c) A close-up of a chakra, a dumbbell-like structure penetrating the nuclear membrane.

Symptom Keywords

• There is a sensation of 'pressure' in the body at the classic chakra locations.

Diagnosing Questions

• Do you get these symptoms when you do some particular physical action?

Differential Diagnosis

• Bacteria: they can cause pressure pain, but usually in the head.

- Trauma: activated pain or injury traumas might coincidentally be at chakra locations. Testing with a trauma therapy is the simplest test.
- Crown brain structure: rarely at chakra locations. Both can cause pain with motion; sometime the crown structure encloses an area creating pain. A partial test of temporarily dissolving crown structures is the best test.

Treatment

- For pressure symptoms, heal the trauma resistance to the 'push' at the boundary. Continue at each stuck spot until there is no more resistance and hence no feeling of pressure.
- Use a licensed Peak States technique to eliminate the chakra organism.

Typical Mistake in Technique

- Not eliminating the entire chakra fungal organism.

Underlying Cause

- A class 2 fungal organism embedded in the nuclear membrane along the center outer axis.

Symptom Frequency & Severity

- Very common, but not usually serious.
- Most people automatically avoid the actions that trigger pain.

Risks

- Not known at this time. Assume that there are the usual risks for trauma psychotherapy.

ICD-10 Codes

- F45, R52.

Column of Self - Bubbles: "I feel confused"

The structure in the nuclear core of the primary cell we call the 'column of self' can have a variety of problems. One rather strange one is the presence of what looks like bubbles of air inside the column. These bubbles give a distinct psychological effect: the person feels confusion along with a sense of fragmentation. This problem varies depending on the size and number of bubbles inside the column of self.

The 'column of self' is a very common class 2 fungal structure that most people experience as part of themselves.

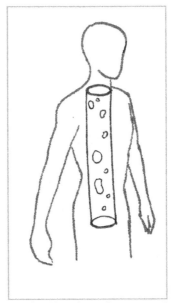

Figure 10.8: The column of self (a fungal structure) can have bubbles in it. This causes confusion in a person that would have been there since birth.

Symptom Keywords

- Confusion in spots of body; fragmentation; focus shatters in areas; internal confusion; the problem is always there; scattered attention; I am confused all the time.

Diagnosing Questions

- Is the feeling of confusion in various spots in your body?

Differential Diagnosis

- Shattered crystals: the crystals cause an inability to focus – if you don't focus there is no problem. It occurs when you focus attention outwardly.

The column bubbles are about confusion that is always there in distinct places of the body, and exists even if you don't think about a concept.

Treatment

• This is currently a licensed Peak States certified therapist process.

Typical Mistake in Technique

• The problem is not fully healed because parts of the column are cracked or detached, blocking these areas from the client's awareness.

Underlying Cause

• Areas of the column of self that didn't fill in fully when it first formed.

Symptom Frequency & Severity

• Occasionally found in clients, but it is rare to have it severe enough to require treatment; usually people have adequate coping strategies.

Risks

• The usual for trauma psychotherapy.

ICD-10 Codes

• R41.0

E-Holes/ E-Cords: "I am revolted by a really evil feeling in you"

This e-hole ("evil hole") problem is due to a gap in the pinecone structure. The gap has a feeling of a negative emotion with an underlying evil twist to it. For example, "I am sad, so I'll make you unhappy too". Each gap will have a different negative emotional tone. Most people fill the gap to try and block the sensation, generally with a bacterial parasite. However, when the person meets another with exactly the same damaged area in their pinecone, they will feel the negative feeling *in the other person*. This sensing is via a bacterial parasite inside the void left in the pinecone that resonates with a bacterium in the other person's void. There are actually no 'cord' connections, as with the class 2 borg fungus, but for convenience we call it an 'e-cord' (evil cord), as both kinds of emotional connections feel similar, and both can be eliminated with DPR (Distant Personality Release).

　　The e-hole problem is common, but noticing it in oneself is very uncommon. Noticing it in another is not as rare, but it requires the coincidence that both people have exactly the same damaged area in their pinecone structures. We see this problem occasionally in couples, although they often don't recognize exactly why they feel uncomfortable with each other.

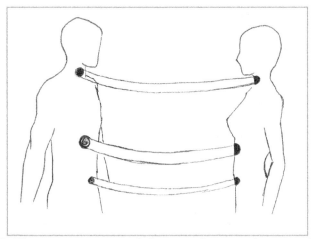

Figure 10.9: The person notices a feeling in others in a location that matches the same evil feeling in their own body. These holes are actually in the pinecone structure.

Symptom Keywords

- Someone else feels evil or gives off an evil feeling; that person feels evil at a specific body location.
- I am uncomfortable around a particular person.
- I have an evil feeling at a particular spot in my body.

Diagnosing Questions

- Where in the other person's body do you sense the negative feeling? Do you have the same feeling at the same location in your own body?

Differential Diagnosis

- Trauma: trauma techniques like EFT or WHH have no effect on the negative feeling in the e-hole.
- Projection: there is no underlying evil in the projected emotion; nor is there a specific body location for the feeling in the other or in oneself.
- Cords: they don't have a specific location in the other person's body, and rarely have an evil undertone to the feeling sensed.

Treatment

- The e-hole is a generational trauma problem.
- DPR can be used to eliminate the connection to another person, but it does not heal the e-hole in the client.

Typical Mistake in Technique

- Sometimes there are overlapping e-holes with different feelings.

Underlying Cause

- Gaps in the interior of the nuclear core's pinecone structure can fill with an evil emotional tone. This is a generational problem.

Symptom Frequency & Severity

- E-holes are common in the general population, but it is rare to find someone else to resonate with so it can be felt.
- The feeling in the other person (and in oneself) can be very disturbing, because of the evil undertone in it.

Risks

- The usual for trauma psychotherapy. In addition, as it involves sensations of evil, it is difficult for some people to acknowledge or face in themselves.

ICD-10 Codes

- No specific code yet identified.

Flattened Emotions: "My feelings, good or bad, are muted"

We first encountered this problem when we rapidly moved attention back and forth between the present and a past moment ('time jumping'). In about four cycles, the emotional content of the past moment is gone, or very muted. Unfortunately, this does not heal trauma. Instead, all emotional content (be it pleasurable or painful) is also muted. This condition does not go away without treatment; and people who have it for a while often describe it as 'being depressed'. This problem can be seen at the triune brain level – the heart brain looks like it is covered in a hard shell, instead of its normal fuzzy, extended appearance.

This 'time jumping' triggers a very early developmental event, which in most people involves trauma that makes them susceptible to this problem. Healing this event quickly restores the clients to a normal emotional range.

We have not yet identified the underlying biology, because our treatment worked so well we did not need to investigate further. However, there is a problem with similar symptoms that may be due to the same underlying issue. In this, the interconnection between the emotional heart brain and the other brains is damaged in the merkaba (a fungal structure). People with this condition can sometimes feel positive feelings again, but only in the presence of people who stimulate that experience in them. This merkaba damage is also the cause of ADD or ADHD in most people. Repairing the parasitic structure eliminates these symptoms.

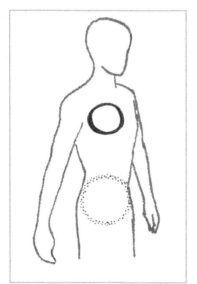

Figure 10.10 (a): The 'flattened emotions' problem causes a triune brain to form a hard surface. (b) Damage to the interconnecting points on the merkaba fungal structure blocks function of the triune brains, ranging from emotional numbness to ADD/ADHD.

Symptom Keywords

- Depression. "Blah". "I don't feel much." Monotone or monotonous voice.
- "My partner is not happy with me." "It used to be different."
- Shallow emotional range (positive & negative)

Diagnosing Questions

- Are negative *and positive* feelings still available but very muted?
- When did this start? (After time jumping or taking hallucinogens?)

Differential Diagnosis

- Bacterial problem: the bacterium covers key parts of the cell. It usually is accompanied with tiredness.
- Bubble: the bubble partially disables a person physically and mentally; flattened emotions only effect emotional range.
- Soul loss: the emotional numbness conceals extreme loneliness or loss.
- Asperger's Syndrome (mild autism): there is a 'glass wall' sensation around a person, or around their inner core, blocking connection to others and/or their own emotions. This is lifelong.
- Heart brain shutdown: people feel like an object, as well as loss of emotions.
- Fungal overgrowth: there is also a feeling of resistance to any actions.
- Inner peace state: you still have the full positive emotional range.
- Brain fusion state: you usually feel partially or fully hollow. The lack of emotions feels appropriate, you don't feel depressed, and it does not feel like a problem.

Treatment

- This is currently a licensed Peak States certified therapist process.

Typical Mistake in Technique

- Not recognizing that the client's 'depression' is actually flattened emotions (because they are not aware of when or how it started).

Underlying Cause

- An early developmental event is triggered (via drugs, time jumping) that causes this problem. Or it was always there since childhood or birth.

Symptom Frequency & Severity

- Rare in the general public. Very common if done deliberately using time jumping.
- We have occasionally seen this problem in people who have used hallucinogens – they have it by the end of the drug experience.

Risks

- The usual for trauma psychotherapy.

ICD-10 Codes

- F34.1.

Fungal Overgrowth: "I don't feel much; I am filled with white stuff"

This subcellular case involves a fungal species inside the primary cell that 'looks' like white cotton candy. It can range in size from small patches to entirely filling the body image of the client. The primary symptom is emotional and physical numbness that can be mild to extreme. This is sometimes noticed as an inability to feel normal positive emotions like love or happiness. It can also give the sensation that the person is physically 'tied down', as if they were Gulliver and the Lilliputians had bound them with tiny strings. It can also be experienced as a feeling of being stuck or restricted, with everything in life taking a lot of effort and willpower. However, this fungal species does not create emotional or other interconnection problems between people (as in the case of the borg fungus).

This fungal overgrowth problem can occur in some people when they regress to coalescence or conception. The sexual feelings experienced there trigger overgrowth of the fungus inside their primary cell in the present. Fortunately, this is not a common experience, and if it occurs, the client usually recovers in up to a few days as their primary cell regains homeostasis. However, in some cases the problem lasts – if so, active intervention is needed.

As of this writing, we rarely see clients who come in with this fungal overgrowth problem. However, we have seen it in two very ill individuals in extended care settings; we don't know if the fungal overgrowth was a consequence or a cause of their inability to leave their bed or maintain weight.

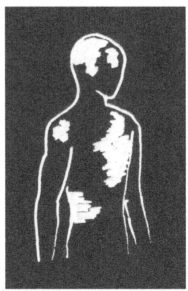

Figure 10.11: A fungal webbing can grow in various parts of the primary cell. It is experienced as if inside the body. It usually 'looks' like white cotton candy to people who can see into themselves at the primary cell level.

Symptom Keywords

- Resistance, effort, can't feel, white inside, tied down, can't see, no perceptions, restricted.

Diagnosing Questions

- Do you have the sensation that your body is filled with white cotton candy, that makes you feel like you can't really sense or feel things? When did this start?

Differential Diagnosis

- Biographical trauma: tapping or regression works. The fungal issue won't respond to simple trauma therapy.
- Copies: copies have a feeling of personality in them; the fungus problem does not.
- Flattened emotions: similar to the fungal problem with regards to emotions. But the fungal process makes a person also feel disabled as far as emotional connection and physical symptoms.
- Soul loss: emotional numbness from extensive soul loss is driven by suppression of extreme loneliness or sadness. The fungal problem does not have emotional content.

Treatment

- This is currently a licensed Peak States certified therapist process.

Typical Mistake in Technique

- Only partially healing the problem, because of the loss of awareness due to the fungus.

Underlying Cause

- A fungus growth, of various species and in various locations in the primary cell. Sometimes triggered when regressed to conception.

Symptom Frequency & Severity

- Relatively common, but most people consider the symptoms to be normal.
- Symptoms can be quite disturbing but in a negative way, as it shuts down feelings and sensations, as if filled with white cotton candy.

Risks

- The problem might be made worse by attempts to heal it in some cases; plus the usual trauma psychotherapy problems can be triggered.

CAUTION

Attempting to heal this problem can drastically worsen symptoms. Only do this process under supervision with backup in case of problems.

ICD-10 Codes

- F70-F79

Image Overlay: "I am remembering something I saw in a photo"

When doing regressions, many people 'overlay' images that they are familiar with, instead of seeing what is actually there. This is rarely a problem; the feelings associated with the overlaid and real image are usually the same, so the healing still works. This phenomenon of overlays can carry over into people's lives, when prenatal events gets confused with real life. For example: the client believes he is just recalling a childhood photo; or during regression a man saw an image of himself moving rapidly on a motorcycle, when in reality he was experiencing himself moving as a sperm. This can sometimes play out in clients when they believe parents or relatives did bad things to them, while in reality they are remembering a prenatal trauma overlaid with familiar people. Unfortunately, in our experience real abuse is far more common than an overlay 'memory'.

Rarely, image overlays in regression can be more bizarre, because the client is trying to block access to a particularly painful event and will use anything at all to do it with. These overlay images are not consistent with the rest of the experience. For example, like a painting, or a vase, or a yellow airplane swimming up the river. The real trauma image is hidden underneath or inside the overlay.

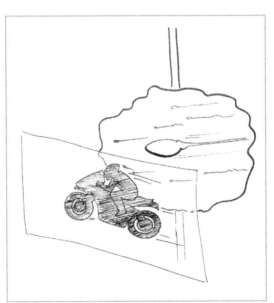

Figure 10.11: (a) An example of a trauma regression. The client experienced himself as zooming along on a motorcycle – in reality, he was reliving the sperm swimming to the egg.

There is another class of unconscious overlays that almost everyone has that does create problems for people. They exist in the present: all women are seen with an overlaid image of the viewer's mother; all men are seen with an overlaid image of the father (sort of like seeing a ghost over the person, like a video effect). This is a problem because people unconsciously feel and act on these inaccurate perceptions in real life. Therapists in particular should eliminate these parental overlays in order to be able to perceive their clients more accurately. This is rarely an issue that clients come in to address, as it is unconscious for almost everyone and they consider it normal.

Overlays are a distortion of biographical trauma that, once recognized, is treated with the usual trauma methods.

Figure 10.11: (b) The most problematic of the overlays is putting one of your mother on all women and your father on all men.

Symptom Keywords

- Seeing a ghostly image overlay someone; all women are like my mother; all men are like my father.
- I am remembering a photo; I don't recall seeing this before, and it is sort of strange; I was abused; my parents did bad things to me.

Diagnosing Questions

- Do all men (or women) remind you of your dad (or mom)?
- Do you have almost two different memories of that person, as if they were very different people?

Differential Diagnosis

- Biographical trauma: the overlay imagery doesn't really make sense or fit into the rest of the client's experience.
- Multiple personality disorder (MPD): in abuse situations, the abuser can have MDP and hence acts in completely different ways without memory of it. Overlay memories usually describe events that simply don't make sense ("he drugged me many nights").

Treatment

- Trauma healing on the emotional feelings and body sensations.

Typical Mistake in Technique

- Forgetting to heal both mother and father projections.

Underlying Cause

- An unconscious attempt to explain prenatal images that are outside the person's experience; or to escape imagery that is simply too traumatic to face directly (for example, parasite images).

Symptom Frequency & Severity

- About 1/3 of clients see overlays occasionally when regressing, but it causes no problem if the therapist recognizes it and continues the trauma healing.
- Therapists rarely treat the mother and father overlay problem, as most clients are not aware of it, even though it is present.

Risks

- The usual for trauma psychotherapy.

ICD-10 Codes

- No specific code yet identified.

Kundalini: "I am very spiritually advanced"

Unfortunately, kundalini has become a catchall term that includes many unrelated phenomena. In this manual, we are referring to the original definition: a small area on the spine that radiates heat as it slowly moves up from the pelvic area, triggering traumatic feelings, spiritual experiences, and an inability to sleep. This may or may not be accompanied with energy flows up the spine. It is also characterized by alternating periods of ego inflation and deflation. We have also seen some clients with this condition unintentionally induce a tingling or buzzing sensation in others nearby, as if the bystanders were next to a high-tension electrical power line. Although many people believe that kundalini is a mark of spiritual advancement, we have not seen any convincing evidence of this. Instead, in our experience it causes years, even decades of torment for the person involved. The cause is simple: the body brain is blaming all the rest of the being for its own issues. Eliminating kundalini is also simple: heal the body brain's feelings of blame using trauma or projection techniques.

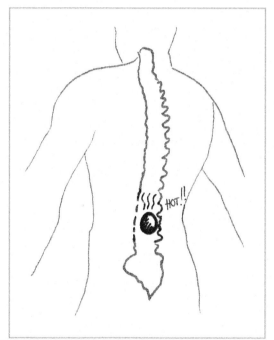

Figure 10.12: During kundalini, there is a physically hot spot on the spine that slowly moves upwards over months.

Symptom Keywords

- Spiritual emergency; I've gone crazy; visions; I'm so amazing; I'm worthless.
- Can't sleep; wired; anxiety.

Diagnosing Questions

- Are you unable to sleep, and are continually flooded with traumatic feelings and spiritual experiences?
- Did this problem start while using spiritual practices or having unusually powerful sexual experiences?
- Is there an area on your spine that feels hot, and is slowly moving upwards?

Differential Diagnosis

- Trauma flooding: there is no heat on the spine, and ego inflation and deflation don't happen.
- Psychosis: there is no involvement with energy up the spine.

Treatment

- Use the Courteau Projection Technique on feelings of blame that the client senses in or between other people; and/or use trauma healing on feelings of blame in the belly. The phrase "It's all your fault!" generally captures the emotional tone of the body brain's projection.

Typical Mistake in Technique

- Missing some of the blame issue in the belly.

Underlying Cause

- The body brain activates the kundalini mechanism because it blames the rest of the organism for its own problems.

Symptom Frequency & Severity

- Very rare in the general population. However, people with this problem are usually severely impacted and often can't work or maintain normal relationships.

Risks

- The usual for trauma psychotherapy.

ICD-10 Codes

- F51

Mitochondria Clumping: "I am the boss"

Damaged mitochondria usually cause vortices to form. There is another problem that they can have: damaged ones can clump together. Because mitochondria share awareness (they are part of the solar plexus triune brain), the most damaged one can act as a 'ringleader' to the rest, acting like a Napoleon, controlling them and causing them to move from their correct places in the cell. This subcellular problem can result in a psychological issue in real life, in an autocratic and controlling identification (and behaviors) with that damaged organelle. This doesn't always have this effect, as it depends on the client identifying with the solar plexus brain.

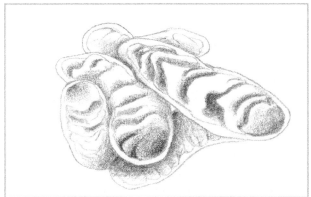

Figure 10.13: Mitochondria clumped together, like a jumble of hot dog buns.

Symptom Keywords
- Superior; rule; others are lesser; I am the leader.

Diagnosing Questions
- Is this feeling coming from your solar plexus?
- Is there a vortex (spinning, dizzy) somehow related with this feeling.

Differential Diagnosis
- Biographical or generational trauma: this problem won't go away with trauma healing. Unlike trauma which can be felt anywhere, this feeling radiates only from the solar plexus.

Treatment
- Find the focus of the feeling. Feel the underlying damage to the feeling. Heal by WHH or the Crosby vortex technique.

Typical Mistake in Technique
- Not identifying the 'ringleader' for healing.

Underlying Cause

- A damaged group of mitochondria create symptoms; the person identifies with their solar plexus.

Symptom Frequency & Severity

- Rare. If present, symptoms can range from mild to extreme, but typically the intensity doesn't vary much.

Risks

- The usual for trauma psychotherapy.

ICD-10 Codes

- No specific code yet identified.

Multiple Personality Disorder (Column of Self Fractures): "I didn't say that!"

In 2006, one of my colleagues said something to me that only moments later she denied having said. Investigating this, we found that, to our great surprise, various degrees of MPD (multiple personality disorder; currently called dissociative identity disorder) existed in about 70% of our students. This problem can range from personalities that could connect then split away, to one or more fully separate personalities. Instead of being rare, this problem was the norm! Interestingly, it can be particularly difficult to spot because we believe memory lapses are normal; and in many cases the personalities of the MPD are similar.

We were able to study this problem because it could be seen in the primary cell in a structure we call the 'column of self'. An MPD shows up as separated parts of the column, or a column that has pieces still attached but separated by cracks. Each piece contains a unique personality with its own memories and attitudes. Given the damage to the column, it becomes a problem defining which personality is the main one if the pieces are all about similar size. The client can detect the presence of an MPD as an area in their body where their awareness 'blanks out'. It took us two years before we were able to come up with a treatment that couldn't be reversed by life events.

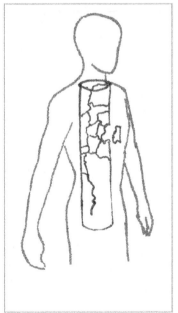

Figure 10.14: Broken off pieces of the 'column of self' contain awareness. When they are separate, the person has MPD (and usually does not realize it).

Another variation on this problem happens during conception. The sperm and egg both bring their own genes and their own columns; one feels like the mother, one feels like the father. As conception completes, the genes, columns, and other structures merge and form the new person out of their substance, with the sense of new self forming along the centerline of the body which expands to the right and left. Most people do not complete this process; instead they are left with three personalities (and three columns) that feel like the mother, the father and their own. The mother and father columns don't seem to act like MPDs, but do cause problems in life. These columns are normally of equal height, and shrink in proportion as the new one is made; but some people have a lack of column material when they start, causing the new column of self to be unable to fully form.

A class 2 fungal organism makes the columns of self. Almost all people have these structures.

Symptom Keywords

- Confusion or irritation due to what feels like inappropriate intimacy from others.
- Behavioral changes or action or dialogue that the client doesn't remember but others can notice.
- I don't recall much (or any) of my childhood.
- From excessive mother father columns: My mother/father is always in me; I ring my mother/father every day; my mother/father is in my life all the time and I am in theirs; I have severed all contact with my mother/father.

Diagnosing Questions

- If you move your awareness around your body, where do you 'blank out'?

Differential Diagnosis

- Biographical trauma: with both trauma and MPD, the person can blank out what they felt or said, but the MPD person also has an area(s) of their body that they are not aware of.
- Triune brain self-identity or projection: it takes me over, but I can still remember how I was. With the MPD, you are not aware of it, or you can sense it in part of your body but reject it (if it is partially attached).
- Egg or Sperm side: You can shift your CoA from your left (egg side) to right (sperm side) to feel differently, but you are still aware of doing this.

Treatment

- This is currently a licensed Peak States certified therapist process.

Typical Mistake in Technique

- Forgetting to address follow-up issues as new memories come in.

Underlying Cause

- Fractured or split off areas in the column of self.

Symptom Frequency & Severity

- Awareness of fully separated personalities is very rare. Partially separated personalities are often automatically rejected or suppressed as being 'unlike me'. Stress can activate or change severity of the splitting.
- This problem to one degree or another is in about 70% of the normal population. This problem is more common in client populations.

Risks

- The usual for trauma psychotherapy. In addition, the memories and feelings of a separated personality can be disturbing to the person who starts to become aware of it.

ICD-10 Codes

- F44.0, F44.8, F62

Over-Identification with the Creator: "I don't need to help because everything is OK"

In this subcellular case, the client has merged their consciousness with Creator awareness, and has partially stayed in that experience. Unfortunately, they can also lose the capacity to see the suffering of others as a problem and any desire to intervene when someone needs help. (For more detail on these concepts, see Volume 2 of *Peak States of Consciousness*.) The usual triggers are meditation or other spiritual practices; regression to early developmental events; and hallucinogens use. This subcellular case is rarely seen in clients because people who have it don't believe they have a problem – in fact, they feel fine to themselves – although we have seen that over time they may start to realize that something is wrong and seek help.

This problem occurs because there is a fungal structure 'above' the head of the person (in the nuclear core) that they merge their awareness into. They then experience their own life from this fungal organism's perspective, characterized by extreme acceptance of all circumstances in the person's life, good or bad; but without any inclination to help others or improve their own situation.

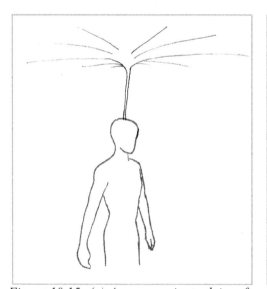 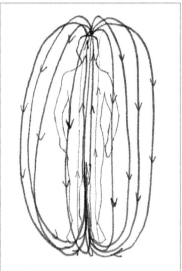

Figure 10.15: (a) Awareness is stuck in a fungal parasite that feels 'above' the body. (b) Normal function is restored by getting (and removing trauma around) the sensation of a flow up the center of the body and back down the outside and then healing.

Symptom Keywords

- Everything is the way it should be; it is their karma; I don't feel involved.

Diagnosing Questions

- If someone were suffering and could use your help, would you feel a drive to help them?
- Does it feel like you can accept anything, and everything is fine as it is?

Differential Diagnosis

- Biographical or Generational trauma: there is an underlying physical and/or an emotional pain with the symptom. Standard trauma techniques will eliminate symptoms.

Treatment

- Focus on generating a flow up the body from the earth, to the sky, then back down outside the body and back up the body in a continuous, fountain-like flow. Once the issue has vanished, use standard trauma techniques on the resistance to having this flow continue.

Typical Mistake in Technique

- Follow- up is needed to make sure the problem doesn't return, as the client won't notice any painful symptoms from it.

Symptom Frequency & Severity

- Rare in the general population.
- Rarely seen in therapy because the client doesn't believe they have a problem.

Underlying Cause

- Awareness is partly stuck in the Creator structure inside the nuclear core.

Risks

- The usual for trauma psychotherapy.

ICD-10 Codes

- No specific code yet identified.

Selfishness Ring: "In reality, I do most things for my own benefit"

One puzzling aspect of human behavior is why people limit the amount of positive feeling they are willing to enjoy. There are several reasons for this, the tribal block being a major one. But an even more direct limitation is caused by a structure we call the 'selfishness ring'. It is located inside the nuclear core, and causes people to limit their experience of all altruistic feelings; and it twists their actions into self-serving ends. This structure is also associated with what is sometimes called 'armoring'. The ring problem is a spectrum disorder – some people have it worse than others, and the lucky few do not have it at all. The ring is formed during birth; the armoring is formed earlier. A class 2 fungus makes this structure.

It is very unlikely that people will come to a therapist for this problem, as blocking both positive altruistic feelings and actions makes them feel more comfortable. People wanting personal growth or to feel stronger positive feelings might be interested in healing this.

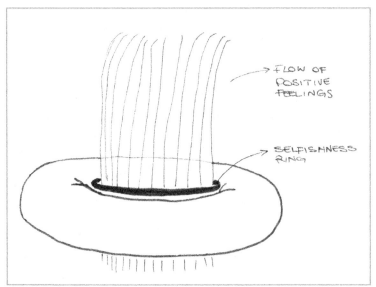

Figure 10.16: The torus has an inner ring that causes awareness to twist away from the flow of positive feelings through the center.

Symptom Keywords

* 'Friends are people I use'. Good feelings are painful. I feel fine feeling calm.

Diagnosing Questions

- Do you feel pain or uncomfortable feelings if you try and feel altruistic, positive emotions?

Differential Diagnosis

- Generational trauma: the ring problem does not make a person feel defective or traumatized.
- Biographical trauma: the ring problem is continuous, not occurring in discrete moments like trauma. The problem has been there since birth, so feels normal.
- Tribal block: tribal block makes a person feel heavy who tries to resist the tribal block to altruistic positive feelings; the selfishness ring does not (it feels painful instead).

Treatment

- This is currently a licensed Peak States certified therapist process.

Typical Mistake in Technique

- Missing other issues around a willingness to change and have permanent, positive feelings.

Underlying Cause

- This ring structure is formed at birth.

Symptom Frequency & Severity

- Almost everyone has this ring, but don't realize it is a problem. It is a spectrum disorder: some people have it worse than others; and some people have a left/right side asymmetry to how it affects them.

Risks

- Not known at this time. Assume that there are the usual risks for trauma psychotherapy.

ICD-10 Codes

- F60.8

Shattered Crystals (Attention Deficit Disorder): "I can't focus"

Inside the cytoplasm can be what looks like shattered pieces of glass or crystal. This is caused by a class 2 fungal problem that occurs in early development. When a person attempts to focus their attention, they find their focus fractures into pieces, like looking into a kaleidoscope. This problem is usually there from birth, but people learn strategies to cope with it. They may keep their attention diffuse; or they bunch the crystals together and avoid using that area of their psyche when focusing their attention.

Severe examples of this problem are often diagnosed as ADD or ADHD. In some cases, the problem is complicated by unusually damaged triune brains that cause the client's attention to be continuously pulled in different directions, as first one then another gains ascendency. Although it is usually present since birth, in some people it is triggered later in life if the corresponding developmental trauma is activated. It is sometimes first encountered during spiritual emergency experiences.

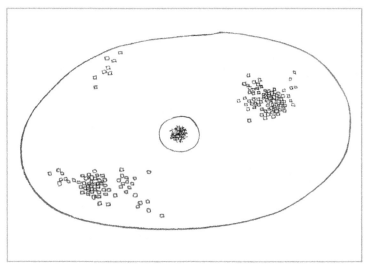

Figure 10.17: Clumps of shattered crystals in the cytoplasm. Most people with this problem have managed to push them into clumps so they can focus if they avoid that area of their cell.

Symptom Keywords

- Can't concentrate, can't focus on "stuff", never been able to learn well, trying to focus is like looking thru broken glass; kaleidoscope.
- An ADD or ADHD diagnosis.

Diagnosing Questions

- When you attempt to focus your attention, does it feel like it fractures into pieces?

Differential Diagnosis

- Brain damage: generally does not cause a focus problem, they can focus but just can't get it. Both cases feel stupid/disabled but brain damage is more mentally and physically specific; both cases can be steady and continuous.
- Bubbles in the column of self: this causes confusion if awareness is put in specific locations regardless of outer activities; while shattered crystals fragment attention or awareness when attempts are made to focus on the outer world or inner activities. Bubbles cause a problem all the time, while with shattered crystals if one does not attempt to focus attention there is no problem.
- Triune brain damage: the clients can focus fully and easily, but their attention is pulled away to different subjects.

Treatment

- This is currently a licensed Peak States certified therapist process.

Typical Mistake in Technique

- Doing the process incorrectly can create or make this problem worse.

Underlying Cause

- The material that helps form awareness is too solid and fractured, so is not absorbed properly.

Symptom Frequency & Severity

- Rare issue in clients. However, a significant number of people have this problem, they just adequately compensate by avoidance or partial focus.

Risks

- The usual for trauma psychotherapy.

ICD-10 Codes

- F80, F90

Triune Brain (Sacred Being) Damage: "There is something fundamentally broken in me"

We have tracked an amazing number of different kinds of subcellular cases, and trauma itself, to damage in the triune brain structures. The 'sacred beings' are the most fundamental form of the triune brains – their awareness extends outward into larger and more complex structures. First to the points of the merkaba in the primary cell's nuclear core, then to cell organelles, then to the anatomical structures in the brain. Most importantly, damage in the sacred beings blocks echoes outwards into these larger structures as they are formed during pre- and post-natal development, and also causes all kinds of traumas, symptoms and subcellular cases in people. Healthy sacred beings have a block shape with rounded edges and corners (unless they are combined in their usual totem pole configuration, or as a single fused block). They should feel hard, smooth, and 'look' shiny black (with a solid gold interior). Most people have both fungal and bacterial parasites inside the blocks. The fungus makes the sacred beings seem like human children.

Working with the sacred being blocks is potentially very dangerous. Much of their damage is due to parasites, and working on them can trigger new damage from parasites. Another problem we've encountered are healing techniques (not from us) that eliminate symptoms by causing the sacred being block to become transparent or soft – this inhibits their ability to function and so needs to be reversed as quickly as possible.

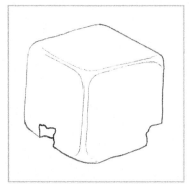

Figure 10.18: The sacred being blocks are where the consciousness of the triune brains reside. These structures can be damaged by generational formation trauma or by parasite actions.

Symptom Keywords

- Core damage; can never be healed; it was and always will be terrible; I am never able to heal this pain.
- There is something fundamentally wrong and irreparable with me.

Diagnosing Questions

- Is there the feeling of a block-like structure under all of your problems?

Differential Diagnosis

- Generational trauma: this trauma is issue specific; one that is about a very personal flaw in oneself. Damage to the sacred beings causes many simultaneous problems, due to this more fundamental, underlying driving problem.
- Parasites: The different species of parasites do not feel sacred, although some class 1 bug-like parasite shells can feel like a sacred being surface.

Treatment

- This is currently a licensed Peak States certified therapist process.

Typical Mistake in Technique

- Stimulating parasite interactions by mistake.

Underlying Cause

- Damage to the sacred beings due to parasite actions or original budding problems.

Symptom Frequency & Severity

- This is a very common problem, especially among client populations. The consequences are usually severe, although most people find ways to mask or avoid much of the problem.

Risks

- Working on these problems must be considered experimental and potentially dangerous. It can trigger more problems, tiredness, lack of ability to connect to the outside world, and a host of other major issues.

DANGER

Working on sacred being damage is potentially dangerous. Only do so under the supervision of someone trained and knowledgeable in how to deal with parasite issues in this context.

ICD-10 Codes

- This can cause a large variety of very different symptoms.

Triune Brain Shutdown: "I've lost an essential ability in myself"

This occurs when a triune brain feels so rejected and attacked by the other triune brains that it shuts itself off – in essence, commits reversible suicide. This causes the person to lose the essential ability of that brain. For mind shutdown you lose the ability to form judgments, as when choosing between two items in a store. For the heart, you lose the ability to feel other people are like yourself and not just objects. For the body, you lose the sense of time passing. Shutdown can be partial or complete, so symptoms can also be partial or extreme. We have seen this problem in people who have used hallucinogens, and at the end of the experience had brain shutdown.

Using the peak ability we simply call 'Seeing the Brains', the affected brain looks flattened, rather than ball shaped; as if it was run over by a car. In the primary cell biological view, the merkaba point that corresponds to the brain is damaged.

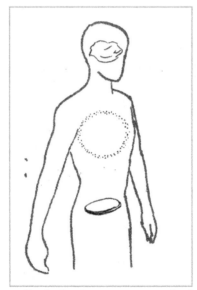

Figure 10.19: Normally the brain awarenesses look like fuzzy spheres. Shutdown brain awarenesses look flattened, like run over by a car. (These triune brain views are of a fungal infection inside the sacred being blocks.)

Symptom Keywords

- "I feel disabled", lack of normal ability.
- I can't make decisions; people now feel just like objects; time seems to have stopped.

Diagnosing Questions

- What triggered this problem? (Look for triune brain conflicts.)

Differential Diagnosis

- Flattened emotion: partial heart brain shutdown can appear like the flattened emotions case. However, with flattened emotions people do not feel like objects. You can also test by seeing if the Courteau projection technique works on their issue.
- Autism: with autism, people also feel other people as objects. However, there is also a feeling of being in a glass box, while with brain shutdown this is not the case.

Treatment

- Use the Courteau Projection Technique.

Typical Mistake in Technique

- The therapist forgets to select several people with the projection and find the common traits.

Underlying Cause

- Essentially, a decision by a triune brain to shut itself off.

Symptom Frequency & Severity

- This problem is very rare, and can be partial or fully present.
- People with it often feel relief that the brain that shut down is gone, but are frustrated with the consequent loss of function.

Risks

- The usual for trauma psychotherapy.

ICD-10 Codes

- F60.2, F60.9.

Viral Net: "I have a pressure or migraine headache"

Many, and perhaps most 'migraine' headaches are caused by a viral activity. These clients have viral particles that combine to form a 'netting' (reminiscent of a lace doily) that surrounds part or all of the nucleolus genes, about half way between the gene bundle and the nuclear membrane. This viral material has an imperative to get to the center of the nucleus, apparently so it can activate its own life function. This viral net squeezes inward, creating a corresponding, usually painful pressure in part or all of the head (since the nucleus feels like their head to most people).

Some clients have this viral net problem continuously (with corresponding continuous head pain), some only temporarily. More disturbingly, clients with the netting can trigger its formation in others who are susceptible. This viral net induction can occur one on one – for example, between a mother and daughter – but is also common in organizations. Folks with this problem evoke symptoms in others by triggering them to participate in emotional drama. This triggering also shows up in groups. The viral netting problem is eliminated with a Peak States certified therapist process; the pressure disappears immediately.

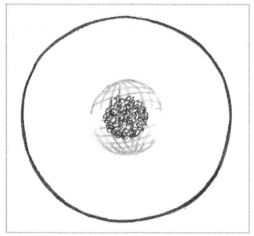

Figure 10.20: A network of what we think are viral strands form a lace network around the nucleolus and squeeze, causing headaches or migraines. The net can fully surround the nucleus or be partial.

Symptom Keywords

- I have a pressure headache; I have a migraine; my head feels squeezed.
- A person stimulates emotional drama and pulls others into resisting or separating from the teacher/boss.
- I betray people that trust me; I disrupt the organization I'm in; I have to be in the center of attention.

Diagnosing Questions

- What triggered this problem? (My parent/ loved one is very upset at me.)
- Has this happened several times before? (i.e., disrupting the group/ organization.)
- Do you have a pressure headache most or all of the time in a specific area of your head?

Differential Diagnosis

- S-holes: needs love and attention all the time, but the head does not feel compressed.
- Biographical trauma: the pain is due to long-term muscle tension. Viral net causes pressure only on the head.
- Body association: I need that exact pain for some reason. Viral net pressure can expand or contract in size.
- Chakra: I feel something pushing in or ripping my bones apart centered at one of the traditional chakra locations. By contrast, the viral net pressure is like a skull cap squeezing the head.
- Bug-like parasites: it feels like being stabbed/ ripped/ burned, but anywhere on the body. There is no feeling of pressure.
- Sound loop: this bacterial organism can cause an outward pressure to the nuclear membrane (head). The viral net only squeezes inwards towards the center of the nucleolus (head).

Treatment

- For some clients, healing trauma located in the solar plexus while having the migraine (or using regression to a migraine event) may reduce or eliminate the symptoms.
- Elimination of the viral net is currently a licensed Peak States certified therapist process.

Typical Mistake in Technique

- Misdiagnosis of the cause of the pressure symptom.

Underlying Cause

- A viral network inside the nucleus that squeezes the nucleolus, giving corresponding symptoms in the head.

Symptom Frequency & Severity

- This squeezing pain is stimulated rather rarely in most people (and generally goes away if the person avoids the person who stimulated the emotional drama in them).
- The people who have the problem permanently and who induce it into others are rare, but very noticeable in their circle of family or work.

Risks

- The usual for trauma psychotherapy.

ICD-10 Codes

- F24, F60.3, G43, R51.

Chapter 11

Subcellular Cases that Block
(or Mimic) Trauma Healing

Client issues can be directly due to trauma, or *indirectly* due to trauma as shown in many of the subcellular cases in previous chapters. Thus, the ability to quickly and effectively heal trauma is a critical skill for the therapist. However, all too often the healing does not work, in spite of the use of proper technique for the therapy.

The previous chapters covered how a trauma therapy fails because of incorrect diagnosis – the client actually had a subcellular case issue, not a simple trauma. ('Simple' in the sense that the symptom is from a stuck mRNA trauma string and so well-known standard techniques apply, not in the sense of how it affected a person's life.) For example, as a rule of thumb when using a meridian therapy, *if change doesn't happen in two or three minutes, you need to stop the therapy and look at reasons why it isn't working.* Given that you are doing the therapy correctly, a review of the previous chapters would suggest that their issue is not a trauma, but rather is most likely to be a subcellular case, often a 'copy'.

In this chapter, we explore other non-standard, mostly unknown or unrecognized reasons that we have found so far that causes a trauma-healing therapy to fail, either in general or in specific issues. These reasons can also be considered 'subcellular cases'; unfortunately, a client can have more than one at the same time. Although many of these cases are not common knowledge, it does not mean that they rarely occur – far from it. The reader is probably wondering which of the cases in this chapter are the most frequent, but that is difficult to say as this varies from issue to issue and client to client. Hence, the therapist needs to learn the characteristics of each one (just as they have to do for the other subcellular cases) to keep in mind in case their therapy process gets stuck or does not work.

As an aside, there can also be a number of ordinary reasons why your trauma healing process with a client does not work. For example, some issues just involve such intense feelings that the client cannot or is not willing to face them. Most therapies include various tricks to help the client in these cases.

(From our perspective, the therapist might want to check if there are generational traumas causing the problem to feel too personal to face.) Or that the trauma therapy chosen just doesn't work well for that particular client or that particular trauma; different therapies tend to work on some kinds of problems more effectively than on others. Or perhaps the client doesn't realize that they are doing the therapy incorrectly. Switching to a new trauma therapy can help in those cases. Clearly, having a good 'toolkit' of trauma therapies and experience in using them is necessary for the therapist.

Empirically, we've found that there are three main reasons why clients don't heal. The most common reason is that the therapist has a 'resonating' trauma, one that is the same or complementary to the client's. The client can feel the therapist's unconscious reaction to the issue, and so may not feel safe enough to continue. The second most common reason is that the therapist unconsciously does not want the client to change. This is usually due to illogical body associations, where the client unconsciously reminds the therapist of someone from their past, is jealous of the other person, etc. Oddly enough, the *least* common reason is the one that we spend the most time on – the technique is not good enough for the problem. On the other hand, there are some very interesting reasons why the client heals even when the technique was *not* adequate or appropriate for the problem: for example, the client just needed to feel safe enough to face the problem; or the therapist is unconsciously helping the client to heal by temporarily inducing a peak state; or the therapist is unknowingly doing a healing-at-a-distant method like DPR, surrogate EFT, or others.

Psychoactive Medications: "I just can't feel it"

In this section, we focus on the effect of prescription psychoactive drugs during trauma healing. Specifically, we report on our experiences with using Whole Hearted Healing (WHH) – it is likely that other therapies have similar issues.

Fortunately, only a few psychoactive drugs can block or dramatically slow down trauma healing. However, unless they are specifically asked, many clients forget to say that they are taking prescription or other drugs. Thus, client intake forms need to specifically check for these substances. For more on the topic of medications, side effects, withdrawal, and other problems, we refer you to *The Whole-Hearted Healing Workbook* by Paula Courteau.

Many drugs can have side effects that induce symptoms of schizophrenia or other serious mental illnesses. Be sure to check your client's drug history and current usage when diagnosing.

Benzodiazepines

Valium (Diazepam), Klonopin, Xanax, Ativan (Lorazepam), Librium, and some others are from a class of drugs called benzodiazepines, which act as a central nervous system depressant. In other words, they slow down the activity of the central nervous system. Matt Fox writes: "When I have tried WHH on clients who are taking benzos, either the results are unusually slow or the client can't get it together enough emotionally to focus on the intervention. I don't like to use either WHH or EFT on clients while they are taking benzos, and advise them to talk to their doctors about getting off them."

SSRIs and Lithium

Our experience, and that of others using power therapies, shows in particular that neither lithium nor selective serotonin reuptake inhibitors (SSRIs, such as Paxil and Prozac) will interfere with the regression process. Note that you can, and should, stay on your medication while doing the therapy.

Tricyclic Antidepressants

The tricyclic antidepressant desipramine càn block people from regressing. This problem showed up in a client who was using the medication at full dose. Nowadays, with the advent of SSRIs, physicians typically prescribe desipramine and other tricyclic antidepressants for chronic pain rather than for depression. The bedtime dose for pain control is only about a tenth of the antidepressant dose and is unlikely to cause a problem. We have shown that it's fully possible to regress and heal effectively even with a somewhat narrowed emotional range. Make sure that the client does not quit their medication unless monitored by their physician.

Psychological Reversal (Guarding Trauma): "I've tapped for hours and nothing happened"

Probably the most common problem that blocks a trauma-healing therapy is actually quite simple when understood. The client has a 'guarding trauma'; a trauma that tells the client that they need another trauma. For example, the guarding trauma might be 'I need to stay on guard or people will take advantage of me', while the trauma that the client is unsuccessfully trying to get rid of might be 'I feel unsafe'. You can also have a guarding trauma that guards another trauma that guards another trauma, and so on. Fortunately, you can heal the guarding trauma, and once that is gone, the 'protected' trauma can now heal in turn. The meridian therapy BSFF uses this approach.

They use a different approach in the meridian therapy EFT to deal with this problem. They call this guarding trauma phenomenon 'psychological reversal', and rub lymph nodes to temporarily disable its effect. This can work well, but in the case of severe guarding trauma, the window of opportunity to heal before the guarding trauma becomes re-activated can be very brief, on the order of seconds; too brief to get much healing done.

Other trauma therapies are less affected by this problem. For example, the regression technique WHH can usually heal a trauma in spite of the effect of any guarding trauma. However, it is still generally easier when there is no guarding trauma present.

At the deepest level of trauma, most people resist healing (positive change) because of suffocation trauma that gets stimulated – this feeling is usually completely blocked from awareness. Having the client deliberately scan for the suffocation feelings as they try to heal can bring this to awareness in some people if it is not too suppressed.

There is a completely different mechanism in the case of psychologically reversed diseases. Examples include cancer, multiple sclerosis, and chronic fatigue syndrome. Here, the client resists or avoids any process that will eliminate their symptoms. This behavior, which can be quite bizarre at times, is because the client's body feels it needs the disease to suppress a more serious (to it) problem – even if the presenting disease will end up killing the client. Treatment for these issues is to eliminate the underlying problem first, then the presenting disease.

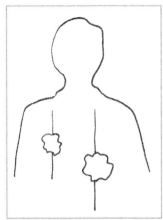

Figure 11.1: About 10-20% of the time a tapping therapy does not work because there is another trauma telling the client not to heal the original trauma. This is shown as two trauma strings superimposed into the body image.

Symptom Keywords

- I just can't do this; I must not let it go; I am not safe without this problem.
- Nothing happens when I try to heal.
- Healing is really slow.
- I can't continue the healing session, I have to do something else now (like feed the cat).

Diagnosing Questions

- Has it been over three minutes since we started tapping with no effect?
- At the end of the therapy process, is there a shadow of the feeling still there, like a memory?

Differential Diagnosis

- Dilemma: you feel pulled different directions, not blocked from healing.
- Body association: often no obvious connection/relationship with the issue, and no belief, just sensation.
- Tribal block: the issue feels heavy.
- Multiple trauma roots: some small change usually does happen as the roots dissolve one at a time.

Treatment

- Find the trauma driven belief(s) about why the client must keep all or part of the targeted trauma. The easiest way is to have the client imagine that the trauma being healed is gone – this evokes the guarding trauma feelings. Once these are identified, you heal them first then return to the original trauma.
- Use EFT's psychological reversal steps to turn off the guarding trauma temporarily.

- Use triune brain therapy so that the triune brains won't interfere with the healing.

Typical Mistake in Technique

- Not realizing there was another guarding trauma.
- The client doesn't notice that there is still some of the problem there.

Underlying Cause

- A trauma can cause a person to block healing on another trauma, e.g., "I need this traumatic feeling to survive."

Symptom Frequency & Severity

- Seldom for most issues. Relatively frequent in chronic or long-lasting issues.

Risks

- The usual for trauma psychotherapy.

ICD-10 Codes

- No specific code yet identified.

Trauma Bypass: "I can heal effortlessly and instantly"

We first encountered this problem in 2005. A person who was a self-proclaimed powerful healer and shaman got very sick. In trying to diagnose why, we found a lot of ribbon-like structures on the underside of the nuclear membrane; each enclosed a stuck gene. Eliminating these structures caused the person to suddenly feel all the traumas that had been blocked by these structures. Later we found that some students who came for training would 'instantly' heal trauma moments – but instead of healing, they were creating these same structures. Some therapies appear to train people in how to do this on purpose. However, although symptoms vanish, this is a bad idea – the stuck gene still cannot be expressed; this is a bit like cutting off your finger to eliminate the itch of a mosquito bite. Although it is possible to eliminate all the bypasses simultaneously, this approach needs to be discussed with the client before treatment. Interestingly, some of the people we've met who do this have told us that they feel that the technique (or self-created internal method) they use to make bypasses is somehow damaging them, although they can't say why. For the most part, these people do not show up as clients; we generally see them only during therapist training.

There is another, much less common biological mechanism that also allows a client to instantly block trauma feelings. In this subcellular case, the client puts a crown brain structure around the trauma string in the cytoplasm. Although the motivation to avoid pain, along with an immediate and genuine removal of symptoms is the same in both cases, treatment is different – the client has to be guided to heal the crown brain's need to create these structures.

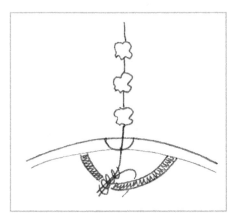 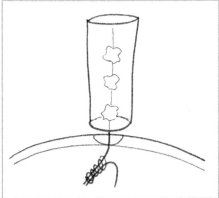

Figure 11.2: Shown are cutaway side views of the nucleus. (a) A bridge-like structure encloses a stuck gene in the nucleus. It blocks awareness of the trauma string. (b) A crown brain structure encloses the trauma string to block the feeling of the trauma ribosomes.

Symptom Keywords

- I can make the trauma go away instantly/fast; it's because I am a powerful _____ [shaman, healer, spiritual type, teacher]
- Therapist can sense incongruence between the client's presentation (behavior, talk) and a deeper level in them.

Diagnosing Questions

- Is trauma healing almost instant and easy for you?
- Did you experience a feeling of calm, peace and lightness at the end of the healing, or did the emotional pain just vanish?
- (For the therapist: does the client appear to be very exceptional in their compassion and acceptance? If so, their healing is likely to be due to a state, not a trauma bypass.)

Differential Diagnosis

- Being Present state: Healing progress is fast instead of instant. Check attributes of the state: are they in-body automatically?; do they exhibit exceptional self-love and self-acceptance?
- Unstable Beauty Way: when the aliveness sensation is present, the symptoms vanish. When the aliveness feeling is lost, the symptoms come back.
- Crown brain structure: test empirically by using the crown brain structure elimination method.

Treatment

- For gene bypasses: this is currently a licensed Peak States certified therapist process.
- For a crown brain enclosure: have the client sense their symptoms and attempt regression. Then have them sense the crown brain structure like a bell around the body. Do crown brain structure healing on the bell. The bypassed trauma can now be healed normally.

Typical Mistake in Technique

- Be prepared for trauma flooding once the structures are gone.

Underlying Cause

- The client creates a 'trauma bypass' structure in the nucleus to surround a stuck gene to block the symptoms.

Symptom Frequency & Severity

- Rare.

Risks

- Trauma flooding can occur once the bypasses are healed. There can be emotional difficulties in accepting the idea of trauma bypasses, as they are in conflict with a self-image of a powerful or skilled healer.

ICD-10 Codes

- No specific code yet identified.

Tribal Block Influence: "Healing slows or stops when I try to heal this moment"

The tribal block phenomenon can also cause difficulty in healing particular traumas. We first noticed this problem when we were having therapy students target specific development events for healing. We were using EFT at the time; we found that the moment simply wasn't healing adequately. Switching to the WHH process, we found the students could heal, but it was far more difficult than it should have been. We tracked this to the tribal block problem; every developmental event's Gaia command was being blocked by it.

Bicultural people have two problems – they have two different types of borg fungus, one from each culture. Especially if the client is trying to reject one of the cultures, the corresponding borg will show up as a uncomfortable sensation attached somewhere in their body. The other culture's borg will have the navel position. Healing this issue is best done by eliminating the borg fungus with the Silent Mind Technique.

This subcellular case has already been covered in a previous chapter; we include it in this section because it can also cause the trauma healing process to become slow or impossible to do.

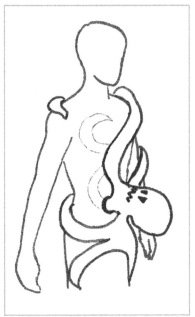

Figure 11.3: A borg fungus that is controlling the behavior of the client can be felt in or on the body. The control point is at the navel. In bicultural cases, the second controlling borg fungus has shifted to another location.

Symptom Keywords

- Nothing is changing; healing won't go to completion; I don't know what is wrong; it is tougher in a group; I feel heavy when I try to heal.

Diagnosing Questions

- When you say the Gaia command and think of the trauma moment, is there an emotional tone coming at your belly button?
- When you focus on a trauma issue to heal, what is the emotional tone coming at your belly button?

Differential Diagnosis

- Guarding trauma: the guarding trauma has its own feeling; but the tribal block makes a person feel heavy, like they were wearing a backpack when they try to heal.

Treatment

- Use the standard one issue at a time Tribal Block technique.
- Do Silent Mind Technique (SMT) to get rid of the fungus that causes the tribal block phenomenon.

Typical Mistake in Technique

- Not staying focused on the issue to be healed, or switching to another issue, while working on the tribal block.

Underlying Cause

- The tribal block is caused by a class 2 (borg) fungal infection, in interaction with other people who are infected by that particular subspecies (family and larger social culture).

Symptom Frequency & Severity

- Different cultures can have more resistance to healing. For example, our Polish students had more trouble with this than most other cultures.

Risks

- The usual for trauma psychotherapy.

ICD-10 Codes

- F43.2

Life Path Trauma: "I can't find what I truly want to do in life"

We first found this subcellular case problem empirically in 2004 – our Australian students were having great difficulty in healing certain traumatic material *if* it had anything to do with their life's purpose, or optimum life's path. When we switched techniques and had them look at their resistance to their optimum life path, these particular traumas were quickly identified and relatively easily healed. The advantage with this 'life path' approach was that they no longer unconsciously blocked awareness and healing of these motivations.

Years later we discovered that these paths were part of a fungal organism living on the inner side of the nuclear membrane. It has a tremendous and generally negative impact on a person's life. Trauma sensations that cause a person to leave the 'bright' path are from locations on the membrane where the path crosses a nuclear pore with its associated trauma feelings. It is optimum for a person's consciousness not to be on this path network at all – but very few people are disengaged from this parasite.

We work with this problem in three ways: for clients who have a decision in their future, heal all the emotional charge on the choices and then choose the one that feels the 'brightest'; use a Peak States process so the client can 'see' the path and deliberately heal poor future choices (although very few clients are willing to maintain an optimal path consistently); or use a Peak States process to eliminate the fungal organism.

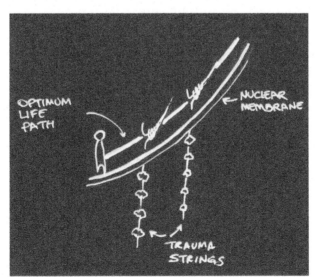

Figure 11.4: The life path fungal organism is on the inner surface of the nuclear membrane. It can also be 'seen' in a 'black space' as paths at your feet that stretch forward in time with many decision points.

Symptom Keywords

- Life path; what I really want to do; fear of the unknown; I can't find the issue; healing is slow or very hard.

Diagnosing Questions

- Does the issue that is hard to find or heal involve what you truly want in your future (a future without you trying to feel special or noticed)?

Differential Diagnosis

- Tribal block: the tribal block makes a person feel heavy if they resist it, and emotionally flat if they don't resist. The life purpose block feels emotionally neutral and more simply blank.

Treatment

- Use the licensed Peak States certified therapist technique for the Life Path.

Typical Mistake in Technique

- Not getting the euphoria feeling fully.

Underlying Cause

- To be on the optimum life path requires healing traumas that can be very difficult to find or face with normal techniques.

Symptom Frequency & Severity

- Infrequent, because it only comes up around issues involving resistance to being on one's optimum life path.

Risks

- The usual for trauma psychotherapy.

ICD-10 Codes

- No specific codes.

Parasite Resistance: "I am afraid to do anything to change"

When the primary cell environment is disturbed or improved due to healing, parasites in the cell may find the changes uncomfortable or threatening and want it to stop. We've found that many people, especially low functioning client populations, resist healing because they cannot tell the difference between themselves and the parasites inside their primary cell. Sometimes the parasites cause painful sensations that the client has learned will stop if they quit trying to change, a bit like a rider whipping a recalcitrant but well trained horse. In other cases, the emotional desire to have the primary cell environment stop changing is actually in the parasite, but the client feels these feelings as if they were their own. (Interestingly, some people don't sense the parasite feelings at all, although most people do to a greater or lesser degree.) Thus, due to the fear of punishment or identity confusion the client avoids or resists healing or change, even in cases where they also want it to happen.

The parasites also influence the person to change their internal cellular environment to make it more comfortable and/or to facilitate their reproduction. For example, and quite counter-intuitively, emotionally positive group experiences facilitate reproduction of a species-wide bacterial infection. Negative emotions also indirectly affect the subcellular environment, making it more comfortable for various parasites. Diabetes is another example of a subcellular parasite influencing the host in order to modify the primary cell environment.

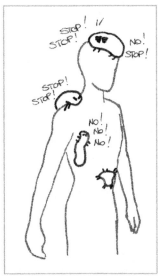

Figure 11.5: Almost all people confuse themselves with the desires and actions of the parasites in their primary cells. Generally these organisms do not want any changes to their environment, leading to similar behavior in the client's daily life.

Symptom Keywords

- Resist, don't want to, don't change, fear, anxiety, stop.

Diagnosing Questions

- Does it seem like there is some sort of voice telling you to stop the healing?
- Does it feel like you are being attacked and that this therapy feels dangerous?

Differential Diagnosis

- Mind chatter: mind chatter sounds like real people speaking. Parasites are much simpler and don't use language – it just seems like it.
- Suffocation trauma: the resistance is from trying to avoid feelings of suffocation.

Treatment

- Still under development. As it is hard for people to recognize that the parasites are not themselves, targeting it for elimination is difficult.

Typical Mistake in Technique

- Not yet known.

Underlying Cause

- Not yet known.

Symptom Frequency & Severity

- Frequent in many people, especially low and medium functioning client population.

Risks

- Unknown.

ICD-10 Codes

- May trigger anxiety in codes F40-48.

Multiple Trauma Roots: "I heal and heal but the symptoms are still there"

When healing simple trauma, be it biographical, generational or associational, we normally see one or at most a couple of genes anchoring the stuck trauma string. When we have multiple stuck genes connecting to an mRNA string, we call the different branches 'roots' because of their visual resemblance to a tree root. The different roots each contribute different traumatic qualities to the later traumas, as if they were summing together. (This corresponds to the psychological experience of 'having more than one root to the problem'.) As we heal and a gene releases its mRNA, the client loses the trauma sensations that were associated with the stuck gene. Unfortunately, we've occasionally seen clients who had many, many roots for a given trauma issue. These people can actually heal one or more trauma roots, yet not realize it because the incremental change in the presenting symptoms are so small. Especially if the therapy is slow on a 'per stuck gene' basis, this therapy can appear to be a waste of time to the client, even though it is working as it is supposed to.

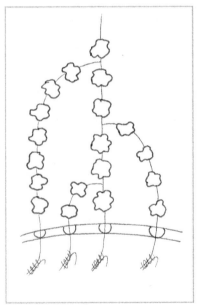

Figure 11.6: This figure shows a four-root trauma string. The uppermost ribosomal traumas will contain a combination of feelings from the four stuck genes.

Symptom Keywords

- No change. Healing makes no difference. Futile. Had this problem for a long time. Nothing works.

Diagnosing Questions

- Do the specific trauma origins actually dissolve; if they do, do they come back again?
- Is there a minute amount of change on the presenting symptom?
- Did a trauma origin actually heal, but the symptom is still there?

Differential Diagnosis

- Time loops: traumas in loops can be eliminated, but then return later. Multiple roots simply don't seem to heal (much).

Treatment

- Use a technique that is very fast on a per stuck gene basis. If the client responds to tapping, just use the 9-gamut spot.

Typical Mistake in Technique

- Quitting too soon.

Underlying Cause

- A presenting issue from a trauma string that has many roots (stuck genes).

Symptom Frequency & Severity

- Fortunately having multiple roots on a trauma string are very rare. There is normally only one root, with an upper maximum of about six. In one very unusual case the client had around 50 roots to a single trauma string.

Risks

- The usual for trauma psychotherapy.

ICD-10 Codes

- No specific codes.

Time Loops: "The trauma came back!"

We originally discovered this problem while looking at the earliest developmental events. After healing a trauma moment with WHH, in a few minutes (to a few hours) the original trauma would be restored exactly as it had been before healing. At first, we though this might be a property of the earliest developmental events. But it turned out that there was a completely different mechanism, one that we now call 'time loops'. As the name suggests, when regressing one can feel that a segment of time simply keeps repeating itself over and over. If the client heals a trauma in this time zone, it simply resets itself back to the way it was. From the therapist's viewpoint, a 'time loop' could more functionally be called a 'trauma reset' subcellular case. This reset is triggered when the client feels anxious or fearful.

The biology of time loops is fascinating – the physical structure that does this trauma reset looks and feels a bit like an egg with a hard shell that encloses bubbles. This structure is inside what we call the 'pinecone' (a fungal parasite) inside the nuclear core. The time loop egg-like structure is actually made in very early development as a defense put there by the parent, against class 1 bug-like and class 2 fungal parasites that eat the developing child consciousness. This shell material also has an emotion, typically anxiety or fear.

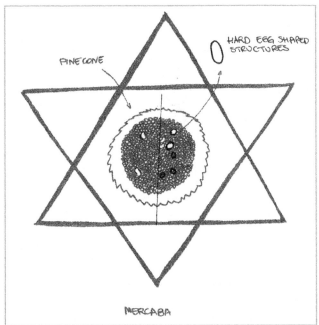

Figure 11.7: (a) Time loops are egg or smooth shaped containers that enclose bubbles in the (fungal) pinecone structure in the nuclear core. The outer structure is a three dimensional merkaba, shown as flat lines in the diagram.

Time looping, like a sports replay on TV, can be felt in regression, once the client's attention is drawn to the sensation. The corresponding physical egg-like structures can *also* be felt in the body in the present. The sensation of a barrier across the upper belly blocking the upper and lower body is a rather common example of a time loop. They can also be felt anywhere in or around the body, and have any size (although in reality they are either in the left or the right of the pinecone structure). They are rare in average clients, but can be common in client populations with chronic issues or paranoia. Time loops can also be inside of time loops like Russian dolls. We've also seen some clients with time loops enclosing their entire egg or sperm side past. Feeling anxiety or fear when focused on the issue will cause a time loop to replace any trauma symptoms that were previously eliminated.

Rarely, there can be another type of biological structure in the pinecone that can cause time loops. Rather than having a hard shell, this structure has a soft membrane without any emotion in it. However, it is attached to a bug parasite that is hidden with a sort of fog or static from the awareness of the client. Eliminating the bug by healing the generational with its emotional tone dissolves both bug and membrane.

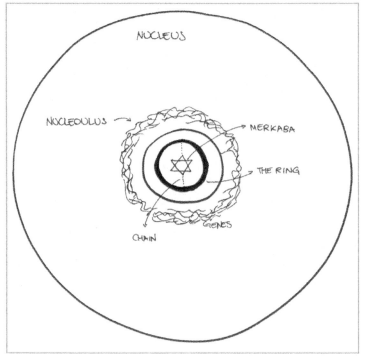

Figure 11.7: (b) A not-to-scale view of the nucleus with the merkaba (a fungal structure) shown in the nucleolus.

Symptom Keywords
- This therapy doesn't work. Nothing ever works for me. The healing reversed itself. The painful emotion keeps coming back.
- I feel a barrier splitting my upper and lower body.

Diagnosing Questions
- Does exactly the same problem keep coming back right after the therapy is finished?
- Do you feel a hard, rounded object in your body?
- If you focus on the eliminated issue, and then try and feel anxious or afraid, do the same symptoms re-appear?

Differential Diagnosis
- Body association: the body recreates symptoms, but uses new methods and traumas to do so; the new symptoms are usually worse; a time loop has no underlying trauma-related cause.
- Copy: the client would need to find new person to copy to restore a symptom; time loops quickly return symptoms (minutes to hours).
- Crown brain structure: these structures also feel hard, but they are angular, like manufactured out of metal parts, not rounded like eggs. And the structure has no emotional tone in its material.
- Guarding trauma: the problem never goes away (never actually heals) vs. time loop trauma that healed and comes back.
- MPD: the client might switch personalities during the healing, hence avoiding healing. If so, they won't recall (or in a very limited way) what was done earlier in the other MDP.
- S-Hole: they only have an energy sucking, annihilating feeling; time loop can reverse any trauma related problem.
- Tribal block: the client will feel heavy; check the navel. Time loops are in regions of the body.

Treatment
- For eggshell time loops:
  - Merge with the *entire* shell of the time-loop structure. Feel the emotional and physical pain, and the desperation of the grandmother to defend the client – the shell will dissolve. Be sure to dissolve all shell fragments, if any. Repeat the healing that was done and reversed.
  - Alternatively, feel the emotion in the time loop shell structure, find the generational trauma that matches, and heal that to eliminate the time loop.
- For membrane time loops:
  - Find the bug attached to the membrane, sense its emotional tone, and heal the generational with the same emotion. If needed, heal any time loops that restore the generational trauma.
- All time loops can be simultaneously eliminated with a licensed Peak States certified therapist process.

Typical Mistake in Technique

- When time loops are suspected, testing for trauma resetting by having the client feel anxious saves time.
- Missing larger, enclosing time loops that need to be healed first.
- Not recognizing a membrane time loop from a hard eggshell time loop.
- Eliminating a time-loop barrier across the body can expose the sensation that the lower half of the body is different than the upper half. This can be healed using the Courteau Projection Technique.

Underlying Cause

- The time loop phenomenon is caused by an egg-shaped structure that is built by the grandmother to defend the developing grandchild consciousness from parasites. This is maintained during development, and shows up in the pinecone structure in the nuclear core.

Symptom Frequency & Severity

- A common problem in people, but very infrequently encountered for any given issue except in clients with chronic problems or problems that therapies don't seem to heal.

Risks

- No known risks if the time loop is healed in the present. Regression can cause a problem due to disturbing parasite homeostasis in the grandmother.

ICD-10 Codes

- No specific codes.

Dysfunctional Homeostasis: "The symptoms came back and are even worse!"

In this very common case, the person's body consciousness (outside of conscious awareness) is actively working to keep certain symptoms or sensations continuously present. This occurs because the body has an irrational association that says 'I have to have this particular symptom or I will die". These associations are formed during traumatic moments when the body felt that its survival was threatened. Normally, as therapists we usually treat clients as if they were a car with a problem, and we just have to figure out what parts need repair. Unfortunately, this approach does not work when dealing with these dysfunctional homeostatic body associations. If you are successful in getting rid of the symptoms, the body will quickly figure out a new way to get the symptoms back, and usually it will overcompensate, making the problem even worse. Thus, these body associations have to be eliminated *first*, or else you'll be caught in a never-ending sequence of new problems. (As an aside, one of the causes of 'trauma flooding' is dysfunctional homeostasis, but one where the body is trying to avoid a sensation, in this case one of peace.)

Figure 11.8: (a) A symbolic representation of the sensate substitute problem. The client holds onto people (or other substitutes) that feel like their surroundings in an early prenatal trauma. Hanging onto these substitutes makes him feel comfortable (although the people who are playing out that role don't look very happy!). (b) The client is paying attention, but her body brain is resisting.

For example, we had a client who had hearing loss. Each time we would figure out the mechanism that was causing it, her hearing would drastically and immediately improve. Yet by the next morning, her hearing loss would be worse than when we started. It turned out she had an abuse trauma where she associated deafness with safety. Thus, finding the reasons why she couldn't hear and eliminating them like replacing broken parts in a car actually made her worse. Her body was actively trying to outwit the healing process.

Symptom Keywords
- The symptoms come back; healing doesn't work; temporary relief only; worse off than I was.

Diagnosing Questions
- After you did the healing and the symptoms were gone, did they return by the next day, and were even worse?

Differential Diagnosis
- Time loops: loops restore the traumas and their symptoms very quickly, as in minutes to hours. But they are exactly the same, and the traumas are exactly the same. The associational problem causes symptoms to return, but healed traumas stay healed.

Treatment
- Body Association Technique.

Typical Mistake in Technique
- Missing some associations; not checking both hands.

Underlying Cause
- A body association that tells the body it needs the symptoms.

Symptom Frequency & Severity
- This problem is infrequent, except in people with chronic problems that have resisted attempts at healing.

Risks
- The usual for trauma psychotherapy.

ICD-10 Codes
- No specific codes.

Trauma Flooding: "New bad feelings endlessly arise"

Occasionally, the therapist will have a client who was doing some trauma healing but when finished, immediately launched into a new and usually unrelated trauma issue. Upon healing that, the client then again goes into a new trauma issue. And this cycle just continues; sometimes with momentary respite after healing, but sometimes with no break at all. Other clients have trauma activation or flooding as a chronic problem, often with simultaneously triggered traumas, but it has nothing to do with trauma healing. Regardless, this is a very serious problem for these clients, and therapists need to know how to deal with it.

First Time Trauma Flooding (After Healing A Trauma)

- Triune brains: Trauma flooding sometimes happens to clients who have an experience of healing trauma for the first time. Their triune brains, who are like delighted children, feel that this is finally a chance to heal, and want to. So they stimulate traumas for the client to heal, a bit like a child can keep asking for chocolate non-stop for hours and hours.

- CoA location: this is a rare problem, but does occur. During the course of healing an issue, the client's CoA has moved down to the area of the stuck genes at the nuclear membrane. Instead of moving normally somewhere else once the healing is done, the client expands their awareness in that area. This causes them to access random trauma strings and their stored feelings all at once. To heal, the client has to be shown how to move their awareness away from the trauma strings, and heal any traumatic need to keep their CoA there.

Pre-existing Chronic Trauma Flooding

- Inner Peace Process: In our experience, the most common reason for trauma being easily or continuously being triggered is due to a biological incompatibility between the mRNA trauma strings and the nuclear pore membrane. Each time an event triggers the need for a protein that has a corresponding stuck gene, there is a feeling of slightly painful irritation at the boundary between the string and the membrane. Over time, these irritations leave a sort of 'anchor' made up of small pieces that accumulate on the nuclear pore. These biographical trauma strings and their corresponding traumatic feelings become much, much easier to trigger as this continues. To heal this problem, we use the Peak States certified therapist 'Inner Peace Process'. This does not eliminate the traumas, but rather eliminates the irritation and anchors at the base of each trauma string, making them much harder to trigger in normal circumstances.

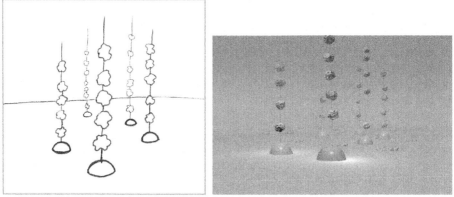

Figure 11.9: (a) Stuck mRNA strings coming out of the nucleus, with 'anchors' at the bottom. (b) A 3D view in the cytoplasm looking down at the nuclear membrane.

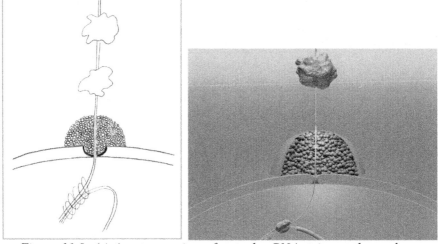

Figure 11.9: (c) A cutaway view of a stuck mRNA string at the nuclear membrane. Note the grains of material at the nuclear pore form the anchor-looking structure. (d) A 3D image of the same drawing.

- Body association: For a client with pre-existing and chronic trauma flooding, the most common reason for this problem is that the client has a negative body association with the feeling of being at peace. In essence, the client's body feels it is unsafe not to have a problem, so they trigger a constant barrage of negative traumas. The key to detecting this problem is to have the client 'feel' (not just have a mental image of) the sensation of having no traumas activated, either at the moment or from their memory of the short peaceful pause after healing an issue.

This will usually activate the underlying driving sensations so they can be healed.

- Suppressing an underlying traumatic feeling: For a client with pre-existing and occasional trauma flooding, we've seen clients who feel they have to have symptoms (for example, the dizziness and nausea of vortices) otherwise they won't get attention (and hopefully caring) that keeps their overwhelming loneliness at bay. To find the issue to heal, have the client look at the moment that the traumatic sensations started at each episode to find the suppressed trigger feeling. And also heal the body associations on their preferred symptoms that they use for this unconscious suppression of feeling (i.e., the sensation of being dizzy is my preferred symptom).

- Kundalini: This triggers a long-term series of traumatic feelings that just continue, no matter how much healing is done. Typically, the trigger is mediation, a strong sexual experience, or some spiritual practices. Unlike normal trauma flooding, kundalini also gives moments of extreme spiritual experiences and feelings; as well as too much energy and tension to sleep much or at all. You heal this subcellular case in the normal manner.

Risks

- The usual for trauma psychotherapy.
- One global treatment for trauma anchor structures involves regression to the Genesis cell developmental event. Clients with a history of heart trouble should **not** be regressed to this event, because there is a potential risk of triggering a heart attack.

CAUTION

Clients with a history of heart trouble should not be regressed to the Genesis cell developmental event due to the possible risk of triggering a heart attack.

ICD-10 Codes

- Not yet determined.

Section 4

Applications

Chapter 12

Issues from Multiple or Indirect Causes

In this chapter, we'll take a look at some common client issues that are caused by simple trauma or multiple subcellular problems. Obviously, any given client issue needs to be diagnosed from the presenting symptoms; but it can be very helpful to have a list of likely subcellular cases in the back of your mind as you diagnose.

More importantly, in some issues the symptoms are not obviously due to subcellular cases. Like seeing the trick to solving a math problem, this chapter includes explanations of the rather odd and indirect ways that subcellular dysfunctions and developmental event trauma can create an issue's symptoms. This understanding is often critically important for diagnosis and treatment.

As a reminder, therapists who intend to work with serious client issues (such as addictions or suicide) have the ethical and usually legal requirement to have appropriate and adequate training.

Suggested Reading

- *Peak States of Consciousness, Volume 2* by Grant McFetridge, Wes Gietz (2008). (Covers pre- and perinatal developmental event trauma).

Addictions

Therapists who work with addictions absolutely need specialized training to work with this client population. However, if we just look at mild addiction problems in well-functioning people, and who want to get rid of their problem, we have found some simple solutions that have worked for many people. For more in-depth information, see our *Addiction and Withdrawal* Peak States Therapy manual.

Cravings

For most people, cravings are caused by body associations that have linked survival to the addictive substance. It can be a bit tricky, but the therapist can usually do the Body Association Technique on the craving and quickly eliminate the problem. In some clients, the cravings are from copies. Note: this approach rarely works with smoking, because it is usually used to self-medicate symptoms from a fungal parasite problem.

Withdrawal Symptoms

The symptoms of withdrawal are usually due to a body association. Simply use the sensations of the withdrawal symptoms in the Body Association Technique to quickly (minutes) eliminate the symptoms. Generational traumas may also be a cause.

ICD-10 Codes:
*   F10-F19

Allergies

Several usually effective techniques already exist for allergies, such as the Tapas Acupuncture Technique (TAT) or Nambudripad's Allergy Elimination Technique (NAET); and we recommend therapists who wish to become competent in working with allergies to study these existing approaches. For example, we've even seen anaphylactic shock in a baby eliminated in seconds using the TAT approach. Our own Body Association Technique can also be used on allergies by targeting the specific allergy symptoms.

However, these techniques do *not* work when the client's liver filtering is no longer adequate for the demands placed on it. This means that the client will be simultaneously allergic to several allergens; the symptoms depend on how stressed the liver is at the moment. Liver damage, or toxic overloading from a systemic candida infection is the usual cause of this problem. A simple diagnostic question to ask is "do you find car exhaust to be noticeable, or bothersome?" – if yes, this indicates a significant lack of liver function.

Anxiety/ Fear

At the deepest level, all people (except ones in the Beauty Way state or better) have an underlying fear that they project out into events in their lives. Unfortunately, at this time we don't yet have a treatment for this parasite-driven problem. Nor do we yet have a treatment for the intense anxiety of obsessive-compulsive disorder (OCD).

Fortunately, most clients have treatable anxiety or fear issues that are due to trauma or subcellular cases. (Note that the therapist often needs to get a more accurate description of what the client's words 'anxiety' or 'fear' mean to do differential diagnosis.) Here is a list of causes from roughly most to least common:

- Holes: unconsciously becoming aware of a hole is *often* the cause of anxiety. In some cases the person has multiple holes coming to awareness.
- Copies: making copies of another person's anxiety or fear is also common.
- Biographical trauma: the fear or anxiety is usually from a childhood or prenatal event. This can also show up in dreams, as old trauma emotions get replayed. A subcategory of this is a 'fear of fear' trauma, as in "I'm afraid it will happen again."
- Body association: the client has associated fear with survival, so is not able to stop being afraid. (i.e., "Someone could hurt me if I stop being afraid.")
- Awareness of parasites: some clients feel fear or anxiety because they unconsciously sense a parasite in their primary cell.
- Column of Self – Void: the client's CoA is approaching or is in their body's core, and feelings of dread and annihilation are arising.
- Generational fear: the client has a generational fear or anxiety.
- Spiritual emergency: the client is afraid or anxious about a non-ordinary event that happened or might happen again, such as kundalini. Treatment is simply to reassure and give reading material on the topic.
- Abyss: the client has fear around moving forward and falling into the abyss.

Sometimes the anxiety or fear is so intense that the client cannot concentrate on diagnosis or follow a process or procedure. If simple tapping does not work, we suggest using the Waisel Extreme Emotion Technique; start the process then have the client walk their body to the location of the most intense fear.

Up to this point, we have diagnosed assuming that the client is feeling anxiety or fear emotionally or kinesthetically in their body. But sometimes this is not the case – instead, the client has fearful or anxious thoughts, but describes their situation as feeling fear. Of course, these thoughts may in turn stimulate anxiety or fear in their body, but are not the source of the problem. These thoughts/voices are eliminated in the standard way. Note too that a client can have more than one problem simultaneously.

ICD-10 Codes:
- F40, F41, F60.6, R45.0, R45.1, R45.2

Contracted, Tense or Frozen Body Areas

In this problem, a client comes in with an area of the body that is contracted, tense or frozen. Typical body-centered therapy would have the therapist briefly and gently push in to the area, so that the client can become aware of images or any other feelings in that area, to bring the causal traumas into consciousness. And this often works. However, the cause of the distortions in the body can be from a subcellular case. For example: we've seen a compressed chest had a large hole in that area. We've seen an expanded chest, like the prow of a boat, also had a large hole there. In both cases, the client was attempting to make a sensation in that area of the body to 'fill' the emptiness of the hole.

ICD-10 Codes
- M62.88

Depression

We've identified quite a number of different causes for depression. This is partly due to the fact that the word 'depression' has different meanings to different people. Thus, the therapist must be very careful when they hear that word to track down the exact sensations that the client is feeling.

- A deep sadness that doesn't leave. This is most likely a simple trauma, copy, or soul loss.
- A dull, lethargic heavy feeling, a feeling of being 'muffled'. Often due to a suppressed thought. Regress to the moment this started and heal the pattern or trauma.
- Feelings of the futility of life, with thoughts about all the bad things that have happened to mankind, like genocide, Nazi crimes, etc. This is treated using the Courteau Projection Technique.
- All feelings are reduced. This can be lifelong or more recent. This is caused by the flattened emotions subcellular case.
- A feeling of reduced mental and physical energy or exhaustion. This can be caused by a 'blanket curse'. Or a bacterial infection that 'smothers' or puts toxins into critical parts of the primary cell.
- Unable to connect to other people, or feel love. Due to heart brain shutdown. Alternatively, can be due to mild autism, but if so, it would have been lifelong.
- A depression that is similar to someone else's. This can be a copy; or if with a family member, it might be generational.
- A heavy, weighed down feeling. This is often a tribal block problem.
- Depression as a common reaction to losing a peak state. The best solution is to restore their state, if possible.

ICD-10 Codes:
- F33, F34.1

Dreams

The client may come in with strong feelings from a dream or nightmare. We've found that dreams are sequences of feelings that exactly match a traumatic event in the past. Their story line and images are irrelevant. However, some dreams feel numinous, ineffable, or sacred. These types of dreams are very rare, and are not (usually) based on trauma, but are rather visionary types of experiences.

To heal traumatic dream feelings, the client can usually regress to the series of feelings (not the story line) and heal them using WHH. They can also use other trauma techniques like meridian therapies on each feeling in the sequence.

The other reason a client might come in about dreams is that they don't dream and are concerned. People in the Beauty Way state don't dream unless they've lost the state – this lack of dreaming is normal. They do review the day's events each night in sleep, but this is not at all similar to dreams.

ICD-10 Codes:

• F51

Hallucinogens

We have seen a lot of clients over the years that have come to us because a serious problem occurred from using a hallucinogenic substance (LSD, psilocybin, etc.). This has not been because the drugs poisoned them (although this is always a risk), but rather because the drugs triggered dormant 'land mine' traumas. These problems, albeit often quite intense, can usually be handled with standard trauma techniques. In fact, in psycholytic (and psychedelic) therapy, the usual treatment for triggered trauma is another drug session along with support techniques between sessions.

Unfortunately, some of the clients we've seen had triggered a cascade of problems during the drug experience; the presenting symptoms no longer resembled the cause, and so the usual 'trauma therapy on symptoms' approach couldn't be used. Even eliminating the initial triggering trauma wouldn't reverse the subsequent problems in many cases. This is usually due to the fact that the client has triggered a subcellular case whose symptoms are not from a trauma. In approximate order of frequency, the most common subcellular cases are:

• flattened emotions;
• mind chatter;
• shattered crystals;
• over-identification with the Creator;
• body distortions and frozen musculature;
• and primary cell parasite issues including pain and loss or damage to personal identity.

We've also seen other problems triggered by using hallucinogens that we don't yet know how to treat. For example, one young man entered a state of long-term psychosis. Another particularly disturbing example was in a normal healthy adult who acquired irreversible and debilitating multiple sclerosis only hours after using LSD. It is fortunately that serious problems are the exception, not the rule, given the large numbers of people using psychoactive substances.

ICD-10 Codes:
• F1x.7

Headaches

There can be many reasons for headaches. Diagnosis requires a close look at the symptoms. At this time, our techniques are not perfect – some people have problems we can't yet treat. Below are some of the usual causes we've seen for this symptom.

The problem of pressure headaches, from the sensation of pushing in or pushing out or both can have several causes.

• An injury moment might have caused the musculature into a contraction. Later, if this biographical (or generational) trauma is activated for any length of time, it can cause pain as the surrounding structures are stressed or dislocated by the contraction. (Incidentally, this trauma effect is particularly noticeable in spinal column alignment.)

• Another cause is the presence of a bacterium of a particular species inside structures of the primary cell pushing against boundaries in the 'head' region of the primary cell structure. Standard body associations and bacterial generational healing can usually deal with these issues. (See the bacterial parasite case page 138.)

• Yet another possible problem is a 'pulling apart' pressure in the center of the forehead, or a downward pressure on the top of the head. These pains are caused by movement of the fungal chakra organism on the nuclear membrane. The fungus is triggered into a defensive response by conscious or unconscious muscular contractions in the region of the body that correspond to the area of the nuclear membrane where the chakra fungus is attached. (See the chakra case on page 185.)

• Many, and perhaps most 'migraine' headaches are caused by contractions of a 'viral net' inside the nuclear membrane. When severe, this problem gives the 'sensitivity to light' symptom associated with migraines. (See the 'viral net' case on page 216.) Some people respond well when the far less obvious solar plexus symptoms are eliminated.

• Much milder symptoms in the solar plexus or other part of the body can be an indirect trigger for the headache. Have the client look for these subtle feelings and heal them to test this possibility.

A headache can also be described as a stabbing or ripping pain. This less common cause of head pain is due to bugs that are injuring a primary cell membrane whose location corresponds to the head area. (See the bug-like parasite problem on page 142.)

And headaches (an in fact any pain) of all sorts can be due to the activation of a 'copy' of someone else's headache. (See copies on page 119.)

Other common causes of headaches are reactions to toxic substances like sulfites or MSG; and withdrawal symptoms from caffeine. In these cases, use the body association technique on the symptoms. Rarely, other medical problems may need to be considered, such as a ruptured cerebral aneurysm (with a point source of pain that rapidly expands; a headache sometimes described as "like being kicked in the head").

ICD-10 Codes
• G43, R51

Pain (Chronic)

Often, chronic pain can be healed with simple tapping or other trauma techniques. This is because the pain, especially back pain, is often due to trauma that causes muscles to contract in the present, causing symptoms over time. In other words, the contracted muscles pull the spine out of alignment. These traumas were usually moments of injury or anticipated injury that get 'frozen' by the trauma, and for some reason get activated in the present. This is why chronic pain in the back can be temporarily adjusted by a chiropractor, but then returns – the trauma-driven contractions are still present. Treatment can be done by stimulating the traumas into awareness by briefly pushing in to the area of the body where the pain is, and having the client watch for a trauma image or a memory surface. However, finding the trauma this way is not consistently reliable. Another often effective approach is to have the client heal their emotions *about* having the pain – such as "I'm falling apart because I'm old', 'I hate my body for hurting', and so on. Although a bit slow as there can be many reasons for this, the SUDS of the pain usually drops quickly with each emotion that is eliminated, giving clear feedback as the process continues. And generational trauma should also be checked – this can cause pain directly, as well as set up a cluster of biographical trauma pains because the painful area formed incorrectly during development.

Incidentally, pain from an injury can often be reduced or eliminated using meridian tapping if used soon enough. For example, one man immediately used EFT after hitting his finger with a hammer; the pain vanished fully, and his finger did not even bruise. In another example, a person cracked a rib, and tapping on a chest point made the pain vanish. Apparently, the musculature must automatically act to brace the injured zone - an hour later someone gave him an unexpected bear hug, causing him to scream in pain, but the pain instantly vanished again once he was released.

Pain is also often from copies. These types of pain don't respond to trauma therapies, and are often the reason why the tapping process doesn't have any effect.

Pain can also be from crown brain structures. Interestingly, these structures can feel like they attach different parts of the body together, for example from the arm to the hip. Thus, when a person with this condition swings his arm, there is a feeling of pain at the anchor sites. Clearly, these structures are motionless inside the primary cell and not actually in the arm, but they respond to movement as if they were in the body.

Pain can also be from various parasites in the primary cell. The most common problem is due to class 1 bug-like parasites that cause sensations of ripping, burrowing, or emit burning acid-like fluid to damage membranes or structures in the cell in response to the person's attention on the bugs. The next most common problem is due to the fungal family of parasites – due to negative interactions with another person, the borg fungal parasite can insert a painful 'curse' that feels like a nail is stuck in one's body. (It can also emit a liquid that feels toxic and irritating.) Or a chakra fungus can contract and cause a pressure pain at a chakra location. And less common, but still a problem for many people, a bacterial parasite might move or push against the nuclear or cell membranes causing pressure pain. (They can also secrete nauseating, toxic fluids into the cell.) And a viral net can form inside the nuclear membrane, causing the sensations that one's head is being compressed, which in the extreme causes migraine symptoms. Each of these parasite issues is treated differently, and training and caution is required when working with these issues.

DANGER

Life-threatening injuries can sometimes occur when working with primary cell class 1 bug-like parasites. Training is required. In addition, do not go into the parasitic cause with clients – this can cause them to obsessively focus on the bugs, stimulating them to continuously rip or damage cell membranes. Very large bugs can kill the client if they rip open too large an area of the cell membrane.

In areas of the body with holes, people often contract (or inflate) the muscles in those areas to give a sensation to counteract the feeling of deficient emptiness. As this is chronic (the hole is continuously there), this can lead to muscle pain and distorted musculature. For example, a hole in the chest can lead to either a collapsed chest, or an extended chest a bit like the prow of a boat. In areas of the body that were injured, we often find a hole there that inhibits healing. It is as if the body can't feel into the area of the hole to repair it. This leads to injuries that don't heal properly, and indirectly to some kinds of pain. Often, there is also soul loss in the injured area, which can also inhibit proper healing. When treating a client's injury, the therapist should assume soul loss and a hole will be present in the injury zone, and allocate time to heal them as a standard part of the treatment.

In terms of peak states, there is a state of consciousness where pain does not normally exist – a person who is injured just has a momentary flash of pain, and then it vanishes, leaving either no pain or just a feeling of pressure. This is not some kind of numbness or repression, but a state of more than usual health.

Finally, it is important to realize that pain can also be a warning or a symptom of large-scale injury to the body, not just damage in the primary cell. As in the saying "everything looks like a nail to a man with a hammer", because of a therapist's orientation it becomes habit to assume everything is 'psychological', or (from our viewpoint) due to problems in the primary cell. However, this is *not* always the case. For example, shoulder pain can be due to an inflamed gall bladder. Or belly pain can be due to an inflamed or ruptured appendix or passing kidney stones.

CAUTION
Be sure to consider possible medical causes for the pain.

Chronic Pain Summary (in approximate order of occurrence)
- Biographical trauma (involving muscle contraction)
- Biographical trauma (about the feeling of the pain)
- Generational trauma (the painful area didn't grow quite right)
- Body association (the body feels it needs the pain)
- Copies (of pain)
- Crown brain structure(s)
- Class 1 bug-like parasite (ripping, tearing, burning)
- Curse (nail or arrow-like pain)
- Medical condition (e.g. inflamed gall bladder, infection, etc.)
- Hole (triggering muscular contraction in that region)
- Chakra contraction (pressure pain in a chakra site or sites)
- Bacterium movement (painful pressure)

ICD-10 Codes
- R52

Premenstrual Syndrome (PMS)

PMS symptoms can be very severe. We've found that in most cases the cause of the problem is generational, and standard techniques will quickly eliminate symptoms. This can be identified quickly by asking if ancestors, siblings or relatives have the same PMS symptoms. But the therapist should also rule out copies and body associations that might be causing the symptoms.

This generational healing approach also works on menopausal symptoms.

ICD-10 Codes
- N94.3

Relationships (Intimate)

Nothing can be so satisfying – or so painful – as a romantic relationship, be it a new or long standing. Intimate relationships can trigger a huge variety of traumas and fundamental structural issues that involve early developmental events (such as conception) where different parts of us are supposed to connect or fuse together. High-functioning couples tend to have just one issue that needs treating, while more typical clients can have a variety of issues all at once.

Peak state issues compounds these difficulties. Although most people don't realize it, they are also unconsciously looking for a relationship that only a lucky few get – what we call the Optimum Relationship state. People with this state are best friends, find each other endlessly fascinating, almost never have an upset with each other, continuously feel and enjoy the presence of their partner, and enjoy continuously high levels of physical intimacy into old age. To acquire this state is beyond the scope of this diagnostic manual; instead, we cover here what clients usually expect from the therapist. Two other peak states are also relevant: the male/female archetype state, where the person embodies the essence of being male or female; and the more advanced version, the god/goddess state, where the person embodies the essence of a god or goddess. These states are also aspects of relationship that a person usually unconsciously craves, adding the subtle feeling that something else is also missing to most people's intimacy. Other problems can exist with these states: if one partner has the state and the other does not, it can lead to either addiction by one partner to the other (no matter how much else is dysfunctional in the relationship); or frighten a partner due to abuse or other trauma issues being triggered when the other partner accesses these states.

Below is a list of typical client relationship issues in approximate order of frequency:
- Cords: the client is distressed by what they feel in their partner. Use DPR or SMT. This is usually the main problem in high functioning clients' relationships.
- Simple biographical trauma issues – the partner triggers various difficult feelings in the client. This is dealt with by using any of the standard trauma techniques, especially the meridian therapies that are commonly used for self-help.
- Biographical and generational trauma: the relationship triggers abuse or other extreme trauma memories. The most common problem is from conception where the male sperm felt disapproved of, and the female egg felt abandoned. These feelings are extremely toxic to relationships. Also, the male often unconsciously feels he will be annihilated from

intimacy, so often withdraws after closeness, a reflection of the sperm-death trauma during conception.

- Body association: the client is sexually addicted to some particular emotional tone in the partner. This can be a serious problem, because it can both cause inappropriate relationship choices, and causes the client to unconsciously push the partner into fulfilling the need of the unconscious addiction. The partner can also remind the client of their parents or even their placenta. This is healed with the Body Association Technique.

- Tribal block: the client is playing out a culture-specific role imposed by the tribal block. For example, after childbirth a woman can lose sexual feelings due to this being considered 'appropriate' in her cultural group.

- Projection: the client is projecting on the partner. This problem can show up in clients who have a dysfunctional pattern in their past intimate relationships (other than one due to a body association). A common projection is the partner as placenta. Use the Courteau Projection Technique to heal these.

- Multiple personality disorder: the partner seems to be two different people (although this can be subtle, as sometimes the other personalities are very similar). One way to tell is to notice if the partner has significant blanks in their memories. This is treated with a Peak States process.

- Selfishness ring: the client resists the partner because the relationship evokes positive feelings that are too intense for them. (Gay Hendricks calls this the 'upper-limits problem'.) This is currently a certified therapist process. This reaction can also be due to various types of trauma.

- E-holes: The client avoids the partner because they suddenly feel 'evil' to them.

The range of intimate relationship issues is huge. For example, some interesting albeit infrequent variations: the partner unconsciously controls sexual arousal in the other person; the partner loses attraction to the other person due to becoming subconsciously aware of the presence of a parasite in the partner; and many more.

At the end of relationships, the most common problems are (in approximate order of frequency):

- Soul loss: the client feels sad or lonely due to this problem. This is by far the most common problem.

- Simple trauma: the end of the relationship is throwing the client into a past traumatic event, or feelings of being not good enough due to generational trauma.

- Cording: the clients are still connected through cords that evoke feelings and behaviors that are inappropriate.

- De-compensation: the relationship was keeping other problems from awareness in the client. Examples are feelings of extreme loneliness; sensations from holes or e-holes; the column of self self-identity problem; loss of the addicting emotion; etc.
- S-holes: the partner was addicted to the other person because they 'fed' their need for love to fill the emptiness of their s-holes.
- Peak states: relationship upset occurred because the client moved into a new peak state, triggering jealousy in the partner; or it triggered the partner to harm the client via parasites to eliminate the new peak state. Dealing with this is a certified peak states process.

ICD-10 Codes:

- F52

Suicidal Feelings: "I need to die"

Due to the inherent risks and complexities involved, the description of the biological cause and the techniques to eliminate suicidal feelings are covered in great detail in a separate book, *Suicide Prevention* by Thomas Gagey M.D. and Grant McFetridge Ph.D. The short description here is only for therapists already trained in our techniques.

DANGER
Working with suicidal clients should only be done by therapist trained in suicide, and who have ensured that the client has continuous supervision during the weeks of treatment. Without this, attempting to use the material in this book is both foolish and potentially lethal.

The Background

Suicide, suicide attempts, and suicidal ideation are a tremendous problem for both the client and the therapist. In the US, about half of the therapists will have a client commit suicide and die during care; and about half of these therapists will also have a second client suicide. Several organizations around the world teach the public (and therapists) how to recognize suicidal people, and what actions to take to try and help them.

The Trigger for Suicide

To our surprise, our research work has uncovered what looks like the primary (and probably only) cause for suicidal feelings and actions. It turns out that life events, or various types of therapies, can trigger the person into suicide. This occurs because the person has accessed placental death trauma from their birth memories. These memories are often very strong, partly because of current standard birthing practices that cut the baby's umbilical cord too quickly, creating a huge PTSD (Post Traumatic Stress Disorder) level trauma. When these memories are triggered, the person's present day awareness is flooded with the feelings they experienced at birth.

The reason that this event triggers suicide is because of the nature of the birth process itself. For the baby to be born, the placenta has to die - and this biological imperative is imprinted into the trauma experience. When triggered in the present, the client has the strong feeling that they have to die; not realizing that these feelings are coming from the past. This can be demonstrated on most people who are feeling suicidal by having them touch their belly button while feeling the urge to die. They immediately realize that the sensations are only radiating from their navel; many then say "I don't want to die, my navel wants to die!" This can be a tremendous and immediate relief for suicidal clients, and we recommend this technique as a temporary intervention.

Because suicide feelings are due to placental death trauma, it can manifest in several ways. Typically there is a lot of emotional distress with the impulse to suicide, both from the birthing event and from their current life response to the problem. But some people trigger this birth memory, and it did not have much emotional content. In this latter case, the person involved will calmly go ahead and try and kill themselves as if it is the most natural thing to do; and may plan ahead to try and outwit people they think might want to stop them.

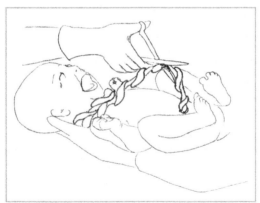

Figure 12.1: The primary cause of suicidal feelings is traumas that contain the feeling of the placenta dying during birth. There can be many of these traumas during the birthing process, but the most severe is usually from cutting the cord too soon.

The Problem of Therapy

Life circumstances are the usual trigger for suicide traumas becoming activated. Unfortunately, therapy of almost any type can also act as a trigger to these suicide-causing placental death birth traumas by accident. Regression therapy can also trigger this problem during a session, but has the advantage that a trained therapist can notice that the client has triggered a birth memory and watch for this problem. Because most therapists do not understand the placental trauma cause of suicide, most therapies do not teach about this problem or what to do if it occurs. However, all therapies could watch for triggering these traumas if they knew it even existed.

Treatment

There are two main issues with trying to treat suicidal feelings. Although the main suicide trauma occurs during the cord-cutting event (due to the current medical practice of cutting the umbilical cord far too soon), for many people there are usually many other traumas that also contain the suicidal impulse. This occurs because the birth event takes quite a while, and the placental need to die can be coupled into many trauma moments during birth. For example, one person had the impulse to hang himself; this was due to the placental death feeling getting connected to the traumatic birth experience of having the umbilical cord wrapped around the baby's neck *in utero*. This is a huge problem for treatment, because the therapist can heal the presenting trauma, making the client feel far better and more energized. But later, perhaps hours or days, their life circumstances keep triggering these birth events (for example, due to a divorce) and the client now has the energy and motivation to kill themselves from a trauma that was not even visible during treatment.

For these reasons, a trauma therapist who works with suicidal birth trauma has to exercise extreme caution to make sure that the client does not kill themselves during or after treatment of the presenting symptoms. This can be done, but needs to be done in the appropriate physical settings - treatment via phone is unsafe. In emergency situations, having the client touch the navel to localize the suicidal sensations is often successful. Emergency treatment on the phone can also be successful IF the client is in a situation where there are people who can monitor the client 24/7 for about two weeks, and are aware that the problem can return and actually be even worse, because the client now feels more energized and able to act.

Some clients have suicidal thoughts but are not suicidal. This can be quite confusing to these clients, because they have no suicidal desires or sensations in their body. Instead of having an activated placental death trauma, they are hearing a 'voice' that is saying suicidal things. Of course, any given client may have both the 'voice' problem and the suicidal feelings from placental death trauma - therapists must check for both problems to ensure the safety of their clients.

Too, copies with suicidal feelings in them can also occur. And in some cases, generational traumas involving suicide can also arise. And equally importantly, the therapist needs to eliminate any body associations on the sensation of needing to die (the suicidal feeling).

Working with suicidal clients requires formal training for the therapist and available, continuous support for the client. Conventional training, such as 'Applied Suicide Intervention Skills Training' (ASIST) is necessary so the therapist can recognize signs of this problem and understands the legal ramifications.

Prevention

The long-term solution to the epidemic of suicide in Western countries is both simple and something that families can immediately do to safeguard their children - do NOT let the hospital staff cut the umbilical cord immediately after birth. Cutting the cord about 20 minutes after birth appears to be adequate; longer can be better (see the technique called 'lotus birth'). These children won't usually have the burden of being triggered into suicidal feelings later in life unless they had earlier perinatal birth traumas that also coupled to the placental death impulse.

The other reason to not cut the cord immediately has to do with the child's mental health. When the cord remains uncut for significant amounts of time, the child will typically (in about 4 out of 5 births) retain a peak state we call 'wholeness', making the child (and later the adult) far more mentally healthy than normal.

Suggested Reading

- *Suicide Prevention - Peak States® Therapy Vol. 3* by Thomas Gagey M.D. and Grant McFetridge Ph.D.
- *Therapeutic and Legal Issues for Therapists Who Have Survived a Client Suicide: Breaking the Silence* by Kayla Miriyam Weiner
- "Applied Suicide Intervention Skills Training" (ASIST)
- *Lotus Birth: Leaving the Umbilical Cord Intact* by Shivam Rachana

Symptom Keywords

- Suicidal; considered ending it; a plan to kill myself. (See ASIST coursework on this topic.)

Diagnosing Questions

- Have you felt suicidal, or thought about how to kill yourself in the last year? Ever?
- Were there any emotional feelings along with a desire to die?
- If you put your hand on your navel, does the feeling radiate from there?

Differential Diagnosis

- Copies: the suicidal feeling also has some one else's personality.
- Generational traumas: the 'grandparents' also feel suicidal.
- Voices: there are no suicidal feelings – the client has a suicidal 'voice' (thoughts) speaking from a fixed position in space, usually outside their body.

Treatment

- We do not recommend treating this problem unless the therapist is qualified and licensed, with appropriate and *continuous* support in place for the client for two to three weeks.
- Start with the navel touch technique; heal all suicidal traumas (and associations, generationals and copies); assume that the client will be triggered into suicide in the next 1-3 weeks as more material surfaces.
- All relevant biographical traumas can be eliminated simultaneously with a licensed Peak States certified therapist process.

Typical Mistake in Technique

- Not fully healing the presenting issue or feelings.
- Healing the presenting trauma can make the client feel more energetic, so they actually carry out suicidal intentions later if new suicidal traumas arise.
- Not realizing the client is concealing their intention to commit suicide later.
- Not recognizing that suicidal sensations don't have to have dramatic emotional content.
- Misdiagnosing suicidal thoughts as suicidal feelings.

Underlying Cause

- Birth trauma that contains the feeling that the placenta has to die.

Symptom Frequency & Severity

- This can range from occasional to continuous.
- The intensity can vary over time.
- There may or may not be strong emotions involved with the suicidal compulsion.

Risks

- Clients with this problem should be considered at risk, and other problems should not be addressed while the client is currently or recently feeling or considering suicide.

DANGER

Clients who have expressed suicidal ideation, plans, attempts, currently or recently should be considered at risk. Other therapy issues should not be started. Healing the presenting symptom birth trauma may miss other relevant trauma or subcellular cases like copies.

DANGER

Focusing on suicide-inducing trauma can subtly activate other, similar traumas from the same placental death time zone of birth. In some clients, healing the presenting trauma can energize the client, making them appear fully healed, but the client now has the energy to follow through with suicidal impulses from other placental death traumas.

DANGER

Some placental death traumas can trigger a calm, unemotional drive to commit suicide. Extreme care must be taken when working in this time zone, as the client will appear rational yet think it is perfectly normal to commit suicide immediately.

ICD-10 Codes

- R45.8, Z91.5

Chapter 13

Spiritual Emergencies and Related Problems

In the last few decades acceptance of 'spiritual' phenomena outside of conventional western beliefs and models has continued to increase, both in the professional literature as well as in popular books and movies. These days most people know what you are talking about when you mention a near-death experience, a past life, an out-of-body experience, and so on. Unfortunately, these experiences are in direct conflict with our modern scientific, biologically-based worldview. People generally deal with this conflict either by ignoring and denying the conflicting phenomena, or by splitting their world into roughly two completely independent parts; an everyday one where they go to the doctor for medicine, and a non-physical, 'spiritual' world that is considered to be impossible to really understand.

However, therapists don't have the luxury of just ignoring these non-ordinary phenomena. Albeit infrequently, they have to deal with real people in their office suffering from 'spiritual' problems that may be outside of their own belief system. Although many may simply ascribe their client's problems to various mental illnesses and suggest antipsychotic medication, others try to understand and treat their clients to the best of their ability. This is why we strongly recommend all therapists get training in spiritual emergencies - for example, all certified Peak States therapists are required to take a course in this before we will certify them - so they can recognize these problems and know what the current state of the art is for their treatment.

We also encourage therapists to pursue a variety of healing, shamanic and spiritual practices. Our work describes the basis for these phenomena, and so becoming familiar with them in other contexts is extremely valuable both as a therapist and as someone living and working with exceptional states of consciousness. However, spiritual practices can also trigger spiritual emergencies; and in some cases the particular spiritual practice actually causes the problems.

Fortunately, and with a real sense of relief, with an understanding of prenatal developmental events and subcellular cases these 'spiritual' experiences and emergencies can now be understood for the first time within the context of western biological models and cultural beliefs. This chapter (written for therapists who are already trained in this material) gives a very brief outline of completely new ways to effectively treat some of the most common issues: problems involving extreme spiritual states and experiences; experiences of existential evil; problems with peak states; and issues involving spiritual teachers. However, for in-depth coverage and other spiritual emergency issues, we refer you to *Spiritual Emergencies - Peak States*® *Therapy, Volume 4*.

Suggested Reading

- *A Sourcebook for Helping People with Spiritual Problems*, by Emma Bragdon (2006).
- *Spiritual Emergency: When Personal Transformation Becomes a Crisis* by Stanislav Grof M.D. (1989).
- "DSM-IV Religious and Spiritual Problems" by David Lukoff (online course).
- *Peak States of Consciousness*, volumes 1-3, by Grant McFetridge *et al*.
- *Spiritual Emergencies - Peak States*® *Therapy, Volume 4* by Marta Czepukojc and Grant McFetridge.

Evil Sensations

Although infrequent, some clients do come in to therapy due to experiences of feeling terrifying evil in themselves or someone else. By this, we are referring to the kind of sensations that a person might get when watching a movie like "The Exorcist" – where you feel like you will be forever contaminated by the sensation. There are a number of mechanisms involving the sensation of evil; below are pointers in how to deal with the various ways this occurs in clients.

As an aside, areas that lack the material that consciousness is built from radiate a sensation of evil; this is normally blocked from awareness. Unfortunately, virtually all human beings have this particular problem, as it is the result of damage from a bacterial species during the creation of the original sperm or egg awareness in the parents. Healing this is a Peak States certified therapist process.

CAUTION

Some therapists should not work with these problems, as it can overwhelm their compensation mechanisms and increase their own problems in this area. If you intend to work with this issue, we recommend that you get training with people who have experience and can give you practice with appropriate clients.

Evil is Encountered During Regression

The client encounters feelings of evil in themselves, their ancestors, their past lives, or their parents or grandparents. Treatment is simple acceptance and the allowing of change (a key part of the WHH technique).

During regressions, a client may sometimes enter a 'hell realm' when they enter a biological passageway in membranes. For example, entering into the coalescence room through its wall often causes this problem, but it can occur in other stages of early development. The solution is to have them stay in the 'center' of the passage, ignore their usually very horrifying surroundings, and continue through to complete their passage through the barrier. Alternatively, the client can also be encouraged to switch to 'biological view' to see whatever physical problem is driving their experience so they can heal it directly.

Evil is in One's Own Mind Chatter

In a mild form, the 'voice' gives thoughts that are evil. In an extreme case, this causes the classic demonic possession problem. This problem can occur unexpectedly during a session, or the client can come in with the problem. Treatment is to eliminate the single voice with its association of evil with survival using Body Association Technique; global treatment is the Silent Mind Technique (SMT).

Attracting Evil People and Situations

The client attracts evil people and situations. This usually has nothing to do with the negativity of the person involved. It is caused by a body association that tells the body it needs to have the sensation of evil nearby to survive. It is easily dealt with using the Body Association Technique.

In rare cases, this problem is caused by a different mechanism. This client has unusually good peak states; others are drawn to try and harm the client due to the painful lack they feel when around or focused on the client. This behavior in the lacking person is driven by a variety of causes. Unfortunately, this is an intrinsic issue with having peak states. Like having wealth, having the client downplay or conceal their peak states around others helps reduce this problem. Also, eliminating the client's class 2 borg fungal parasites also helps minimize this problem, making the client emotionally 'invisible' to others who have the feeling of lack.

The Client Likes the Feeling of Power in Acting Evil

The client likes a feeling of being powerful (usually driven by feelings of powerlessness underneath) and does evil actions. This can be driven by trauma; by people with heart-brain shutdown who experience others as objects; or in people whose self-identity has been partly merged with the class 2 borg fungus. In this last case, people lose the capacity to connect with empathy, and instead interact with manipulation, abuse or harm – they have a fungal parasite perspective on others. We estimate around 20%-30% of the general population has this problem to some degree (although it can vary over time). A variation on this is interacting with members of a culture that feels evil to the client. Both cases are treated in the same way, by using SMT to eliminate the borg fungus.

You Encounter a Person who Feels Evil

This is usually either a cording problem, or is due to an e-hole. It can be quickly eliminated using Distant Personality Release (DPR), but this technique can be difficult for many clients as they have to be able to unconditionally love the evil sensation. Another approach for the cording is to identify the trauma string the cord is attached to and use trauma healing on it. If the cause is an e-hole, have the client heal the resonating e-hole in themselves using a generational trauma technique.

There can be other, more serious reasons for this problem. This evil-feeling person's core consciousness is unusually damaged, and the evil inside them is being sensed by unconscious merging or by parasite organisms that the evil person extends their consciousness through into others. Working with this type of client requires an approach that is beyond the scope of this manual.

You Feel Evil Somewhere in Your Body

The cause can be a copy, in which case it has the feeling of someone else's personality. In this case, you use the treatment for a copy; tapping or regression will not work. It can also be due to an e-hole: in this case, use the standard subcellular case process.

Another possible cause is from a curse. If so, there will be a feeling of the personality of the other person in it. Few curses actually feel evil (anger is far more common), as they reflect the feeling of the person who triggers the borg fungus into this action. The problem can feel like an arrow in the body, or can feel like a blanket on the body. In either case, DPR works quickly. SMT is a global fix for this problem if the issue keeps reoccurring.

Yet another possible reason is a sensation of nausea and evil in small spots or in larger areas of the body. This can be caused by black-looking toxic material inside the primary cell, usually emitted by some combination of class 1 bug-like (emotion), class 2 fungal (nausea), and class 3 bacterial (toxic) organisms. Simple tapping with EFT can sometimes eliminate this issue. Alternately, you use standard parasite processes to heal this problem. Start with body associations on the toxic feeling; then if there are any emotional tones in the area, heal the corresponding generational traumas to eliminate any class 1 bugs; then heal any generational traumas that have the save evil sensation. Unfortunately, current techniques may not be adequate to eliminate this issue in some cases – Institute clinic processes may be needed.

An Opening to Hell

This counter-intuitive experience may be triggered when the client is around a group of people who are celebrating, dancing, praying, etc. The client may feel unusually tired when in the activity (to unconsciously suppress the experience); reluctant to be in these group activities at all; or may 'see' a large, round, black opening in the floor under the group of people that feels evil and appears to lead to hell.

This experience is caused by the client becoming aware of a class 3 bacterial parasite in their nuclear core that lives 'below' them – the tunnel is part of the organism's body. It becomes activated in groups because people's positive feelings 'feed' the parasite so it can reproduce. This particular parasite exists in almost everyone, but fortunately is usually suppressed out of consciousness. Although generational healing can reduce this problem, we suggest you contact a Peak States clinic for treatment.

You Sense the Presence of an Evil Ancestor

Clients sometimes notice the presence of their grandparents nearby, and if they feel evil, this can cause great distress, partly because it is sometimes hard to ignore. Or they might be feeling an earlier ancestor who feels evil. In either case, use the generational trauma technique.

You Are Surrounded by a Feeling of Negativity or Evil

In this case, people feel negativity or evil in an area around the client, to a radius of up to 10 or 15 feet. The client doesn't usually sense it themselves. This problem is caused by a cloud of bacterial organisms that live at the inner edge of the primary cell membrane that have been 'imprinted' with these negative feelings. Interestingly, some people can sense them in the region outside the client's body. These organisms can be eliminated by first getting the client aware of the problem, having them do any body associations, then heal generational traumas on the sensation of the bacterial organisms (soft, toxic, blobby).

ICD-10 Codes

- F44.3

Peak Experiences, States and Abilities

By definition, a peak state corresponds to sensations, feelings or abilities that make you more able to be in the world. However, odd as it sounds, there can be negative issues that clients have with peak experiences, states, and abilities:

- They have a trauma associated with the peak state sensations or emotions. For example, they are afraid to feel happy, making themselves miserable with the new state. Or the new state or ability can feel too overwhelming. Simple body associations and trauma healing is usually enough to resolve this.

- The peak state or ability is too out of the ordinary so they assume that there is something mentally (or physically) wrong with them. This might lead to totally inappropriate hospitalization, medication or electroshock therapy. For example, many people in the Beauty Way state are told that there is something wrong with them because they don't have any trauma or negative emotions. Simple explanations with reference to appropriate textbooks is generally enough to solve this problem.

- The client had a peak experience, state or ability and it vanished. Depending on the state and the person, this loss can be devastating. The client may have spent a tremendous amount of time and money trying to get it back. The best resolution is to restore the state, if this is a state that our current techniques are adequate for.

- The client is addicted to a peak experience in their work or leisure activities. This problem is extremely common, and many people with this issue don't even realize it. For example, a person who destroys their knee joints because they want the 'runner's high' so much. Or they keep an inappropriate job because occasionally it rewards them with a momentary peak experience feeling. The best resolution, if possible, is to use our Peak States process to turn the experience into a permanent state.

ICD-10 Codes

- Not yet determined.

Spiritual Emergencies

Spiritual emergencies involve non-ordinary or spiritual experiences that cause either distress, inability to function, or both. They are often experiences from various spiritual, mystical or shamanic traditions that become a crisis. (A spiritual emergency is not the same as a crisis of religion or faith, nor is it a psychotic episode.) For the original in-depth discussion on the variety of different kinds of spiritual emergencies, see Dr. Stanislav Grof's *Spiritual Emergency*. Or see Dr. David Lukoff's instructional website about the DSM-4 V62.89 category called 'Religious or Spiritual Problem'. Or see our own textbook on this topic, *Spiritual Emergencies* by Marta Czepukojc and Grant McFetridge.

Probably because the Institute is focused on peak states of consciousness, we tend to see more people in spiritual emergency than most therapists. In our experience, most spiritual emergencies are simply primary cell subcellular case problems that have risen to conscious awareness because of meditation practices (or less frequently, triggered by intense experiences like childbirth, sex, extreme trauma, experiences of extreme beauty; or rarely for no apparent reason). Sometimes there is nothing to heal; rather the state or experience is so out of the ordinary the client believes they must be mentally ill. For example, direct experience of the Sacred Being state caused one client to needlessly stay in a psychiatric hospital for years. Regardless of whether there is something to heal or not, giving the client references to books that describe their spiritual emergency is a tremendous relief to clients and should be done as soon as possible.

If the client's spiritual experience does not match one of the standard cases, therapists can often still solve the problem by having the client switch from a 'spiritual view' to a 'biological view'. Because the client is generally experiencing the event from the spiritual view to avoid pain, it can take some gentle coaching to help them make the switch. Once that is done, the underlying biological damage can usually be identified and healed using standard techniques.

Categorized Spiritual Emergencies (in approximate order of frequency in therapy):

- Channeling: This is usually a case of schizophrenic voices and is eliminated as described in the 'mind chatter' subcellular case.
- Racial and collective experiences: the client feels the pain of a subset of all past humanity. For example: the suffering of all prisoners who were tortured; the agony of mothers throughout time who died in labor; and so on. This is not a generational trauma, as it has a different biological cause. Treatment for this problem is to use the Courteau Projection Technique.
- Kundalini: The client feels energy rising up their spine, triggering an unending series of traumas. This phenomenon is easily eliminated using the process in the subcellular case list.
- Possession: This is usually a case of ribosomal voices, and is very quickly treated using body associations or EFT tapping. However, as of this writing we've had a client that we could not help; it was some other mechanism we haven't yet identified.
- Alien Encounter: We've seen a number of people whose 'alien implants' were actually simple crown brain structures.
- Mystical Experiences: These can have multiple causes. They can be positive peak experiences or states that trigger traumatic reactions; experiences of the primary cell; or experiences of parasitic primary cell organisms, particularly fungal ones which are usually interpreted as being experiences of God.
- Shamanic Crisis: This is often reliving of very early developmental event trauma.
- Near-death Experience: Some NDEs are hellish in nature. Treat a positive or negative NDE by healing any traumas triggered by thinking about it; this is usually sufficient to bring the client to peace.

Miscellaneous Spiritual Emergencies from Subcellular Cases

There are a variety of other uncategorized spiritual emergencies in the literature. The following are found in this manual as subcellular cases:

- Abyss – the client is aware of the abyss, with a possible visual image, causing extreme angst.
- Chakra problems – the client feels pain and other sensations caused by the chakras (a fungal organism living on the nuclear membrane).
- Image Overlay – although usually applied to trauma images, one example of this is when the client sees ghostly images of the parents superimposed on people of the appropriate gender.
- Internal Archetypal Images – the client perceives a numinous, ancient god or monster inside their body.
- Curse (Negative Thought Form) – the client feels like someone has 'cursed' them, causing them injury.
- Over-Identification with the Creator – the client feels that they have Creator-like equanimity, but at the expense of human compassion.
- Past Lives – the client experiences trauma from past lives.
- Triune Brain Sacred Being Damage – the client sees or becomes a sacred being, and usually has intense sacred feelings.
- Void in the Column of Self – the client feels existential dread when they become aware of the void in their core.

ICD-10 Codes:
- F23

Spiritual Teachers/Therapists and Their Issues

As part of our therapist training, we always teach about the problems of working with spiritual teachers and therapists as clients. This is because our work with peak states attracts spiritual teachers, and our work with cutting edge therapy techniques attracts therapists. From a diagnostic and pricing viewpoint, therapy usually takes about three times longer for a therapist than for a typical client. First, this is because most therapists got into this line of work due to some major life problem that they were trying unsuccessfully to heal. Thus, they have probably already eliminated all of the straightforward traumas, and so their problem is probably going to be unusual and complex. But the biggest time loss with this group is that they will try and explain their issue with what they've been taught or believe. Most of our trainee therapists have a very hard time keeping the therapist client on track with symptom descriptions and sensations, instead of the abstractions and explanations that they are eager and usually driven to share.

In the case of the spiritual teacher, therapy generally takes about five times longer than for the average client. Like the therapist, the spiritual teacher will also usually have already done all the easy healing, and also will have the same issue of wanting to explain their problem in terms of their particular beliefs. However, they tend to have another major issue: as part of their persona, they tend to find it very difficult to admit that they have a problem. Thus, getting an accurate symptom description is very hard, especially if it conflicts with their self-image. Of course, many people have this issue; but spiritual teachers tend to be much better at forcing their deception on the therapist via various parasite mechanisms (such as cording). For example, one well-known spiritual teacher was concealing a core feeling of inadequacy, and would trigger borg fungal spray into anyone who became aware of it. Hence, in our experience with this group, their problems tend to be severe, concealed, and very difficult for them to face. All this takes more time (and effort) on the part of the therapist than would be expected from a person who usually seems so nice and compliant.

To give some examples, we've seen spiritual teachers that are filled with bypasses; ones who have unusual levels of both good and evil in their being, and switch between them; ones who use their genuine psychic abilities to manipulate and harm others so they can continue to feel special and unique; ones who conceal deep, core feelings of inadequacy and incompetence; ones who have students so they can use them for their own selfish ends; ones who induced sexual feelings into others via the male/female archetype state to get attention; and so on.

Induced Peak States

Another issue we've seen with spiritual teachers in general is one that seems at first to be very positive. The teacher has one or more genuine peak states, and has learned how to induce them in others. The problem here is that this is addictive to many people, especially people who are 'searching' due to their own underling emotional issues or a serious, long-term illness. Thus, you get the phenomenon of the client who 'follows the guru' like an addict to keep getting that peak experience. This is financially lucrative to the teacher; there is no incentive to actually have the student acquire the state in question, and a disincentive to have it happen due to their own emotional issues around feeling superior. The bottom line: genuine spiritual teachers both act and feel completely ordinary, and have students who successfully learn how to master the material and maintain stable states on their own.

As part of our regular training, we address this problem in a very interesting way. We have the student focus attention on their spiritual teacher of choice who feels 'amazing' to them in some way or other. We then have them eliminate all of the different trauma issues or subcellular cases that have been activated by this teacher that gives the sensations. Sometimes it is simple projection or trauma issues; but far more often, the deception is an active one – the teacher is cording with the student to give them the superior or exceptional feeling; or they have the s-hole problem and they project a 'loving' feeling to the susceptible student; or they use a parasite connection to harm others who would see past their deceptions or who might learn their abilities or gain their states.

These latter parasite issues can be a serious problem for the therapist who is working with this group of people.

Spiritual Paths or Groups

One other interesting point that we also make with our students: every spiritual or psychological practice we've looked at mostly attracts people who have the same particular unconscious flaw that resonates with the practice and the teachers. For example, one well-known practice attracts people who are trying to escape all emotions; another practice attracts people who are trying to escape all sexual feelings; another attracts people who want to manipulate others; another attracts people who have a need for power; and so on. The flaw is extremely difficult for a person to detect in themselves; the best way is to assume that this problem exists, and ask someone who is not interested in the practice but is familiar with people doing it to look for the common underlying issue.

Spiritual Practices that Damage the User

We've seen a number of clients over the years who have used various spiritual practices or techniques that caused them harm, such as strange body sensations, pain, paranoia, voices, and other issues. Of course, even standard meditation techniques can trigger spiritual emergencies or other problems in clients. But here we're referring to techniques that directly interact with and unintentionally damage the primary cells of some users.

The first step is to get the client to stop using the technique – as obvious as this sounds, many of these clients can't believe that the practice could be causing their problem, often because their spiritual teacher said so. If the client does not recover in a week or so after stopping the practice, then the next step is a full diagnostic workup.

This problem is not confined to just 'spiritual' techniques, since many 'psychological' techniques also interact with the primary cell. As mentioned earlier, some psychological techniques get their intended effect by damaging the client's primary cell. Sometimes the resulting symptoms are subtle; other times they are severe enough that they eventually drive the client to get help.

The Problem of Merging

As you've read, many members of our species unconsciously (or consciously) try to harm others via the various species of parasites - especially if the other shows overt signs of having peak states, or in fact any unusual talent, ability or wealth. However, these parasite issues are a particular problem with most healers and spiritual teachers, because they can usually 'merge' consciousnesses with their client or student. The teacher/healer will likely be unconsciously 'activated' by what they feel in the other person; worse, teacher/healers tends to be much better than average at harming others via parasites. Or, of course, the reverse is also true – the client/student might harm the teacher/healer during this 'merge'. This covert but unfortunately quite real problem is one of the reasons why the Institute does not teach merging skills to therapists.

So what to do? First, teacher/healers born with a stable, life long Beauty Way state won't identify with or use parasites, no matter what they might feel about the client. So the issue of harming others does not arise for these people. Other than that, the best long-term solution is getting rid of all these parasites, which is the current focus of our research.

ICD-10 Codes

- Not yet determined.

Section 5

Appendices

Identifying Stuck Beliefs in Therapists

When we start a new module we first have the student therapists look for and then heal any emotional issues about the material they'll be learning. We've seen over and over again that unless their emotional reactivity or stuck beliefs are eliminated, learning and acquiring skill can go slowly or even stop completely.

The hard part is getting the student to become aware of their issues; we find that providing them a list of possible triggers helps this process along. So over the years we've recorded what our students have found in themselves (shown below). We have them go through the list and check off the ones that have emotional charge for them, or jot down on this page what personal ones they might have found or realized they had. Obviously, many of these issues don't make any sense from a logical perspective, and the student is sometimes reluctant to admit that they have an emotional reaction to them.

Another way to find issues is to use the trick of saying a positive statement or phrase about the topic. Notice the counter-feelings or statements that come into awareness. They often start with 'Yes, but...' or 'No, because...'. Some examples are:

- I lead (direct) the client confidently.
- Diagnosis and healing is fast and simple.
- I am calm before working with my client.
- I will always remember to ask for a SUDS rating.

Yet another way to see if you have a stuck belief or core trauma is to look at others to find counter-examples to your convictions or beliefs.

Once they are identified, and since these issues are almost always due to simple trauma or core beliefs, the students usually only spends a couple of minutes per issue to work through their material. After identifying issues in class, we often give them the healing task as homework.

However, this scheme is not foolproof. Many students still suppress awareness of some issues, which means they still occasionally crop up during class or with clients. But it does help a lot, and is well worth doing.

Beliefs around charging and 'Pay for Results'

Therapists often have fears around changing to a pay for results billing system. But other issues also crop up.

- I feel guilty that I charge so much for such a simple/ fast process.
- I feel guilty charging extra to compensate for clients I can't help.
- What if the client gets healed and says they didn't?
- I don't understand what the client really wants – I am missing the real issue.
- I am afraid the client will have a too high expectation of me.
- This is too complicated.
- I am afraid of legal actions.
- Finish the session as soon as possible so I can get the money.

Beliefs about the contract and initial interview

- I am afraid I can't figure out the right issue.
- I will always remember to ask for a SUDS rating.
- I don't understand what the client really wants.
- I am missing the real issue.
- I am more interested in addressing underlying issues, rather than the presenting problems.
- I am afraid that I will lose control of the session.
- I am afraid that the client will have too great of an expectation of me.
- I won't have any ideas, so the client will be stuck, and I will be embarrassed, and the client will think I am incompetent.
- I am afraid I will be embarrassed in front of the client.

Beliefs about diagnosing

These are common beliefs that interfere with the therapist's ability to diagnose. Read through the list and identify any of them that trigger feeling; then see if you have some of your own not on the list below. It would be a very good idea to heal these issues in yourself before trying to diagnose clients.

- It is too complicated.
- It has to take a lot of time (to be thorough, etc.).
- I am afraid that I will be triggered by client issues.
- I am afraid that I will let myself be mislead by the client.
- I won't remember the cases and their symptoms.
- I am afraid I'll do it wrong and will harm the client.
- I may have difficulty understanding (language, style) of the client.
- I am distracted by the story the client tells.
- I will forget the clues to look for.
- I'm afraid I'll draw a blank.
- I am afraid of leading the client.

- I will misdiagnose.
- I won't be able to help them.
- I have resistance to so much structure in diagnosing and healing.
- I am afraid I will 'copy' the client's problem.
- I will lose focus during diagnosis.
- I am afraid I will appear incompetent or stupid.
- I will forget something.
- I am not good enough.
- I have performance anxiety.
- I am confused because I don't understand the underlying structure and mechanisms.
- I need more information.
- I am reluctant to direct the session.
- I am afraid I won't be able to get back on track if I loose control of the session.

Beliefs around safety and ethical issues

- I am afraid the client will leave if they read the informed consent form.
- Why should I use a disclosure form? No one else does it.
- I am afraid I will scare the client away.
- I need to be the center of attention (or need money), so much so that I will do dangerous/ unethical/ unhelpful things to keep people drawn in.
- Healing is always a good idea.
- You never get more than you can handle.
- I'm so advanced/ capable that nothing bad will ever happen to me.

Issues involving client-therapist relationships

See if the following common therapist issues either trigger you (trauma) or feel true (possible generational trauma, core trauma, and/or biographical trauma).

- I am afraid of leading clients.
- I have fear of legal action.
- I am afraid of the client's issues.
- I have fear of meeting other experts.
- I can't help/ feel inadequate to help.
- I am afraid of being ridiculed.
- This is too complicated.
- I don't know what to say/ ask.
- Fear of failure, or of making the client worse.
- I can't/ afraid to direct the client.
- I am interesting instead of interested.
- I lose focus on the issue.
- I excessively help/ mother/ sympathy.

- I won't earn enough/ not valued.
- I don't get enough (or any) clients.
- I lack motivation to do related tasks like advertising.
- I would be crushed if I hurt a client.

Issues involving peer or expert relationships

- I am intimidated by others who are highly competent.
- We are all competing for the same clients.
- There is not enough to share.
- I don't want to be seen as inadequate.
- They will take advantage of me.
- I am better (worse) than other professionals.
- I won't work in a team setting with other professionals because (they will judge me, I am not good enough, they are all stupid...)
- I think I am better than the medical profession.

Personal issues about being a therapist

- I think I made a mistake to become a therapist.
- It is too much responsibility to be a therapist.
- I am overloaded by family and clients.
- I am in conflict about who has first priority, family or clients.
- I would be crushed if my client committed suicide.
- I want to be famous/powerful/influential.
- I only teach workshops/ I don't need to be an expert.
- I am not an academic/ medical profession looks down on my work and on me.
- I have to prove myself.
- I am only worthwhile if I am helping others.

Issues about specializing

- You have to work hard for money.
- If it is easy and fun for me, I don't deserve to be paid.
- Only if it is hard to do does it have value. If it is fun and easy, it has no value.
- I don't recognize my talents because they are so easy and effortless. Isn't everyone like me?
- I can't do what I really want to do because if it fails I would be totally crushed. So I'll pick a lesser option that doesn't matter as much.

Common training or healing issues

Beliefs about healing in the client or in the therapist can interfere with the client's healing. It is also very useful to heal the therapist's resistance to accepting pain or feel difficult emotions in themselves (and by extension in their clients).

As an aside, healing these sorts of issues can also be used for clients who want learning enhancement. However, in severe cases check for brain damage problems.

In-class learning or training problems
- Not enough time.
- The material is too complicated.

Beliefs about healing
- Healing is slow.
- Healing is painful.
- Healing is tiring.
- If the client doesn't heal, it isn't supposed to happen.
- It is not the right time to heal.
- The client is not ready to let go.
- I have to understand to heal this.
- Only Jesus/ doctors can heal.
- I need support for healing / I can't heal by myself.
- I can never get to full calm / finish a session fully.
- Healing is dangerous.
- I feel frustrated when I can't heal something.
- I am not doing the healing, I'm a channel for God.
- I believe that the client has to want to change.
- The reason the client does not heal is because they don't want to change.
- I can't remember how to do it.
- I can't completely let go of my issue.
- I have to remember my issue for the next time.

Essential healing for advanced therapists

Our clinic therapists receive much more training than our certified therapists. Some of the personal issues we've found that they must face in order to do their jobs well are listed below. We require that the therapist come to peace and get to the point that their issues have no emotional charge, significance or interest to them anymore. Strangely, even though they know they are required to do this so they can be better therapists, most of them still delay or completely avoid facing their own personal issues. This is very bizarre behavior especially in a therapist, but experience has shown that this is the norm and not the exception.
- Chronic or dominant personal issues (like life long loneliness, fear, paranoia, superiority, and so on). These cause the therapist to miss or be unable to heal similar issues in their clients. The therapist sometimes

needs outside help to even notice what they are. These include phrases like "I'll always be sad"; "Loneliness is just my life" and so on.

- Mother issues (including projection of the mother on all women).
- Father issues (including projection of the father on all men).
- Other family issues, such as ones involving siblings or relatives. Random clients will trigger these issues in the therapist.
- Any need to have secrets. This problem is a doorway to delusion and mental illness, and absolutely must be faced and eliminated.
- Fear, concern or avoidance of death. We've found empirically that mental health is proportional to this issue – the harder a person wants to hold onto life (or avoid death), the sicker they are.
- Look for problems concealed by compensations. These compensations are activities or symptoms that you can't live without. (This is sort of like using a crutch all your life to handle, numb or avoid some personal feelings.)
- See if the therapist can't allow themselves to feel continuously good or have peak states of consciousness. This may also show up as never fully healing an issue.
- Heal issues about other people. (Who do you really dislike? Who do you really like? Both are problems.)
- Facing resistance to knowing and doing what the therapist truly wants to do in their life. For example, do they always choose second best so they won't be crushed if their first choice fails?
- Look for any spiritual teachers, leaders or other people who feel exceptionally 'special' or 'powerful' or 'loving' to them. Heal these feelings until only calm remains. (This does not mean that the person can't admire the actions of others; it just means that they feel this way about the other person because of trauma or projection.)

Appendix 2

Examples of 'Pay for Results' Contracts

In this appendix we'll look at several different styles of 'pay for results' contracts. They vary from simple and informal to very detailed, depending on the therapist or the client's needs. For the most part, therapists simply use their own template and plug in information while doing the first interview (and perhaps diagnosis), so that the whole process is done in a few minutes and they can hand or email the agreement to the client on the spot. Whether the therapist asks for prepayment or payment after some set time interval is up to them or can also vary from client to client.

Your contract serves several purposes. Obviously, it defines the criteria for success and your fee; but just as importantly, it helps minimize disagreements after treatment about whether you actually healed the issue or not. This can happen because of the apex phenomenon – many clients literally cannot remember that they had the problem you healed. The contract helps to address this (as does video or audio recordings of the initial interview). Less frequently, clients sometimes have unrealistic expectations, and having the exact success criteria in black and white can help address this when they complain that their 'real' (and sometimes completely new) problem is not gone. If their 'real' problem is not gone, even though it was not in the contract, smart therapists will usually offer to treat that problem or give a refund (writing down the new success criteria) even though they actually healed the client's issue. Remember, word of mouth is your best friend – and if you were not experienced enough to realize what the client was really trying to ask you to heal in the first place, then this becomes a cheap and valuable training experience.

If a client contacts the Institute because of a contract dispute, the first thing we will do is ask to see the contract so we can check if the agreed upon criteria have been met. If the therapist did not write one (perhaps because they could not believe the client could ever forget their issue!), the therapist is automatically required to give an immediate refund. If the agreement terms were not met the therapist is also required to give an immediate refund. In this later case, this can happen because the results criteria were too broad and vague; or it was not something that a therapist could really deliver or verify; or they offered to do too much and failed in part of the agreement. Therapists quickly learn to write more focused contracts when this sort of thing happens.

In some cases, the client will offer a donation for time spent even if there was no success. As long as this is from their heart and not subtly coerced or via some kind of emotional blackmail, it is acceptable. A helpful and meaningful way to respond to their kindness is by putting this towards pro bono clients.

Institute certified therapists also use contracts with two different types of success criteria: ones where the client and the therapist come to a mutual agreement on what is to be healed; and ones using an Institute licensed process with predefined criteria (to ensure quality control around a given disease process).

A typical contract usually includes the following:
- The treatment price.
- The client's exact wording describing what they want healed (this can be very important later!)
- It can be helpful to include the client's current SUDS rating about their issue. This is useful later to show the client that yes, they really did have emotional upset about that issue.
- The appointment time.
- How to contact the therapist in case of emergency.
- How payment is handled (if it is held on deposit, payable after treatment, or some other arrangement).
- The length of time you give the client to verify that the problem is gone before payment is due (if needed).
- What happens if the symptom returns (they can get a refund or more treatment to see if the problem can be eliminated).
- Verification that they signed liability and informed consent and have no remaining questions; and filled out the patient history form.
- Verify their permission to use any testimonial (with or without their name as they specified).

Example: General therapy contract using symptoms

This is an example of a client who wanted distinct physical symptoms (and associated feelings) eliminated. Note in this case a trauma phrase would not be relevant or appropriate. These sorts of contract range from pain, to back alignment, to PMS symptoms, and so on.

> Dear -------,
>
> For our pay-for-results criteria, we agree to treat and eliminate your fear and anxiety about being sick, throwing up and having intestinal cramps in public places. You will test the treatment by driving distances and being around people away from home.

Plan on three sessions, spread over two weeks (and one more if needed).

If we eliminate the issue, the fee is $-----. If you decide to cancel treatment before the third session (if needed), the cancellation fee will be $200. Payment is to be made 3 weeks after we see substantial results – if that does not happen there is no fee.

If you have any problems related to the therapy process after we start, feel free to call me at home at any time. If I am not available, contact my colleague ------- at -----------.

Thank you, and we look forward to working with you.
Signed -----------

Example: General therapy contract using a trauma phrase

Many contracts just use a simple trigger phrase to identify the problem in the client's mind.

Dear ------------,

I am confirming the session on Saturday at your 12:30pm (US Central timezone).

Attached is the liability form. Please read, sign, witness (anyone will do), and email it to me or mail it to -----------.

For our pay-for-results criteria, we agree to treat the following, and eliminate all the feelings around the phrase involving the husband and previous intimate relationships:

"I have to take care of the person or I'm going to die." The feelings are panic and anxiety, with numbness on and in the mouth triggered by these emotions. My current level of distress (SUDS from 0 to 10) is _____.

You will then test the treatment by sending divorce papers to your husband shortly after the first session. We agree to re-treat you the following weekend, if needed. We may do a third short session if needed.

If we do not heal the issue in three sessions, there is no fee. If we eliminate the issue, the fee is $-----. If you decide to cancel treatment before the third session (if needed), the cancellation fee will be $200.

Sincerely,
Signed -----------

Example: Predetermined criteria contract for the Silent Mind Technique

The Silent Mind Technique is a licensed process that certified therapists use with clients to eliminate all ribosomal voices. For this process the Institute specifies predetermined criteria, although the therapist can adjust them as needed to fit the client's wording and situation. There are also several other Institute processes with predetermined criteria.

> Dear --------,
>
> As we discussed on the phone today (July 27, 2014), we still need one or two recent pictures of you for our files. A phone photo would be fine. We'll need it before we start treatment.
>
> Thank you for signing the liability and informed consent forms, and filling out your patient history form.
>
> We're scheduled to work with you at your 6pm (8am in Australia). As we discussed, we'll need to do the treatment three times - the first time should get rid of your voices, but by the next day they may return. We do a second treatment 2 to 4 days later, and then a final check (and minor treatment if needed) in about 2 weeks to make sure the problem does not return.
>
> This is a charge for results' agreement - this means if we don't meet our agreement, there is no fee. Note that we do not agree to eliminate other issues. For example, your childhood abuse will not be treated with this process. As we also discussed, we do not know if your visual hallucinations will be eliminated or not. You should not expect that they will go away with this treatment.
>
> AGREEMENT
>
> We agree to eliminate the client's autonomous voice chatter; i.e., background thoughts you hear when you are trying to meditate (that can sound like other people's voices). We will test the results by having the client meditate for a few minutes and listen. These voices feel like they are in fixed locations in space, and have fixed emotional tones.
>
> After the process, the client will have the sensation that their head feels empty, quiet, open and large (like they are now standing on an empty stage). Note that the client will soon become used to this feeling and it will be hard to notice it later.
>
> The fee is $------- payable in 3 weeks after the change is stable. If the voices return, there is no fee.
>
> If treatment is successful, you might have a reaction to losing your voices. Although infrequent, some clients have feelings of loneliness after their voices leave. If you have this issue, please let us know so we can treat it in the follow-up sessions. Some find that people they are close to (spouses in particular) feel like you are more distant or aloof, even though you have not changed. This is a normal outcome, due

to the fact you don't unconsciously connect to them in the same way. This issue passes with time as they adjust to your new condition.

If you have any other problems arise as an immediate outcome of treatment, contact us immediately. In Australia, phone ------------.

Sincerely,

Signed -----------

Example: Predetermined criteria contract for CFS (chronic fatigue syndrome)

This process is currently only available through the Institute's clinics. As we develop new treatments, there is usually a lag of a year or two as they go through more testing and optimization before they are released to our certified therapists.

Dear -------,

As we discussed on the phone, here is a contract for our treatment for your chronic fatigue syndrome symptoms. Please review it for changes before treatment starts at 2pm on -------------.

For a sum of $------- payable after three weeks without symptoms, we agree to treat your chronic fatigue syndrome so that: "the overwhelming fatigue will be gone, to normal levels, like I had before the disease started less the fact I haven't had exercise for a long time and I'm older than when this started." (My CFS symptom is: debilitating fatigue = bedbound.) Be aware that we are not treating other symptoms, and you should not assume that they will go away with this treatment. This agreement also does not include any issues that resulted from the chronic fatigue, or other issues that occurred before or during your illness.

You have already signed a liability agreement; and read the disclosure form on the PeakStates Therapy website, and have understood what you read without further questions.

As I mentioned, after the symptoms are gone (assuming we are successful), we will do two more sessions to make sure the healing is stable. The first will probably be in the first week, the second either the following week or the next after. It is not uncommon to have the problem return after the first successful treatment - this is why we plan on the follow up treatments, to eliminate anything we missed.

We may also use your write-up on our website to help others recognize the symptoms we treat, but that we won't use your name without your permission.

If you have any questions, or don't agree to these conditions, please let me know before the treatment starts.

Sincerely,

Signed ----------

Informed Consent Form

Therapist's Name:
Mailing Address:
Office Phone:
Office Email:
Office Hours:

Hello,

      We're going to start our work together by going over this informed consent form. Many countries have laws requiring that we do this; but it is a good idea to do anyway, as it may answer some of your questions, or address ones you may not have even thought about before. As we cover each item, I'll have you check it off to show that you and I discussed it to your satisfaction. I'll keep the original form, and give you a copy for your records.

What are my qualifications and orientation as a therapist?

When you need your car engine fixed, you need to go to a mechanic who knows all about engines – you don't go to the transmission guy. In the same way, therapists also specialize, and are better at some things than others; and some things they just don't have the right training for. Thus, I am what is known as a trauma therapist, specializing in healing traumatic memories that you may or may not realize cause you problems. Later, during our discussion of 'pay for results', we'll go over your issue to see if I feel I can help you with your particular problem; but for now, here's a description of my formal background:

- Academic qualifications: _____
- My formal certification as a therapist or counselor is by (in) _____
- I am certified by _____ to use their techniques.
- Professional membership(s): _____
- Therapeutic orientations: _____

❑ We've discussed what my therapist's qualifications and therapeutic orientation, and I understand what the therapist is saying.

What issues won't I work with?

There are certain issues that I will be sending you to see another therapist for. The most important for you to know about is the issue of suicide. If you have suicidal feelings, have attempted to commit suicide, or have made plans to commit suicide, you need to see someone else who specializes in this problem. If this comes up during our work together, I will end our sessions and refer you to another therapist (or other professional) who works with this issue.

Another problem that might come up involves physical problems like heart conditions. Because therapy might bring up strong emotional and physical reactions, if you have any medical conditions that might put you at risk, we cannot start therapy.

❑ We've discussed the areas that my therapist won't work with, and I understand and agree to this. Additionally, I don't have any of the suicidal issues that we discussed, nor do I have any physical condition (like heart troubles) that might be triggered by therapy.

Confidentiality and its exceptions

During our sessions, I may be taking written notes, or audio or video recordings. This helps me remember what we accomplished or still need to do; and can help remind you too, because one of the common effects of modern therapy is forgetting what one's issue used to be (the 'apex effect'). This material is confidential and is not for other people, even after we finish working together. However, there are some exceptions:

a) If a child is or may be at risk of abuse or neglect, or in need of protection;

b) If I believe that you or another person is at clear risk of imminent harm;

c) For the purpose of complying with a legal order such as a subpoena, or if the disclosure is otherwise required or authorized by law.

d) If you are in couples therapy with me, do not tell me anything you wish kept secret from your partner.

e) I may also disclose information for the purpose of a professional consultation, or for a professional presentation or paper, in which case your identity will remain confidential. *(Note: if you are a client at an Institute clinic, your full information is available to other Institute staff as needed.)*

f) I may also be sharing anonymous data (length of time, effectiveness, unusual problems) from our sessions to help improve the quality of the processes we are using.

g) You should be aware that email or cell phones can be monitored by others, so don't communicate in this way if you wish confidentiality.

❏ We've discussed exceptions to confidentiality, and I understand and agree with these terms of therapy.

Benefits and risks of trauma therapy

The trauma-based therapy that we will be doing is intended to heal the specific issue(s) that you and I decide on in our 'pay for results' agreement. Trauma therapy may also bring deeper personal insight and awareness; solutions to, or better ways of understanding and coping with problems; improved relationships; significant reductions in feelings of distress; and greater insight into personal goals and values.

You should know, however, that trauma therapy usually requires that you be willing to examine and discuss difficult topics or times in your life, to experience stronger than usual emotions, and to try out new and different behaviors. The therapy may feel challenging and difficult at times. Uncomfortable feelings and experiences may be addressed (in that you may feel anger, sadness, guilt, grief, loss, frustration, etc.) as well as physical discomforts or pains (nausea, aches, pains). During treatment, you may feel worse before you start to feel better. And I simply may not be able to help you, or, in rare cases, make you feel worse than when we started. However, you ultimately get to decide what we discuss and work with. If you feel uncomfortable or not ready to discuss a particular issue at any point, this is completely okay.

In your session, we'll almost certainly be using one or more state-of-the-art therapies such as EMDR, EFT, TAT, TIR, or WHH, depending on your issue and other factors. (They work far better than older trauma techniques.) You should also know that these techniques, although widely used, are still considered experimental and may cause you problems that have not yet been recognized. Also, the techniques you might learn in therapy are for your own use and not to be taught to others, be they partners, family, friends, therapists or clients. This is for their safety, because formal training is needed in case something goes wrong; and also because some of these techniques are trademarked.

There are other different types of therapy you might want to pursue instead. For example, you might simply need a counselor to help you come to a decision in your life, and not someone to heal the feelings you have around the situation. If you decide to continue, we'll look at the issue you want to heal, and decide if it is something we can agree on treating, and ways to measure success. And of course, after this discussion, you may realize that not doing anything is the right thing for you at this time.

❏ We've discussed therapy's benefits, risks, and other options available to me, and I understand and choose to continue with trauma therapy.

Benefits and risks of trauma therapy (alternate)

NOTE TO STUDENTS: this section is a more detailed version of the previous section. It has the advantage of being more specific, and helps you remember the specifics yourself. It has the disadvantage of more detail that can be irrelevant to your client. Remember to choose which section you want to use.

This is the part of the informed consent form that may come as a surprise to you (unless you're a therapist yourself). First of all, you should know that *any* therapeutic technique *may* trigger certain kinds of problems; and some therapies potentially have additional specific problems. Clearly, I would only like to only use therapies that have no risks; but they don't exist. After we discuss the benefits and risks, it is up to you to decide if the possibility of healing your issue is worth the known or anticipated risks of trauma therapy.

So, what are some of the risks? We'll start with a problem that you may not have realized could even be a problem – that the therapy is successful and your issue goes away. Why might this be a problem? After all, that's why you are here, isn't it? Well, what sometimes happens is that you not only lose your issue, but you also change in other ways. For example, you are an actress who needs to frequently exhibit sadness on stage – and now you just can't evoke it at will anymore. Or previously vivid or traumatic memories may fade which could adversely impact your ability to provide detailed legal testimony regarding a traumatic incident. Or your interests and personal goals shift, causing you to want to quit your job or change careers. Or how you feel about your spouse or friends suddenly changes, and you have to deal with the interpersonal problems that causes. Or you may have adjustment problems to feeling very different inside, or have a spiritual experience that conflicts with the teachings of your religious affiliation. Obviously, these problems aren't restricted to therapy – they can happen due to any growth experience, like travel, education, or meeting new people. It just happens a lot faster and more frequently in therapy.

During sessions, you will most likely encounter strong emotions, difficult memories, or physical pains; and that during or after treatment, new emotional and physical sensations or additional unresolved memories may also surface. These experiences typically occur in any therapy, and you should either be prepared for them or do not start therapy. Additionally, if these feelings aren't eliminated by the end of your session, you might find yourself having trouble driving after your session due to the distractions of strong feelings, sensations, or tiredness; or having to deal with these feelings afterwards at home and work. Fortunately, in most cases these feelings fade, even if you aren't treated for them, as the memories get pushed aside as you live your daily life. However, if you find that these feelings remain a problem that is too uncomfortable to wait until your next session, you should contact me for more timely help. In rare cases, a sequence of traumatic memories might arise, as if a block in the flow of a stream were removed. Depending on the situation, this might require healing the new issues; or you may simply need to stop further healing until this flow dies down.

In your session, we'll almost certainly be using one or more state-of-the-art therapies such as EMDR, EFT, TAT, TIR, or WHH, depending on your issue and other factors. (They work far better than older trauma techniques.) If we use WHH, TIR, or EMDR, you should know that, as strange as it sounds, you may relive very traumatic prenatal experiences – this is to be expected with these techniques. You should also know that these techniques, although widely used, are still considered experimental and may have problems that have not yet been recognized. Also, the techniques you might learn in therapy are for your own use and not to be taught to others, be they partners, family, friends, therapists or clients. This is for their safety, because formal training is needed in case something goes wrong; and also because some of these techniques are trademarked.

There are a few more risks that we should discuss. What if you decide to leave therapy before it is finished? In this case, you can expect that you'll probably feel worse than when you started, at least for a while. Another problem is that the therapy may not work and your problem remains. Unfortunately, there are no guarantees that any therapy will be able to help. Although this won't lead to a financial burden for you, because we only 'charge for results', this can be very upsetting for some. And, just as you've most likely already experienced at home, you might feel worse than you did when you started as a result of focusing on the problem.

The last risk I want to cover is that, during therapy, in rare cases we might end up making you feel worse, not better. This can happen because your issue has a deeper, more traumatic source that we simply couldn't heal, or that another issue was triggered, or for reasons no one can explain. Although this rarely happens, it is a possibility. If so, we typically find that the new problem fades with time as it re-submerges into your unconscious, but it might not. I also have specialists available to me who we would call in to help. There is one case in particular that we need to talk about - what happens if suicidal feelings arise in the course of your treatment. In this case, I will end treatment and refer you to a therapist who works with this issue.

In summary, you now know a lot more about the risks of therapy, some that are common sense, and some that many people don't realize even exist. As an informed consumer, you are the only one who can judge if the risks of intervention that we've discussed are ones you are willing to accept. If this sounds like more than you are willing to risk, I recommend you see a counseling therapist, not a trauma therapist.

❑ I understand the benefits and risks of therapy that we have discussed, and agree to the use of the therapies described.

Benefits and risks of Peak States processes

There is another kind of therapy, where the focus is on gaining certain 'peak states' of consciousness. For example, you can get a continuously quiet mind, or a feeling of peace that is greater than normal.

So, what are the difficulties or risks with using these processes? First, they involve healing prenatal trauma. If you don't heal them fully, you may feel badly for a period of time ranging from hours to days, and perhaps longer, until these memories re-submerge and leave your awareness. Secondly, these processes are relatively new and experimental. Long-term effects, if any, have not been studied or researched. This means that there is always the possibility that problems may occur that we have never seen before, and do not know how to deal with. By analogy, this is like a new drug that after a few years turns out to have side effects that only affected some people. If problems happen, I will call in specialists to help, but even they may not be able to solve your problem. Given this, why would you ever want to use such a process? The reason is the same as why you would use a new drug – it can do things that you really want done, and there are no obvious problems (at least so far).

Obviously, due to safety concerns only a therapist who is trained in these techniques should be using them. If you go ahead with this type of treatment, you must not share the techniques with others, including your spouse or other therapists you know.

❏ We've discussed the Peak States processes benefits and risks. I understand that there may be problems that remain after the treatment is finished. [Circle the choice that applies to you below:]
- Yes, I am willing to accept the risks and any consequences that may arise, and use these processes. I agree to not share the techniques to anyone else.
- No, I am unwilling to accept the risks or be fully responsible for what happens, and so will not use the processes.

Practical details

If you decide to start therapy, we will start by writing up a 'pay for results' agreement for your therapy. Sessions are typically two hours long, but can run overtime; and we'll agree on a schedule that works for both of us. If you miss three sessions without canceling or with less than 24 hour notice, or cancel therapy before completion (up to five sessions), you may forfeit your deposit (if any). I do not do insurance billing.

I encourage you to phone if any emergency situations arise from our work between sessions, but other concerns should be addressed in your regular therapy session. My phone number is at the end of this document. When I am unavailable or on vacation, I will provide you with a contact number of someone who can assist you.

If you have a life-threatening emergency, you must either call the Suicide and Crisis Hotline at _____, phone emergency services at ___911 in the US and Canada___, or go to the nearest emergency room. I provide only non-emergency therapeutic services by scheduled appointments. If I may need additional or more intensive services, I may refer me to another organization to receive extended services.

❑ We've discussed practical details of our work together, especially about emergencies, and I understand and agree to these terms.

Reviews, referrals and ending

In counseling, it is your right at any time to:

a) Have a review of your progress and of any of the topics in this form;
b) Be provided with a referral to another counselor or health professional;
c) Withdraw consent for the collection, use, or disclosure of your personal information, except where precluded by law;
d) End the counseling or therapeutic relationship by so advising the therapist or counselor. (This may forfeit part or all of your deposit, but the amount will be less than or equal to the standard $100/hr rate of the time you've already spent in therapy.)
e) Access or obtain a copy of the information in your counseling records, subject to legal requirements.

Your right of access to or to obtain a copy of your personal information continues after the end of the counseling relationship.

I reserve the right to terminate therapy at any time. This may occur, for example, if I believe that I simply can't help you. If this happens, there would be no charge to you for our work up to that point and your deposit (if any) would be returned.

❑ We've discussed my rights around the termination of therapy, and I understand and agree to these terms.

Concerns or complaints

If you have a concern about any aspect of your counseling, I would prefer that you first address it with me. If you feel that this is impossible or unsafe, or if your concern is not resolved through our discussion, you should contact the Institute for the Study of Peak States at +1-250-413-3211. If this doesn't resolve your complaint, you should then contact the local governmental body that regulates therapists in your country.

❑ We've discussed how to deal with any complaints or problems I have with my therapist, and I understand and agree to these terms.

Signature

"My signature below confirms that I (the client) have read the above, had an opportunity to discuss it with the therapist, had sufficient time to consider it carefully, and had my questions answered to my satisfaction."

_____   _____
Name of Client   Name of Therapist

_____   _____
Signature of Client   Signature of Therapist

_____   _____
Date signed   Signature of Witness (if any)

_____
Revisions
2.1 April 17, 2010

Practice Examples for
Subcellular Case Identification

In this section, we give brief examples to be used to quiz students on their familiarity with the subcellular cases. In a classroom setting, the instructor can roll play as the client to help the student in the identification process.

"I feel depressed"
    What do you feel depressed about? Reply: Everything
    Where do you feel it on your body? Reply: I don't understand the question, I feel "blah".
    Diagnosis: flattened emotion

"I feel depressed"
    Body posture and facial expression look sad. (Grief, heavy all over, low energy, life's not worth living)
    When did it start? Reply: My partner left me.
    Do you feel tired? Reply: Yeah, all over. (This was not useful in differential diagnosis)
    Diagnosis: soul loss

"I want to go to this cool gathering, but I also feel pulled to stay home…"
    Diagnosis: dilemma

"I am feeling heavy"
    It has been there the last couple of months.
    Possibilities: tribal block, blanket curse, copy.
    Diagnosis: tribal block

"I saw something"

I got a problem, but I don't really want to talk about it. I was attending a tantric workshop. I was doing an exercise and my girlfriend was on my lap. A really weird thing happened. She died. I'm a good Christian. It was like she was in my arms, and she was dead. Then I came back, I feel so sad.

Diagnosis: flash of a past life

"War injury"

I keep going to surgery where I had a bullet in my leg, but I still feel pain there.

Feel the bullet; is there a message? Reply: Yeah, I hate you.

Diagnosis: curse

Allergy: sneezing

Possibilities: body association, generational (had it all my life, everyone in my family has it), copies.

Diagnosis: generational trauma

"Dude, I feel sick, terrible, all the time" (speak like an addict)

Diagnosis: heroin withdrawal symptom.

Woman, late 40, happy, cheerful, have what look like chicken pox on her body

Didn't know she attempted suicide. (They are cigarette burn marks.)

Diagnosis: schizophrenia

"Problem at work"

I have a real problem at work. I'm not able to do my job well. Weird shit happens. I am unhappy. I'm thinking of quitting.

When did it start? Reply: Started in this new job. I hate working there, I like the work, but difficult with coworkers. No physical pain.

Diagnosis: cording

"I have the strong urge to go driving"

It is sometimes problematic in going to work, because I want to keep driving.

Diagnosis: positive trauma

"I'm in the office, I feel really sad."

When did it start? Reply: In the fall.

What happened at fall? Reply: Nothing in particular. It started last fall too, and went away in spring. I just can't get over the sadness. I am sad every winter.

Does it feel like you are missing someplace or someone else? Reply: No.

When was the first time you felt like this? Reply: The fall that I moved from the prairies to BC.

Diagnosis: Seasonal Affective Disorder.

Note: In this client it was healed with simple tapping. (It could also be from a body association.)

"Nervousness"

Diagnosis: hole

Inappropriate sexual attraction

Diagnosis: body association on their emotional tone.

Knee problem, injury, difficult to move

Diagnosis: crown brain structure

"My wife complains that I don't have much emotion"

Diagnosis: flattened emotion or inner peace state

"I want to be a therapist"

Diagnosis: seeking a peak experience through the job

"I can't quit thinking about my ex-partner. I keep imagining that I'm still in relationship with her."

(This could have been a very tricky case, but fortunately there was more information.) During a meditation retreat, as he was thinking about her again, his self-image or identity vanished and was replaced by the terrible feeling in his chest, that of a terrible, bottomless deficient emptiness in his heart region.

Diagnosis: hole (He was imagining he was still in relationship to help block the feeling of emptiness in his chest.)

Case Studies for
Differential Diagnostic Practice

The following cases were with real clients (with identifying information removed) who healed by the end of the session. These cases can be used by an instructor in a classroom setting, when the teacher can read the story, pretend to be the client, and have students see if they can diagnose the problem.

Presenting issue: Wants financial abundance.

    Story: The client wants to have consistent financial abundance. When he thinks about earning money, doing the task, and that his survival depends on it, he feels heavy and anxiety.

    Diagnosis: Tribal block.

Presenting issue: Create a school and doing something I love, and make money.

    Story: The client is inspired to create a school called Children Play School, but feels "I don't have what it takes". Feels a block, resistance, fearful, lack of confidence, hopelessness (fear it will never happen) to build a school.

    Charge for result contract: Remove the feeling of resistance (fatigue, nauseous, weak).

    Trigger phrase: You don't have what it takes (!!) to pursue this project/ to create this school (SUDS=9)

    Diagnosis: Tribal block.

Presenting issue: Constant unhappiness.

    Story: Client is healed but is not satisfied and comes up with endless more issues to complain about. Unbeknownst to the client, she is addicted to suffering. As soon as she starts to feel calm, either in her life in general, or in a healing session, she starts to unconsciously find another issue or drama to suffer about.

She reports that happiness is terrifying. She is afraid of being happy. Mother was being triggered when she was triggered. Yes, this feels personal.

Trigger phrase: "safe to let go of my suffering"

Diagnosis: Body association (feeling of peace).

Presenting issue: I want to feel joy and exuberance.

Story: Client says "I want to feel joy and exuberance", but it is a cover-up for feeling "I'm not enough, I'm deficient." Many clients who want peak states, or positive feelings, are actually trying to use it as a strategy to fix a problem they have had all their life and cannot solve.

"Why do you want to have access to joy and exuberance?" Reply: "I think it would help me not feel bad about myself and to easier talk with people."

"What prevents you from feeling good about yourself?" Reply: "Most of the time I see myself as inadequate."

Trigger phrase: "I'm not enough"

Diagnosis: Generational trauma.

Presenting issue: Wants full sexual expression.

Story: Client avoided talking about sex during the session but clearly wanted something. Finally, she spoke about that 7 years ago, she already had a diminishing sexual desire. 15 years ago she was in school busy, too exhausted to have sex with her husband. When asked to sense her husband, the client feels he is "detached".

Charge for result contract: "Remove the block to sexual expression with my husband."

Trigger phrase: "I have to give up" (SUDS = 8)

Diagnosis: Cording. (Used DPR to treat.)

Presenting issue: Not being present.

Story: How does the problem feel to you, emotionally? Reply: "I'm mostly afraid of what people are like, unpredictable. I feel sadness. I have an inability to relate because I'm not in the same reality as with other people."

What are some of the way it shows up? Reply: "Perception of this world being fuzzy. Can't quite grasp what is going on. If I focus really hard, I can. It's like in the dream. As a kid, like to play, don't like to come into reality, went into other plane."

When was the last time it happened? Reply: "I was not able to get a sense of what was going on. It has to do with reality being fuzzy. My senses aren't clear. Process of seeing and interacting."

Diagnosis: Bubble.

Presenting issue: Wants to earn more income.

Story: "I feel panic at solar plexus, and fear, anger, and nervousness. I have fear and anger that I'm not going to get enough."

Do you have a feeling of resistance? Reply: "Yes."

Feels heavy? Reply: "Yes."

Trigger phrase: "We are not going to pay you anymore." SUDS: 9

Diagnosis: Tribal block.

Presenting issue: People are immature.

Story: "I am arrogant, I look at people whining about their problem, I think, "you little wimp", and I have a condescending attitude. I go into judgment. I am from a culture of hard working fishermen, a very macho culture."

Charge for result contract: Eliminate the macho response to immature people.

Trigger phrase: "Do it now!"

Diagnosis: Tribal block.

Presenting issue: Anxiety.

Story: "I have anxiety when I wake up in the morning, with feelings of dread. I also have fear of not being successful, indecision, scattered-ness, not able to make decision, feel torn, lack of self-worth, self-confidence. I'm normally high functioning, but not lately, maybe menopause."

Charge for result contract: Get rid of the constant underlying anxiety when I wake up in the morning

Trigger phrase: "I might die alone"

Diagnosis: Generation trauma and body association.

Results: Client was symptom free for few days, but returned with the same anxiety when waking up in the morning. Client wakes up fine but quickly has an anxious thought that causes them to feel anxious and exhibit physical bodily symptoms (racing heart beat, irritable bowl syndrome)

Charge for result contract: same as previous session.

Diagnosis: Mind chatter; treated using the Body Association Technique.

Presenting issue: Not happy with my career.

Story: "I feel blocked, I sabotage myself, and I am working/writing for others instead of for myself. I have to work hard to make money."

Charge for result contract: When thinking of working/writing for myself, instead of for my boss, I no longer feel blocked, or feel I am holding myself back.

Trigger phrase: "When I'm in the spot light, I get put down."

Diagnosis: Tribal block.

Presenting issue: Bothersome voices for most of my life.
Story: "I have really negative self talk. It is subconscious talk, parental voice stuff. I have done hypnosis but it seemed to scramble my voice even more. The language choice is odd, and it is also like an ego voice. I cannot get it to stop, and it can start to spin. Sometimes it's loud, and wants to take over. I am ruminating with negative self-talk, there is a tinge that it is not just my voice."
Charge for result contract: Eliminate 3 voices: Ego voice that's angry and fearful; Mother's voice that's negative, mean, controlling, hatred; Subconscious mind voice that's desperate, stubborn, defiant.
Diagnosis: Mind chatter; treated using the Body Association Technique (one-hand).

Presenting issue: Block to breathing easily.
Story: The client has a metallic, inorganic structure (cage, girder, straight jacket, iron clamp, alien implant) in her belly for 13 years. As a consequences she cannot breath freely, feels she does not own her body, feels suffocated, despair, hopeless, and rage. In regression, the client's memory is blocked at moment of trauma. The client talked about various other events. It took some effort; the therapist used a modified form of TIR to pin down the exact moment of trauma. The client was in an argument at age 34 where her spouse was throwing plates around. She felt anger and hatred.
Diagnosis: Crown Brain Structure.

Presenting issue: Wants to date.
Story: The male client finds it difficult to go on a date. When he thinks about dating attractive women, he has physical symptoms of anxiety, gagging, tightness of the chest, and panic.
Trigger phrase: "I will be broken hearted". SUDS=10.
Diagnosis: simple trauma. Tapping healed the problem.

Presenting issue: Feel badly about borrowing money.
Story: A construction worker has a pattern of earning money, then, when the job ends, he does not go out and find new work. Instead, he feels badly about the need to borrow money from others. He has positive feelings around his choice of not working, along with a sense of entitlement, arrogance, and a cocky attitude.
Trigger phrase: I feel inadequate around my work".
Diagnosis: Simple trauma. Tapping healed the problem.

Presenting issue: Don't want to go back to Europe.

Story: The woman, in her forties, has moved to Canada from Europe. She feels badly when she thinks about going back to work in her original home country in Europe, and has felt this way for the last ten years. She feels that culture is very difficult and unpleasant to be around. She has continuous sensations of pain pressure, and heaviness in her neck when she thinks about going back. She feels controlled and limited there.

Diagnosis: Severe cross-cultural tribal block problem. Healed using the Silent Mind Technique.

Presenting issue: Feeling controlled.

Story: A middle-aged woman's symptoms started last week. She is easily angry, even violent, and feels invaded by everyone around her. She says it is a 'control issue'. "I react to certain people in my space." "Don't want negativity in my space." "There is pressure outside to change or be different."

Trigger phrase: "Fuck you!"

Diagnosis: Tribal block.

Presenting issue: Can't survive here.

Story: A woman was very attracted to come live on an island she had once visited, but when she moved there after several years of planning, it was a disaster. Financially she could not make it, and her savings were vanishing. It turns out that she had an abortion about the time she had originally planned to move to the island.

Diagnosis: Soul loss.

Presenting issue: Financial success.

Story: The client was not happy because he didn't have enough money to do the things he wanted to do. "It's like a thermostat, I only have about a certain level of income."

Trigger phrase: "I'm kept from experiencing life". SUDS=8.

Diagnosis: Tribal block.

Presenting issue: Husband does not pay me attention.

Story: "I feel sad, because my husband, even through he talks to me, he does not give me attention. Therefore I need to talk to someone else who does." The client's attention is always on her concern about "if other people like me or not". "If they give me attention, I feel good and I like to talk with them."

Trigger phrase: "Love is my life's purpose".

Diagnosis: S-hole. "After my healing, attention or love is no longer the driving force behind my talking with people.

Presenting issue: Loss of sexual attraction to husband after childbirth.

Story: A high functioning woman lost her sexual attraction to her husband three years ago after the birth of their child. "He is pushing me away". "I don't see in his eyes his desire for me."

Diagnosis: Cording.

Appendix 6

Quiz

General questions about diagnosis

1) What is a 'trigger phrase' and how does it differ from a description of the client's presenting problem?
2) How long should you listen to the client's story?
3) What category of problems can be triggered by meditation?
4) What is a very disruptive problem that can be caused by awareness increasing by using meditation?
5) What does 'differential diagnosis' mean?
6) If a client abruptly loses their symptoms during healing, what can be the cause?
7) How do you check if a trauma is healed?
8) What are some of the first diagnostic steps?
9) What is one way to spot generational traumas that are causing or helping to make your client's problem worse?
10) When should you always suspect that the tribal block causing your client's problem?
11) If a client has great peak states, can they still have problems, and if so, why?
12) Can clients know the cause of their unusual problem?
13) When healing a client who has different stuck gene problems (biographical, generational, associational), which would you typically start with and why?
14) What is the difference between a core issue and a dominant issue?
15) What is a trauma phrase?
16) What is a sensate substitute?

Questions about specific subcellular cases

17) What is the difference between an e-hole and a hole?
18) What is the difference between an e-cord and a cord?
19) Why do people move their consciousness into bubbles?
20) What is a subcellular case diagnosis for channeling?

21) Therapists assume that a client's experience is always negative, usually caused by trauma. What are a couple of things that a client can experience that are positive?
22) No emotions in a client can be caused by?
23) What subcellular case can trigger a child's temper tantrum?
24) What causes a fixed belief in a client?
25) What is one way to identify the parasite class (or combination of classes) your client is experiencing?

Questions about safety and ethics

26) What is a temporary, easy way to help many suicidal clients almost instantly?
27) What developmental events contribute to suicidal feelings and why?
28) What are some of the problems that can be triggered using trauma therapies?
29) What do you do if you encounter a problem you cannot heal in a client?
30) What preparations should you do before doing a skype therapy session and why?
31) Do you talk to clients about subcellular parasite issues and why?
32) Is it ethical to charge large fees for very quick healing processes?
33) What are some psychological problems that are due to medical issues?
34) What are the two main parts of 'pay for results' agreements?
35) Why are standard billing practices unethical? (Give one reason.)

Questions about the Institute

36) Does the Institute encourage or discourage the use of non-Institute techniques?
37) If a person is certified by the Institute, are they still required to use 'pay for results' even when they use non-Institute techniques?

Quiz Solutions

1) What is a 'trigger phrase' and how does it differ from a description of the client's presenting problem?

Answer: The trigger phrase is designed to stimulate the client's emotional reaction, not describe the problem or story.

2) How long should you listen to the client's story?

Answer: typically only 3-5 minutes.

3) What category of problems can be triggered by meditation?

Answer: Spiritual emergencies.

4) What is a very disruptive problem that can be caused by awareness increasing (perhaps by using meditation)?

Answer: Holes can come into awareness.

5) What does 'differential diagnosis' mean?

Answer: a symptom can be caused by more than one problem. You use other symptoms that are different between the multiple causes to identify the correct cause.

6) If a client abruptly loses their symptoms during healing, what can be the cause?

Answer: They might have a strong 'Being Present' state: or they may have created a trauma bypass; or they may be exceptionally self-loving and accepting; or they are deceiving themselves (need to check for this).

7) How do you check if a trauma is healed?

Answer: Check for a feeling of calm, peace, and lightness in the event moment; and being in-body at the trauma moment when first returning to it.

8) What are some of the first diagnostic steps?

Answer: Get the trigger phrase and the SUDS. Decide if it is simple biographical or generational trauma. Look at the moment the problem first started. Does tapping work on the client?

9) What is one way to spot generational traumas that are causing or helping to make your client's problem worse?

Answer: Is the feeling very 'personal' (this can be hard to explain); or do you feel that there is something intrinsically wrong with you, that you are just defective; or the problem runs in the family line.

10) When should you always suspect that the tribal block causing your client's problem?

Answer: When the client is trying to change or grow; is a high functioning person; or they want a peak state; and/or they feel heavy in their life.

11) If a client has great peak states, can they still have problems, and if so, why?

Answer: Yes. They still have traumas. This is a particular problem among spiritual teachers (for example, famous Zen Buddhist teachers who were also alcoholics). Some people in the Beauty Way state can still find that beer, wine, or hard liquor tastes good; in the extreme, also be an alcoholic.

12) Can clients know the cause of their unusual problem?

Answer: Sometimes.

13) When healing a client who has different stuck gene problems (biographical, generational, associational), which would you typically start with and why?

Answer: Typically you start with the generational trauma first, because it usually has the most impact on a person. (It also causes structural problems in the primary cell that in turn can cause other symptoms.) Then you heal body associations, and then the biographical trauma. This corresponds to healing the genes from the bottom triune brain going upwards (perineum for generational, body for associations, heart for biographical), not randomly or from the top down.

14) What is the difference between a core issue and a dominant issue?

Answer: The client does not feel a core issue, but can see its effect in their lives. The dominant issue causes relatively constant discomfort and suffering, and is the major problem for the client.

15) What is a trauma phrase?

Answer: A trauma moment has a short one to four word phrase of the belief or decision formed during the trauma experience. It is a word translation of the body sensation at that frozen moment in time.

16) What is a sensate substitute?

Answer: The client finds a substitute in the world or in their primary cell that feels the same as something that was outside of themselves during an early pre-birth trauma. This is usually a body association driven by feelings of trying to survive.

17) What is the difference between an e-hole and a hole?

Answer: A hole is an area of deficient emptiness in the body. An e-hole is a missing area but filled with a negative feeling that has an evil overtone to it.

18) What is the difference between an e-cord and a cord?

Answer: A cord connects complementary traumas between people, and gives the sensation that the other person has a personality. The e-cord also connects people, but only gives the feeling that the other person feels evil (in a particular location in their body).

19) Why do people move their consciousness into bubbles?

Answer: It gives the person an illogical feeling of safety.

20) What is a subcellular case diagnosis for channeling?

Answer: Ribosomal voices.

21) Therapists assume that a client's experience is always negative, usually caused by trauma. What are a couple of things that a client can experience that are positive?

Answer: Intuition, especially the 'calm knowing' type; peak experiences or states.

22) No emotions in a client can be caused by?

Answer: Brain shutdown or rarely a peak state of inner peace.

23) What subcellular case can trigger a child's temper tantrum?

Answer: Ribosomal voices, due to the change in the parent's emotional tone.

24) What causes a fixed belief in a client?

Answer: Biographical trauma makes beliefs driven by emotional charge. Core traumas make beliefs that have no emotional content.

25) What are some intrinsic parasite qualities?

Answer: Bugs 'taste' metallic; fungus makes a person feel nauseated; and bacteria makes a person feel poisoned or toxic. Most people automatically block these intrinsic parasite qualities but can usually sense them if directed to do so. However, this should be done sparingly if at all – it is best to keep the client interacting as little as possible with parasites.

26) What is a temporary, easy way to help many suicidal clients almost instantly?
Answer: Have them touch their navel.

27) What developmental events contribute to suicidal feelings and why?
Answer: Placental death – the placenta has to die during birth, but trauma locks this feeling in place and it can be stimulated in the client later in life.

28) What are some of the problems that can be triggered using trauma therapies?
Answer: Trauma flooding, decompensation, uncovering worse traumatic feelings or subcellular cases, new parasite symptoms.

29) What do you do if you encounter a problem you cannot heal in a client?
Answer: Try to help your client find someone who can help them: refer them to specialists you have found just in case of this possibility; if Institute certified, contact the Institute clinic staff.

30) What preparations should you do before doing a skype therapy session and why?
Answer: Make sure you have alternate ways to continue the session if the internet quits; have someone else physically present who can intervene if there are problems; use standard informed consent and liability forms so they won't panic if this happens.

31) Do you talk to clients about subcellular parasite issues and why?
Answer: In general discussing this issue is a bad idea, because it can panic the client or make them unnecessarily concerned, and has no bearing on treatment; or it can cause them to try and invent dangerous ways to heal this problem on their own.

32) Is it ethical to charge large fees for very quick healing processes?
Answer: Yes. Your contract was for the service delivered, not for your time. The client has already decided the value of your service. It also allows you to charge less for clients who take longer, if you choose to do this (fixed fee billing).

33) What are some psychological problems that are due to medical issues?
Answer: Brain damage; prescription drug side effects; candida fungus in the gut.

34) What are the two main parts of 'pay for results' agreements?
Answer: Before treatment starts, determine criteria for success; and specify the total cost of services. If the criteria are not met, there is no fee. This allows the client to decide if the cost/benefit tradeoff is worth it to them.

35) Why are standard billing practices unethical? (Give one reason.)

Answer: (There are several ethical problems the student could focus on.) The client's underlying motivation, even if it is not expressed, is the hope that their time with the therapist will solve their problem(s). Unsuccessful, partial or random healing feeds that hope without meeting the implied contract. Standard practices essentially prey on vulnerable people, using the client's underlying agenda to get money without delivering on the unspoken agreement.

36) Does the Institute encourage or discourage the use of non-Institute techniques?

Answer: We encourage the use of any and all techniques that work. However, some techniques get their effect by damaging the client and must be avoided.

37) If a person is certified by the Institute, are they still required to use 'pay for results' even when they use non-Institute techniques?

Answer: Yes.

Parasite Classes
and Their Subcellular Cases

Class 1 Bug-Like Parasites:
- Bubble (in combination with a fungal organism)
- Bug parasite problems
- Damaged (veiled) peak states

Class 2 Fungal Parasites:
- Chakras problem
- Column of Self
- Cord
- Fungal parasite problems
- Life paths
- MPD (Multiple Personality Disorder)
- Curse (blanket or arrowhead)
- Past life trauma
- Over-identification with the Creator
- Ribosomal voices
- Shattered crystals
- S-hole
- Time loops
- Tribal block

Class 3 Bacterial Parasites:
- Asperger's Syndrome (in combination with a fungal organism)
- Bacterial parasite problems
- Copy
- E-hole
- Grandparents around the body
- Sound loops
- Trauma bypasses

Finding Techniques

This manual was designed to help therapists trained in the Whole-Hearted Healing regression therapy and in Peak States Therapy to diagnose clients. Specific techniques are *not* explained in this manual. Instead, we refer you to existing published manuals, or to our training courses. Below is a guide to where some of these techniques can currently be found (as of 2014):

Body Association Technique: (not yet published).

Courteau Projection Technique: *The Whole-Hearted Healing™ Workbook* by Paula Courteau.

Crosby Vortex Technique: *The Whole-Hearted Healing™ Workbook* by Paula Courteau.

Distant Personality Release: *The Basic Whole-Hearted Healing™ Manual* by Grant McFetridge and Mary Pellicer.

Silent Mind Technique: *Silence the Voices* (not yet published).

Tribal Block Technique: (not yet published).

Waisel Extreme Emotions Technique: (not yet published).

Whole-Hearted Healing: *The Basic Whole-Hearted Healing™ Manual* by Grant McFetridge and Mary Pellicer.

'Pay for Results' Fee Calculation Guide

When using the 'pay for results' system, how do you calculate your fee for services? In this appendix we'll cover the simplest, least risk method that charges your clients the minimum possible fee while still meeting your financial goals.

First, your fee is quoted *up front* in the contract offer you make the client during the initial interview. If you succeed in meeting the contract terms, you get paid that amount – if you don't meet the terms, or only succeed partially, you don't get paid at all. Nor do you charge separately for diagnosis or consultations with clients that don't accept your contract offer, nor charge clients you were unable to heal. Although this sounds impossible for many therapists used to hourly billing, numerous professions use exactly this 'pay for results' billing method. In fact, you encounter this billing method almost every day! After all, you expect your grocery store to only sell fresh, healthy food; not mixed in with old, rotten or spoiled merchandise…

10.1: Compute your fixed fee

In reality, most therapists in general practice who use the 'pay for results' model simply use the same standard, set fee for every ordinary therapy issue. Essentially, "one size fits all". No matter what problem the client has, they charge the same amount. Flat fee billing minimizes financial risk for the therapist, because risk and reward are spread evenly among all clients. Typical minimum fees for general therapy range around $250 - $350US, but vary with country and cost of living.

Interestingly, in our experience most 'pay for result' clients are fine with a fixed fee – they are only really concerned with eliminating their issue. (It is generally just therapists or other 'healthcare practitioners' who have a problem with this billing method.) Clients recognize that they are paying for your expertise, not your time. In fact, for them shorter is better – clients are tired of suffering and just want the issue gone as rapidly as possible. Like with car repair, clients are happier if it's done in an hour rather than a day. Quoting a fee in advance also allows them to evaluate the cost/benefit and budget for their treatment. Again, since this is 'pay for results', their chief worry that they are going to waste a large amount of money for nothing is no longer an issue. This fee structure also means that half of the clients are charged less, and the other half more, as compared to an hourly rate fee system. This really helps the slower clients and is not an excessive burden on the faster ones.

So, how do you set your fixed fee? Like those grocers, you have to price your services to cover the clients you heal and the ones you don't. Although you can't predict which particular clients will heal (and make you money), over time your successes and failures average to a reasonably steady rate. With this, we can now write down a simple way to figure out your needed fee:

Eq. 10.1 $\text{Fee} = (\text{desired hourly rate}) \times \left[\dfrac{(\text{total of all client contact hours})}{(\# \text{ clients healed})} \right]$

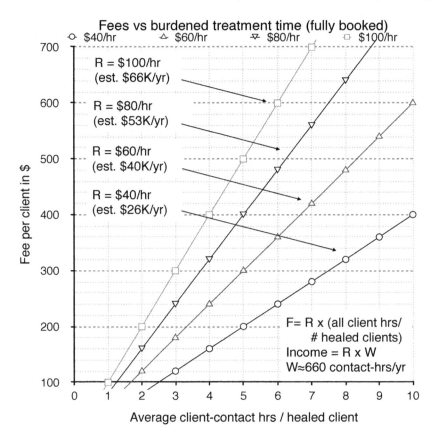

Figure 10.1: A plot of the fixed fee (equation 10.1) for four different hourly rates. Estimated annual incomes were computed assuming 660 contact-hours per year.

Figure 10.1 shows the relationship between fixed fee versus hourly rate from equation 10.1. The plot's name 'burdened treatment time' means this average also includes the time spent on clients we did not succeed in healing, as well as time spent in all initial interviews. It also assumes a full client load.

Note that the fees you set give you an income based on your *client-contact hours*. Other overhead time you spent, say cleaning your office or writing advertising material does not directly influence your fee. In private practice, it is customary that overhead time is covered by the equivalent hourly rate you chose. Of course, what you charge is up to you (within the constraints of 'charge for results').

Nothing says you have to charge your standard, fixed fee if the client's issue was handled quickly, meaning you could charge less if you wanted to - but you have to watch out, as your income depends on having some clients heal quicker to make up for the ones who heal more slowly!

Example 10.1: Math, yuck! Just tell me how much to charge...

A fixed fee of about $350US is a reasonable estimate for a typical beginner using subcellular psychobiology techniques. Over time, you can use equation 10.1 and adjust your fee to better fit your skill level and client issues.

So how did we get a $350 beginners fixed fee? Here are the (hopefully) reasonable parameters we used. You want a $50,000US/year income and you work 660 client contact hours a year, which means you need an equivalent hourly rate (R) of $76/hr. Your average diagnosis time (T) is 0.5 hours; your average general therapy treatment time (A) is 2 hours; your maximum cutoff time (C) when you should quit is 4 hours (we'll explain that later); the percentage of clients who start treatment after your initial interview (Pt) is 80%; and your success rate (P) on the ones who start is 70%. Thus, in terms of figure 10.1, you have 4.6 total contact-hours per healed client.

Given these numbers, you would have to work on 256 clients in a year, which means you have to see 6 new clients each week (if you work a 5-day work week with 15.2 client-contact hours per week spread out over 217 work days for 43.4 weeks a year). If you can't get that many new clients, you'll have to either accept a lower annual income (e.g., for 10% fewer clients your income would be 10% lower) or raise your fee to compensate (e.g., for 10% fewer clients you raise your fee 10%).

10.2: Monitor your financial performance

The simple equation 10.1 says that to figure your fixed, 'one price fits all' fee, all you have to do is keep a running total of the time you spent on *all* your clients, while keeping track of how many you were actually able to heal. The only thing you need to know ahead of time is your desired hourly rate R (say \$75/hour). As the weeks pass, you just keep adding to these totals to make sure your fee is about right.

We can also rewrite that equation so we can make sure our desired hourly rate is holding steady. Simple, eh?

Eq. 10.2

$$R = \frac{(\text{total of client fees})}{(\text{total of all client contact hours})} = \frac{\text{Fee x (\# clients healed)}}{(\text{total of all client contact hours})} \quad \text{in \$/hr}$$

Actually, over time your success rate increases and then plateaus as you become more skilled; and continues to bump up as new techniques are developed and subcellular cases are identified. If you are a beginner, therapists we've trained to use subcellular techniques quickly improve during their first 20 clients. Thus you find you can decrease your fee yet still meet your hourly income target. Experienced therapists get more capable but often start accepting (or attracting) tougher clients that take longer. Thus, their increased speed can be counterbalanced with harder clients, sometimes requiring a fee adjustment to keep their equivalent hourly rate on target.

10.3: Make Choices About Your Practice

10.3.1: Estimate your client contact hours (W)

As a therapist with a private practice, you need to decide how many client hours you want to do per week. You also have to account for time you have to spend on the business (making calls, appointments, advertising, chatting with potential organizations, keeping records up to date, billing insurance, paying bills, etc.) If you work a full 8-hour day, it is reasonable to assume 2 hours a day for these other tasks.

Time off is another issue. You need time off, and the clients often don't come in during certain periods of the year. For example, summer months and the month after Christmas are unlikely to have a full caseload. Thus, although it varies widely, the most you can probably expect is 10 months of full-time work at 30 hours per week of patient contact time, and 40 hours per week total work time. Thus we work about 217 days or 43.4 weeks at 5 days per week. This gives a maximum of 1,320 contact hours - and more likely you'll have a lot less contact hours, because you probably won't have a continuous back-to-back stream of clients. Figuring on a half-time caseload is probably a reasonable maximum estimate (although it may be a lot less especially when you start out). With this estimate, you'll only have 660 client-contact hours per year doing private practice (with another 220 hours for other tasks). This number is low for a therapist employed at a facility, but probably realistic for a therapist in private practice.

If we work about 660 contact-hours per year, this means we have about 3 contact-hours per working day. (Figuring another 220 hours per year for other tasks, this means a total of about 4.1 hours per working day.) This half-day schedule is not unreasonable, because the number of clients who want our services is usually the limiting factor, and this trauma-healing work is very demanding on the therapist. It also allows the trauma therapist to run overtime far more easily, something that happens a lot with this work. It also allows the therapist to work longer on weeks with a lot of clients, and shorter on weeks where there are fewer clients.

10.3.2: Determine your desired equivalent hourly rate (R)

With 'charge for results' you set a price per job, rather than charge by the hour. However, averaged over a number of clients, you can look at your income as if you had a job paying an equivalent hourly pay rate R – the total money you've earned divided by the total time you've spent with all your clients (i.e., $/hr). This idea is helpful in several ways. It lets you compute fees based on the pay rate you want; allows you to compare your income to those of other therapists; and gives you an easy way to figure out your annual income.

First, you can choose your equivalent hourly rate R by comparing yourself to other ordinary therapists' hourly rate. Find out what psychotherapists in your area are charging (both the low end and the high end). You then decide where your skill level and your ability to connect to people put you on the local hourly pay range. (Often, being able to make people feel good about themselves and their relationship with you is more important to being able to charge higher fees than being competent in healing clients). Once you have a figure, find out if it meets your annual financial targets - compute what you'll earn at the end of the year to see if it is enough.

The second way to choose your equivalent hourly rate R is to start from the annual income you want, and then compute what you have to charge to meet that target. Obviously, there is some give and take on this - you'll want to find out what the typical range of fees in your area is, so you can see if what you want is reasonable.

$$\textit{Eq. 10.3} \qquad R = \frac{I}{W} = \frac{\text{(desired annual income)}}{\text{(annual client contact hours)}} \quad \text{(in \$/hr)}$$

According to a 2009 American Psychological Association survey, the median income for a licensed Master's level in private practice in clinical psychology was $40.5K (SD=27K); for an average of 660 client-contact hours, this means R=$61/hr. The median income for a Masters level in private practice in counseling psychology was $55K; for an average of 660 client-contact hours, this means R=$83/hr. There was also quite a variation of income based on years of experience.

Whatever rate you choose, remember that you offer your general clients two exceptional features that make your services far more valuable than those of your colleagues. First, your 'charge for results' policy removes the client's financial risk. This is the single most valuable thing you can offer a client (especially ones with chronic problems where they have wasted their usually very limited savings in futile attempts to be healed). Secondly, your skill with subcellular psychobiological techniques means that you can help many typical therapy clients who are suffering greatly and cannot get help anywhere else.

> *Example 10.2: What should my equivalent hourly rate be?*
> Because your practice is new, you decide that your base rate should be in the middle of the range of psychotherapy fees in your area. This turns out to be $75/hr. If you figure a half-time caseload and the same average equivalent hourly rate R of $80 per hour, you can expect a gross annual income of $75/hr x 660 hrs = $49,500.
> Instead, if you decide that you want an annual income of $100,000 (which is unreasonably high for most general practice therapists, but more possible for therapists who specialize), you'll have to charge an equivalent hourly rate R of $100,000/660hrs = $151 per hour. However, since you're offering very effective therapy with a 'charge for results' policy, you may be worth it - but it will take some time to get you well enough known for this fact to make a difference to your client base.

10.3.3: Charge different rates for different services

This appendix was written to allow you to get a feeling for what you will earn based on a simple, 'one hourly rate for everything' model that most 'pay for results' psychotherapists use in general practice. In other words, the formulas assume that you are charging the same equivalent hourly rate R for all client issues.

However, if a general practitioner also occasionally treats some specialized, particular issue – for example, eliminating schizophrenic 'voices' – they might use a different, higher fixed fee for just that particular problem, especially if it is a pre-defined, standard but time consuming process. Essentially, it is in a time category of its own and should be billed as such.

Also, some of the unique services that a certified Peak States therapist can offer (such as peak state processes or treatment of 'untreatable' conditions) are far more valuable to clients than standard therapy and can be billed at a higher rate. Although this may sound rather mercenary, you've spent a lot of time and money learning this cutting edge material that can help your clients when nothing else can – and the client can decide if the cost is worth it for him. And remember, you don't have a monopoly, since the Institute is doing its best to spread this new way of working as fast as we can. Thus, your client can simply 'vote with his feet' and find another certified therapist whose fees are more reasonable, after all.

10.3.4: Specialize

Experienced therapists generally move into a specialization that they feel passionate about. This can make it much easier to get the needed stream of clients, especially if the therapist can work over the internet, gets referrals for their specialty, or has more than one office location. Specialization also usually pays better than general therapy (experts charge more for their expertise and training) and allows longer treatment time without increasing financial risk.

The fixed fee structure is especially appropriate for therapists who are primarily specialists. They usually set higher than average fees for their work; and since a specialist can accumulate experience in predicting the duration of their treatments, it is also far easier for them to vary their prices to fit the client's issue if they choose to.

Specialists also do a better job (higher success rate) in their area of expertise than a general therapist; and most importantly for long-term job contentment, they wake up looking forward to working and having more fun!

10.4 Cutoff time

However, there is just one little problem...

It has to do with how long you spend trying to heal clients before you give up. You know that some clients are just not going to heal, usually because the state of the art is just not yet good enough to help everyone. So the longer you spend with these clients, the more time you waste not earning any money or treating the clients you could help. Since these impossible clients don't come with little signs on their chests – they're mixed in with the ones who you can actually help - how do you deal with this?

The answer is to have a 'cutoff time'. This means that you quit trying to help your client if the total time you've spent with them goes past this limit. Thus, the other essential part of setting your fees is to pre-determine when to quit and accept that you can't help your client (nor earn a fee).

OK you say, but how to pick it? Well, it turns out that the cutoff time you choose has a real impact on your fee. Too short, and you have to charge way too much to account for all the clients you cutoff. But too long and again you have to charge way too much to account for the many hours you wasted on clients you couldn't help anyway. So there is a 'sweet spot', a cutoff time just right for you that makes your fixed fee as cheap as possible while at the same time giving you the best equivalent hourly rate (your average earning in dollars per hour of client-contact time).

But doesn't the cutoff idea mean that some of your clients might still have healed if you had just kept going? Is this ethical? First, very few clients slip through (only about 8% or so based on a Gaussian distribution). But regardless, you don't just dump the clients you can't help into the street! You pass them on to specialists who work with the tough cases, such as our Institute clinic staff. This means you need to network with your colleagues to find out who has a hope of helping these more difficult cases. Generally, if the specialist succeeds in treating your client, he shares some of his earnings to you for the referral, a win for all three of you.

One final point - as you become more experienced, you begin to recognize during your diagnosis the clients who you know you simply can't help. For example, perhaps they have a disease you don't know how to treat, say OCD, and are not interested in paying for what you can treat, perhaps a reduction in feelings about having the problem. Thus, with time your overall treatment speed and success rate increases because you know when to not even try.

In the next section we're going to cover how to choose an 'optimum', statistically derived cutoff time – but that doesn't mean you have to use it! Say for example you want to always try and help the few clients who take a lot more time than usual; Equation 10.1 and 10.2 will still allow you to calculate the required flat fee. Your income may now wobble a bit more than if you'd use the optimum choice, but probably not by much. And your fee may have to be higher than it would be if you'd optimized, but again, probably not by too much. Or you may just want to skip all the measurement jazz and just arbitrarily pick parameters you think seem about right. You can still compute a fee, and then over the next month or so adjust it to fit real life.

10.4.1 Predict the statistically optimum cutoff time, fee, and number of clients

Many experienced therapists already have a good feel for when they need to give up trying to heal a client. However, beginners and even experienced therapists can benefit from knowing when the statistically derived cutoff time to quit is, to help them understand the intuitive time tradeoffs they are making. Of course, you can use any cutoff time, and compute fees to match, but this little process usually helps you get close to your 'sweet spot'.

For this, we're going to ask you to do some steps without understanding the math behind it. [If you still want to know and have a good grasp of math and statistics, we refer you to our in-depth article at PeakStates.com.]

One mistake that is easy to make – this cutoff time does *not* include your diagnosis time. The cutoff clock starts when you start treating the client. Think of diagnosis as a completely different activity, even if you launch into treatment right after finishing the contract.

Tip - don't forget the 'rule of three' time: Because of the not uncommon problem of missed or inadequately healed traumas, therapists generally do follow-up sessions after all symptoms are eliminated to make sure that the issue didn't return. This is usually scheduled for a few days after completing treatment, and then usually a phone appointment after 2 to 3 weeks to recheck the healing. Be sure to include this 'extra' time in your session length measurements.

Step 1: Get your client times

Record the times it takes you to heal the next 10 successes you have (more is better up to 20 - but 10 is usually good enough). For the tougher clients, work with them an extra hour or so more than you would have normally before you give up; this gives the math better data. Also record the times it took to do diagnosis on everyone who came through the door up to the last client you healed successfully.

> *Example 10.3a:* You've recorded all your diagnosis times in minutes: 25, 35, 40, 26, 37, 22, 40, 28, 38, 15, 17, 50, 28, 40, 20. You've recorded your treatment times in hours: 0.5, ∞, 4.0, 1.5, 2.5, 1.0, 3.0, 1.5, ∞, 2.5, 2.0, 2.5. The infinity symbols are for those clients you just couldn't heal.

Step 2: Compute the mean and standard deviation

Use a calculator or web program that gives you the mean (m) and standard deviation (s) of the *treatment* times you recorded (not the diagnosis times). Use the 'sampled standard deviation' if it gives you a choice. The 'ideal standard deviation' is close enough if it doesn't. For this calculation, you ignore the clients you couldn't heal.

> *Example 10.3b:* The hand calculator gives a value of m=2.1 hours, and s=1.02 hours on the 10 treatment times.

Step 3: Compute your cutoff time

Using a 'rule of thumb', the cutoff time C = m + (1.35 x s). This is an average that doesn't quite fit every case, but is close enough for most therapists.

If you want to see if more precision matters:
(1) if most of your clients heal early or in the middle of your time range (in statistical terms, Gaussian or positively skewed distributions), use C = m + s x [2.04 x ((# clients healed) ÷ (#clients attempted) - 0.13)];
(2) when most of the clients take about the same long length of time and not many heal fast (a negatively skewed distribution), use C = m + (1.5 x s).

Eq. 10.4 $C = m + 1.35 \times s$

> *Example 10.3c:* C = 2.1 + 1.35 x 1.02 = 3.48 hours. Rounding to the nearest tenth hour, C = 3.5 hours.
>
> Since we have very few slow healing clients, we try the more exact formula: C = 2.1 + 1.02 x (2.04 x 9/12 – 0.13) = 2.1 + 1.02 (1.4) = 3.53. The difference is negligible.

Step 4: Add up the diagnosis times

Add up all of the diagnosis times for every client that walked in your door (= Td). Note the total number of people that walked in the door (= Na).

> *Example 10.3d:* You converted that to hours, and added them up. Td = 7.69 hours. The number of people who walked in the door Na = 15.

For fun we compute the average diagnosis time T = 7.69 ÷ 15 = 0.513 hours, not too bad but it could be a bit faster with more experience.

Step 5: Add up your treatment times

For this step, you first need to add all the time you've spent trying to heal your clients. Here is a tricky bit – all the measured times *longer* than the cutoff time you replace with the cutoff time in the sum. (This makes the calculation like it would be in the future, when you actually use your calculated cutoff time with your clients.)

> *Example 10.3e:* Now let's add up all the times. We already did the total diagnosis time in step 2, so we know Td = 7.69 hours. Now we've got to add up all the treatment times, so Ttreatment = 0.5 + 1.5 + 2.5 + 1.0 + 3.0 + 1.5 + 2.5 + 2.0 + 2.5 + 3.53 + 3.53 + 3.53 = 27.6 hours.
>
> Notice that we remembered the tricky bit and replaced our client with 4.0 hours with the shorter cutoff time, and also replaced the 2 we couldn't heal at all (those were the ones which we recorded as ∞) with the cutoff time.

Step 6: Compute your fixed fee

From equation 10.1, your fee F = (equivalent hourly rate) x (total of all client hours) ÷ (# clients healed).

> *Example 10.3f:* Let's assume you want to earn $75/hour (a yearly income of about $50,000). Putting this all together, F = $75 x (7.69 + 27.62) ÷ (9) = $293.

Step 7: Calculate how many new clients you need

From equation 10.5, and using 660 client contact hours per year, our required number of new clients per year is your forecast annual contact client hours divided by the average time you spend per new client. Thus, N_Y = (W x Na) ÷ (Td + Ttreatment) – that's equation 10.5.

> *Example 10.3g:* N_Y = (660 x 15) ÷ (7.69 + 27.6)] = 660 hours/year ÷ (2.35 hours/client) = 280.5 new clients per year. For 43.4 weeks per year, this means you need 280.5/43.4 = 6.46 new clients per week.
>
> This is quite a lot, so you may need to adjust your prices upwards to fit the smaller, actual average number of new clients you attract to your practice. (See section 10.6.)

Feel free to ignore this next part...

At this point, all the steps for Example 10.3 are finished and nothing more is needed. But for those somewhat more interested in math, the steps you did for example 10.3 (as well as fees and incomes for other cutoff time choices) are illustrated graphically below.

The computations of the mean and standard deviation in Step 2 for Example 10.3b are plotted in Figure 10.2 below. The statistically optimum cutoff time for Example 10.3c is shown at about the 1.4σ point on the graph.

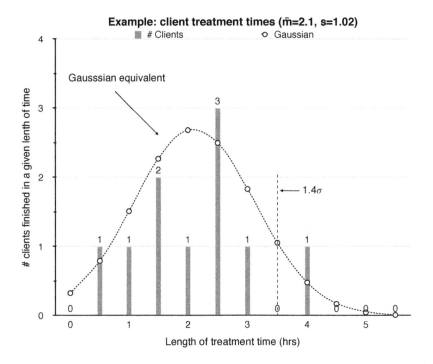

Figure 10.2: (a) From the example data is a frequency plot of the 10 client treatment times. Superimposed on this plot is a Gaussian curve with the same mean and standard deviation. The statistical optimum 'sweet spot' cutoff point is shown as a dashed line at 1.4σ.

In Step 6 of Example 10.3f we computed the fixed fee we need to quote to clients for the statistically derived cutoff time. But we can also compute the fees and the equivalent hourly rate we would get with the data that we actually measured for every possible cutoff time. This is shown in Figure 10.2.b on the next page.

It is interesting to be able to see visually that the lowest client fee gives the highest hourly income over the range of cutoff times. Notice that the statistically optimum choice for cutoff – the 'sweet spot' - fell in a dip. This was probably due to the small sample size; we would anticipate that with more clients, the curve would 'smooth out' and make this choice closer to optimum.

Also note that for this particular client distribution you could pick a cutoff anywhere from 3.5 to 4.0 hours and get nearly the same financial results. Using the longer time would also let you finish healing a few more percent of your clients; or you could vary the time somewhat when you actually quit working with a given client and still get about the same financial return. Past the 4-hour point, your failure rate (the percentage of clients you cannot heal) causes your income to drop (for a given fee) - and if your failure rate were higher that the 17% we used in this example, your income would drop faster with respect to cutoff time.

The figure also includes the results of Step 7 for the number of clients per week (for 660 client contact hours per year) you would be treating for a given cutoff time. Notice that the number of clients is roughly the same per week for reasonable choices of cutoff times.

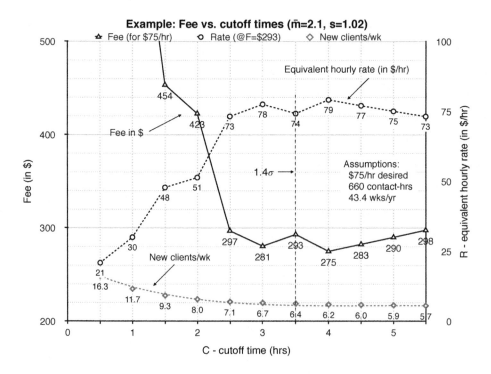

Figure 10.2: (b) For example 10.3 we show plots of fee (for an equivalent hourly rate of $75/hr), equivalent hourly rate (for a fixed $293 fee), and new clients required, all for different choices of cutoff times.

10.5: How Do You Calculate Fees If You Have Less Than A Full Caseload?

Up to this point, the fee formulas in this appendix all assume you've got a full case load. Unfortunately, this may not be true for typical trauma therapists. In this section we'll look at this issue.

Probably the biggest surprise for new therapists is how many more new clients they will have to see to earn a living. This is due to the fact that with the newer trauma therapies – and even more so with the new subcellular biology techniques - clients are either healed quickly or you soon realize that you can't help them. Hence, turnaround is quite fast and therapists have to see a lot of new clients to fill up their open time slots. So what do we do if we just can't attract that many new clients consistently?

Working with another institution that sends you clients in your specialization is by far the best answer. Or simply specialize and focus on what you really care about, where you can charge more for your unique contribution to your clients' lives. But given that you don't have an institutional affiliate and still work as a general practitioner, you will either need to raise your fees to compensate, accept that you'll be earning less annual income, or get a second job.

The other option is just to accept that you have an ebb and flow in your practice. The fee you've calculated ignores any missed appointment slots – so if you have a client, that is the right fee, and if you don't, you don't try and make it up by charging more; you just wait till you do get another client. Perhaps you simply work more hours in weeks that you have a lot of traffic in the door. Of course, you still need to pay the bills, so you need to keep track of your hours and income to see if you are meeting your financial goals.

10.5.1: Compute the full caseload number of clients

So just how many clients are we talking about? Let's start by computing how much time we spend *on average* with each person that we meet in our office. This means the total of all client-contact hours – all the diagnoses, all the treatments, all the failures – divided by how many new clients (or old clients with new issues) walked in the door. That's what the 'average time per new client' means in equation 10.5 below. Thus, for N_Y = (# of new clients per year), you can look at your records and calculate the terms in the formulas:

$$N_Y = \frac{\text{(planned client contact hours per year)}}{\text{(average time per new client)}} = \frac{W \times N_a}{(T_d + T_{treatment})} \quad \text{(in clients/year)}$$

Eq. 10.5

$$= \frac{\text{(planned total client contact hours per year)} \times (\text{\# clients in the door})}{\text{(total of all client contact hours)}}$$

To put this issue in more easily grasped terms, we can express N_Y in the more meaningful 'clients per week' by dividing it by the number of weeks we work. That's just the number of new (or repeat) clients that we need to have every week. As covered in section 10.3.1, if we assume you are in private practice and take about 2 months off (during times that most clients are not seeing therapists anyway), we work 217 days or 43.4 weeks at 5 days per week.

Eq. 10.6

$$N_W = \frac{N_Y}{(217 \text{ work days})/(5 \text{ days per week})} = \frac{N_Y}{(43.4 \text{ weeks})} \quad \text{(in clients/week)}$$

Of course, you particular circumstances might be different – we've shown these simple formulas so you can just plug your numbers into them and compute results for your own situation.

10.5.2: Adjust your fees for light caseloads

If you decide you are going to raise your fees to compensate for a lack of clients, the adjustment to your fee is simple – the percent change to the optimum clients is also the percent change to the optimum fee. In other words, if you've got fewer clients, your fee has to go up by the same percentage. The same holds true for time – if you've scheduled for 15 hours of client contact time per week, but on average only use 10 of those hours, your fee is going to have to increase by $(15-10)/15 = 33\%$ to compensate.

Eq. 10.7

$$\text{New fee} = (\text{fee from full caseload}) \times \frac{(\# \text{ clients in reality})}{(\# \text{ clients with full caseload})}$$

$$= (\text{fee for full caseload}) \times \frac{(\text{full caseload hours})}{(\text{actual caseload hours})}$$

Another way to compute your fee is by just adding the time in you did not see clients (but were planning to) to your total client-contact hours. Thus the fee is:

Eq. 10.8

$$F = (\text{desired hourly rate})$$

$$\times \left[\frac{(\text{total of all client contact hours}) + (\text{total time of empty appointments})}{(\# \text{ clients healed})} \right]$$

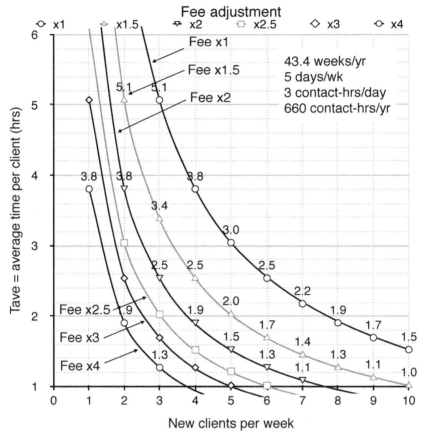

Figure 10.3: Plot of how much you have to multiply your fee if you don't have a full client load (or get a lower income instead). The upper right curve is for a full case-load at 660 contact-hours per year.

Example 10.4: Showing fees versus clients per week

Figure 10.3 illustrates the magnitude of the problem of needing new clients. You've optimized your fee for a full workload. Say your average time per new client (including diagnosis) is a fast 2.5 hours. This means you need to see an average of 6 new clients a week, every week you work that year to stay busy (the full client-load line is labeled Fee x1). But say you can only really average 3 new clients in the door a week? Well, you either earn half as much (6/3 = 0.5), or you have to double your fee to account for all the missed work. You can see this on the plot as the Fee x2 line.

10.6: Other Options – Variable Fees

Therapists who are used to charging by the hour often ask, "Instead of having one fixed fee, how about setting fees based on how long we think the client will take to heal?"

We don't recommend this in general, and here is why. Flat fee billing minimizes financial risk for the therapist, because risk and reward are spread evenly among all clients. New therapists have a (justified) concern that they don't have enough experience to judge how long a client will take to heal, or even if they can help them at all. Unfortunately, failing to heal their higher fee clients has a big impact on income – small errors in your estimates and assumptions matter a lot more than with fixed fee billing. Thus, for many therapists variable fee contracts can be a financial nightmare.

Worse, the estimated time based fees can get prohibitively expensive for the slower half of their client load – and the slowest would be paying two or three times your average rate. $300 is a lot – but $600 to $900 or more is a whole different level of pain for people who may already be struggling to pay bills. Many of these clients simply couldn't afford it even if they have insurance.

Therapists who are primarily specialists might consider variable fee billing, but their situation is different than a general therapist. Specialists usually set higher than average fees for their work; but since they can accumulate focused experience in predicting the duration of their treatments, it is also far easier for them to vary their prices to fit the client's issue if they choose to.

If you decide you want to explore using variable fees, we recommend you make yourself a guide of 'standard times' for the various problems you encounter; obviously, the general therapist would have a far harder time doing this than a specialist, although it is possible. Of course, with experience you can start to get a feel for client's issues and how long they take, and work from your intuition – but if you do, we suggest keeping a close eye on your cumulative equivalent hourly rate!

10.7: A Final Reflection on Fees

'Charging for results' is all about ethical conduct and really living the golden rule – doing to others what you would have them do to you. This appendix has just shown you can do this while still making a living - you now know exactly how to charge the smallest fee to your clients while minimizing your financial risk and maximizing your income.

In practice, you might bend the fixed-fee rules a bit but by this point you should have a good feel for the tradeoffs. For example, you might decide to charge less for some of the 'easy' clients and more for some of the 'hard' clients. Or go longer with a client you think is almost done, and shorter with a client you've figured out you can't help (and need to pass on the a specialist or one of our clinics). Or you might reserve some of your time for charity clients, (a practice we encourage and do ourselves) by charging more than the minimum to cover these unpaid clients.

Obviously, how you bill your clients is up to you and the constraints you have on your practice. One comment we've heard is that the therapist has a lot of insurance billing and can't go to a 'pay for results' policy with them – but have you called and asked the company? After all, it is to the insurance company's benefit to have you work this way! Or you might argue that you don't have to change your billing because it is 'illegal' in the location you live in to give a guarantee. Sadly, we've had a number of therapist use this argument to avoid change; in fact the laws are written to handle the problem of 'snake oil salesmen' who offer cures that they can't deliver. Not about charging for results.

Although how a therapist charges is very personal – for example, some work for free, some only accept donations for their work – we actually encourage our therapists to charge a premium for our new, unique treatments (with a 'pay for results' policy, and no, the Institute does not get any of it). Why? Because we want this new paradigm to spread for the eventual benefit of all people. Introducing new ideas or treatments is very difficult even when there are no paradigm conflicts - for example, it took many years for experienced physicians to accept that ulcers were caused by a bacterial infection, even though it is quickly and easily demonstrated by treatment with tetracycline. Obviously, we hope that over time an altruistic desire to help their clients will make the subcellular psychobiology approach spread. But sadly, the reality is that a huge motivator in much of Western society is just simple self-interest. Thus, we hope to harness this motivation by having treatments that pay more, which we expect will cause people who normally would not use this material to adopt our approaches to their own work. As our models spread, this should in turn allow more people to get help, and give financial incentives for others to develop new treatments for other diseases and problems. And rather quickly bring down he cost to consumers as well as encourage its spread to the various state supported health systems.

Suggested Reading

- "Pay for Results – Statistical and Mathematical Modeling for Fee Calculations" by Dr. Grant McFetridge, at www.PeakStates.com. It derives the equations and statistical models for optimum fees used in this appendix for fixed-fee and variable fee pricing for therapists.

ICD-10 (International Classification of Diseases) and Subcellular Cases

The ICD-10 mental and behavioral disorder categories (F00-F99) below are from the World Health Organization website. We've shown the subcellular cases for codes whose symptoms we've successfully eliminated by using one (or more) subcellular case treatments. We skipped ICD categories if we don't yet know the cause (for example, bipolar disorder and tic disorder); or if we simply have not yet seen clients who had the ICD condition to test our treatments. Many ICD categories have multiple causes; this is because WHO groups symptoms without understanding etiology.

Regardless of the category, practical treatment will usually include healing traumas and 'copies'. This is because they cause such a huge range of cross-category symptoms that they are often the cause of a disorder; or because the disorder created traumatic sequelae that cannot be ignored.

(F00–F09) Organic, including symptomatic, mental disorders
(F00) Dementia in Alzheimer's disease
(F01) Vascular dementia
      (F01.1) Multi-infarct dementia
(F02) Dementia in other diseases classified elsewhere
      (F02.0) Dementia in Pick's disease
      (F02.1) Dementia in Creutzfeldt-Jakob disease
      (F02.2) Dementia in Huntington's disease
      (F02.3) Dementia in Parkinson's disease
      (F02.4) Dementia in human immunodeficiency virus (HIV) disease
(F03) Unspecified dementia
(F04) Organic amnesic syndrome, not induced by alcohol and other psychoactive substances
(F05) Delirium, not induced by alcohol and other psychoactive substances

(F06) Other mental disorders due to brain damage and dysfunction and to physical disease

    (F06.0) Organic hallucinosis

    (F06.1) Organic catatonic disorder

    (F06.2) Organic delusional (schizophrenia-like) disorder

    (F06.3) Organic mood (affective) disorders

    (F06.4) Organic anxiety disorder

    (F06.5) Organic dissociative disorder

    (F06.6) Organic emotionally labile (asthenic) disorder

    (F06.7) Mild cognitive disorder

    (F06.8) Other specified mental disorders due to brain damage and dysfunction and to physical disease

    (F06.9) Unspecified mental disorder due to brain damage and dysfunction and to physical disease

       ▪ Organic brain syndrome NOS

(F07) Personality and behavioral disorders due to brain disease, damage and dysfunction

    (F07.0) Organic personality disorder

    (F07.1) Postencephalitic syndrome

--------- *See subcellular case: brain damage page 178.*

↓   (F07.2) Postconcussional syndrome

    (F07.8) Other organic personality and behavioral disorders due to brain disease, damage and dysfunction

    (F07.9) Unspecified organic personality and behavioral disorder due to brain disease, damage and dysfunction

(F09) Unspecified organic or symptomatic mental disorder

(F10–F19) Mental and behavioral disorders due to psychoactive substance use

See application: addictions page 247.

    (F10) use of alcohol

    (F11) use of opioids

    (F12) use of cannabinoids

    (F13) use of sedatives or hypnotics

    (F14) use of cocaine

    (F15) use of other stimulants, including caffeine

------*See application: hallucinogens page 251.*

↓   (F16) use of hallucinogens

    (F17) use of tobacco

    (F18) use of volatile solvents

    (F19) multiple drug use and use of other psychoactive substances

    Note: the following conditions are subtypes of each code from F10–19:

        (F1x.0) acute intoxication

        (F1x.1) harmful use

        (F1x.2) dependence syndrome

(F1x.3) withdrawal state
(F1x.4) withdrawal state with delirium
(F1x.5) psychotic disorder
(F1x.6) amnesic syndrome
(F1x.7) Residual and late-onset psychotic disorder
(F1x.8) other mental and behavioral disorder
(F1x.9) unspecified mental and behavioral disorder

(F20–F29) Schizophrenia, schizotypal and delusional disorders
See subcellular case: ribosomal voices page 125.
(F20) Schizophrenia
(F20.0) Paranoid schizophrenia
(F20.1) Hebephrenic schizophrenia (Disorganized schizophrenia)
(F20.2) Catatonic schizophrenia
(F20.3) Undifferentiated schizophrenia
(F20.4) Post-schizophrenic depression
(F20.5) Residual schizophrenia
(F20.6) Simple schizophrenia
(F20.8) Other schizophrenia
▪ Cenesthopathic schizophrenia
▪ Schizophreniform disorder NOS
▪ Schizophreniform psychosis NOS
(F20.9) Schizophrenia, unspecified
(F21) Schizotypal disorder
(F22) Persistent delusional disorders
------ *See special case: archetypal images page 174.*
(F22.0) Delusional disorder
(F22.8) Other persistent delusional disorders
▪ Delusional dysmorphophobia
▪ Involutional paranoid state
▪ Paranoia querulans
(F22.9) Persistent delusional disorder, unspecified
See application: spiritual emergency page 270. (Note that this case does not apply to all delusional disorders.)
(F23) Acute and transient psychotic disorders
(F23.0) Acute polymorphic psychotic disorder without symptoms of schizophrenia
(F23.1) Acute polymorphic psychotic disorder with symptoms of schizophrenia
(F23.2) Acute schizophrenia-like psychotic disorder
(F23.3) Other acute predominantly delusional psychotic disorders
(F23.8) Other acute and transient psychotic disorders
(F23.9) Acute and transient psychotic disorder, unspecified

See subcellular case: s-holes page 131; viral net headaches page 216.

(F24) Induced delusional disorder
- o   Folie à deux
- o   Induced paranoid disorder
- o   Induced psychotic disorder

(F25) Schizoaffective disorders
>   (F25.0) Schizoaffective disorder, manic type
>   (F25.1) Schizoaffective disorder, depressive type
>   (F25.2) Schizoaffective disorder, mixed type
>   (F25.8) Other schizoaffective disorders
>   (F25.9) Schizoaffective disorder, unspecified

(F28) Other nonorganic psychotic disorders
- o   Chronic hallucinatory psychosis

(F29) Unspecified nonorganic psychosis

(F30–F39) Mood (affective) disorders

(F30) Manic episode
>   (F30.0) Hypomania
>   (F30.1) Mania without psychotic symptoms
>   (F30.2) Mania with psychotic symptoms
>   (F30.8) Other manic episodes
>   (F30.9) Manic episode, unspecified

(F31) Bipolar affective disorder
>   (F31.0) Bipolar affective disorder, current episode hypomanic
>   (F31.1) Bipolar affective disorder, current episode manic without psychotic symptoms
>   (F31.2) Bipolar affective disorder, current episode manic with psychotic symptoms
>   (F31.3) Bipolar affective disorder, current episode mild or moderate depression
>   (F31.4) Bipolar affective disorder, current episode severe depression without psychotic symptoms
>   (F31.5) Bipolar affective disorder, current episode severe depression with psychotic symptoms
>   (F31.6) Bipolar affective disorder, current episode mixed
>   (F31.7) Bipolar affective disorder, currently in remission
>   (F31.8) Other bipolar affective disorders
>   (F31.9) Bipolar affective disorder, unspecified
>> ▪   Bipolar II disorder
>> ▪   Recurrent manic episodes NOS
>   (F31.9) Bipolar affective disorder, unspecified

See subcellular case: soul loss page 128.

(F32) Depressive episode
>   (F32.0) Mild depressive episode

(F32.1) Moderate depressive episode

(F32.2) Severe depressive episode without psychotic symptoms

(F32.3) Severe depressive episode with psychotic symptoms

(F32.8) Other depressive episodes

- Atypical depression
- Single episodes of "masked" depression NOS

(F32.9) Depressive episode, unspecified

See application: depression page 250. See subcellular case: soul loss
page 128.

(F33) Recurrent depressive disorder

(F33.0) Recurrent depressive disorder, current episode mild

(F33.1) Recurrent depressive disorder, current episode moderate

(F33.2) Recurrent depressive disorder, current episode severe without psychotic symptoms

(F33.3) Recurrent depressive disorder, current episode severe with psychotic symptoms

(F33.4) Recurrent depressive disorder, currently in remission

(F33.8) Other recurrent depressive disorders

(F33.9) Recurrent depressive disorder, unspecified

(F34) Persistent mood (affective) disorders

(F34.0) Cyclothymia

--------- *See application: depression page 250. See subcellular case: soul loss*
page 128; flattened emotions page 192.

(F34.1) Dysthymia

(F34.8) Other persistent mood (affective) disorders

(F34.9) Persistent mood (affective) disorder, unspecified

(F38) Other mood (affective) disorders

(F38.0) Other single mood (affective) disorders

Mixed affective episode

(F38.1) Other recurrent mood (affective) disorders

Recurrent brief depressive episodes

(F38.8) Other specified mood (affective) disorders

(F39) Unspecified mood (affective) disorder

(F40–F48) Neurotic, stress-related and somatoform disorders
See application: anxiety/fear page 248.

(F40) Phobic anxiety disorders

(F40.0) Agoraphobia

(F40.1) Social phobias

- Anthropophobia
- Social neurosis

(F40.2) Specific (isolated) phobias

- Acrophobia
- Animal phobias

- Claustrophobia
- Simple phobia

(F40.8) Other phobic anxiety disorders

(F40.9) Phobic anxiety disorder, unspecified

- Phobia NOS
- Phobic state NOS

See application: anxiety/fear page 248.

(F41) Other anxiety disorders

(F41.0) Panic disorder (episodic paroxysmal anxiety)

(F41.1) Generalized anxiety disorder

(F42) Obsessive-compulsive disorder

See subcellular case: biographical trauma page 105; generational trauma page 111.

(F43) Reaction to severe stress, and adjustment disorders

(F43.0) Acute stress reaction

(F43.1) Post-traumatic stress disorder

------- *See subcellular case: tribal block page 134; column of self - void page 145.*

(F43.2) Adjustment disorder

See generational trauma page 111.

(F44) Dissociative (conversion) disorders

------- *See subcellular case: multiple personality disorder page 203.*

(F44.0) Dissociative amnesia

(F44.1) Dissociative fugue

(F44.2) Dissociative stupor

------- *See subcellular case: ribosomal voices page 125. See applications: evil sensations page 266.*

(F44.3) Trance and possession disorders

(F44.4) Dissociative motor disorders

(F44.5) Dissociative convulsions

(F44.6) Dissociative anaesthesia and sensory loss

(F44.7) Mixed dissociative (conversion) disorders

------- *See subcellular case: multiple personality disorder page 203.*

(F44.8) Other dissociative (conversion) disorders

- Ganser's syndrome
- Multiple personality

------- *See subcellular case: bubbles page 180.*

(F44.9) Dissociative (conversion) disorders, unspecified

See subcellular case: bug-like parasite problems page 142; biographical trauma page 105; copies page 119; chakra problem page 185. Medical causes: systemic candida infection.

(F45) Somatoform disorders

(F45.0) Somatization disorder

- Briquet's disorder
- Multiple psychosomatic disorder

(F45.1) Undifferentiated somatoform disorder

(F45.2) Hypochondriacal disorder

- Body dysmorphic disorder
- Dysmorphophobia (nondelusional)
- Hypochondriacal neurosis
- Hypochondriasis
- Nosophobia

(F45.3) Somatoform autonomic dysfunction

- Cardiac neurosis
- Da Costa's syndrome
- Gastric neurosis
- Neurocirculatory asthenia

------- *See subcellular case: curse page 150.*

↓ (F45.4) Persistent somatoform pain disorder

- Psychalgia

↓ (F45.8) Other somatoform disorders

(F45.9) Somatoform disorder, unspecified

(F48) Other neurotic disorders

--------- *See Chronic Fatigue Syndrome in Peak States of Consciousness, Vol 3.*

↓ (F48.0) Neurasthenia

--------- *See subcellular case: OBE due to trauma (biographical, generational, body association) page 103*

↓ (F48.1) Depersonalization-derealization syndrome

(F48.8) Other specified neurotic disorders

- Dhat syndrome
- Occupational neurosis, including writer's cramp
- Psychasthenia
- Psychasthenic neurosis
- Psychogenic syncope

(F48.9) Neurotic disorder, unspecified

- Neurosis NOS

(F50–F59) Behavioral syndromes associated with physiological disturbances and physical factors

(F50) Eating disorders

(F50.0) Anorexia nervosa

(F50.1) Atypical anorexia nervosa

(F50.2) Bulimia nervosa

(F50.3) Atypical bulimia nervosa

(F50.4) Overeating associated with other psychological disturbances

(F50.5) Vomiting associated with other psychological disturbances

(F50.8) Other eating disorders

- Pica in adults

(F50.9) Eating disorder, unspecified

See subcellular case: kundalini page 199; biographical trauma page 105. See application: dreams page 251.

(F51) Nonorganic sleep disorders

    (F51.0) Nonorganic insomnia

    (F51.1) Nonorganic hypersomnia

    (F51.2) Nonorganic disorder of the sleep-wake schedule

    (F51.3) Sleepwalking (somnambulism)

    (F51.4) Sleep terrors (night terrors)

    (F51.5) Nightmares

See subcellular case: cording page 122; biographical (post birth or conception/ coalescence trauma) page 105. See applications: relationships page 256.

(F52) Sexual dysfunction, not caused by organic disorder or disease

    (F52.0) Lack or loss of sexual desire

- Frigidity
- Hypoactive sexual desire disorder

    (F52.1) Sexual aversion and lack of sexual enjoyment

- Anhedonia (sexual)

    (F52.2) Failure of genital response

- Female sexual arousal disorder
- Male erectile disorder
- Psychogenic impotence

    (F52.3) Orgasmic dysfunction

- Inhibited orgasm (male)(female)
- Psychogenic anorgasmy

    (F52.4) Premature ejaculation

    (F52.5) Nonorganic vaginismus

    (F52.6) Nonorganic dyspareunia

    (F52.7) Excessive sexual drive

    (F52.9) Unspecified sexual dysfunction, not caused by organic disorder or disease

(F53) Mental and behavioral disorders associated with the puerperium, not elsewhere classified

    (F53.0) Mild mental and behavioral disorders associated with the puerperium, not elsewhere classified

- Postnatal depression NOS
- Postpartum depression NOS

    (F53.1) Severe mental and behavioral disorders associated with the puerperium, not elsewhere classified

- Puerperal psychosis NOS

(F54) Psychological and behavioral factors associated with disorders or diseases classified elsewhere

(F55) Abuse of non-dependence-producing substances

(F59) Unspecified behavioral syndromes associated with physiological disturbances and physical factors

(F60–F69) Disorders of adult personality and behavior
(F60) Specific personality disorders
         (F60.0) Paranoid personality disorder
         (F60.1) Schizoid personality disorder
--------- *See subcellular case: triune brain shutdown page 214.*
↓   (F60.2) Dissocial personality disorder
           ■ Antisocial personality disorder
--------- *See subcellular case: s-holes page 131; viral net page 216.*
↓   (F60.3) Emotionally unstable personality disorder
           ■ Borderline personality disorder
↓   (F60.4) Histrionic personality disorder
         (F60.5) Anankastic personality disorder
           ■ Obsessive-compulsive personality disorder
--------- *See subcellular case: anxiety/fear page 248.*
↓   (F60.6) Anxious (avoidant) personality disorder
         (F60.7) Dependent personality disorder
--------- *See subcellular case: selfishness ring page 208.*
↓   (F60.8) Other specific personality disorders
           ■ Eccentric personality disorder
           ■ Haltlose personality disorder
           ■ Immature personality disorder
           ■ Narcissistic personality disorder
           ■ Passive-aggressive personality disorder
           ■ Psychoneurotic personality disorder
--------- *See subcellular case: triune brain shutdown page 214.*
↓   (F60.9) Personality disorder not otherwise specified
    (F61) Mixed and other personality disorders
See subcellular case: multiple personality disorder page 203; biographical trauma page 105.
    (F62) Enduring personality changes, not attributable to brain damage and disease
See subcellular case: body associations page 108.
    (F63) Habit and impulse disorders
         (F63.0) Pathological gambling
         (F63.1) Pathological fire-setting (pyromania)
         (F63.2) Pathological stealing (kleptomania)
         (F63.3) Trichotillomania
    (F64) Gender identity disorders
         (F64.0) Transsexualism
         (F64.1) Dual-role transvestism
         (F64.2) Gender identity disorder of childhood
    (F65) Disorders of sexual preference

(F65.0) Sexual fetishism

(F65.1) Fetishistic transvestism

(F65.2) Exhibitionism

(F65.3) Voyeurism

(F65.4) Paedophilia

(F65.5) Sadomasochism

(F65.6) Multiple disorders of sexual preference

(F65.8) Other disorders of sexual preference
- Frotteurism
- Necrophilia
- Zoophilia

(F66) Psychological and behavioral disorders associated with sexual development and orientation

(F66.0) Sexual maturation disorder

(F66.1) Ego-dystonic sexual orientation

(F66.2) Sexual relationship disorder

(F66.8) Other psychosexual development disorders

(F66.9) Psychosexual development disorder, unspecified

(F68) Other disorders of adult personality and behavior

(F68.0) Elaboration of physical symptoms for psychological reasons

(F68.1) Intentional production or feigning of symptoms or disabilities, either physical or psychological (factitious disorder)
- Munchausen syndrome

(F68.8) Other specified disorders of adult personality and behavior

(F69) Unspecified disorder of adult personality and behavior

(F70–F79) Mental retardation
See subcellular case: brain damage page 178; fungal parasites page 194; bubbles page 180.

(F70) Mild mental retardation

(F71) Moderate mental retardation

(F72) Severe mental retardation

(F73) Profound mental retardation

(F78) Other mental retardation

(F79) Unspecified mental retardation

(F80–F89) Disorders of psychological development
See subcellular case: Asperger's syndrome page 176; brain damage pg. 178; shattered crystals (attention deficit disorder) page 210; see bubbles page 180.

(F80) Specific developmental disorders of speech and language

(F80.0) Specific speech articulation disorder

    (F80.1) Expressive language disorder
    (F80.2) Receptive language disorder
        ▪ Receptive aphasia
    (F80.3) Acquired aphasia with epilepsy (Landau-Kleffner)
    (F80.8) Other developmental disorders of speech and language
        ▪ Lisping
    (F80.9) Developmental disorder of speech and language, unspecified
(F81) Specific developmental disorders of scholastic skills
    (F81.0) Specific reading disorder
        ▪ Developmental dyslexia
    (F81.1) Specific spelling disorder
    (F81.2) Specific disorder of arithmetical skills
        ▪ Developmental acalculia
        ▪ Gerstmann syndrome
    (F81.3) Mixed disorder of scholastic skills
    (F81.8) Other developmental disorders of scholastic skills
    (F81.9) Developmental disorder of scholastic skills, unspecified
(F82) Specific developmental disorder of motor function
    o Developmental coordination disorder
(F83) Mixed specific developmental disorders
(F84) Pervasive developmental disorders
    (F84.0) Childhood autism
    (F84.1) Atypical autism
    (F84.2) Rett's syndrome
    (F84.3) Other childhood disintegrative disorder
    (F84.4) Overactive disorder associated with mental retardation and stereotyped movements
    (F84.5) Asperger's syndrome
(F88) Other disorders of psychological development
(F89) Unspecified disorder of psychological development

(F90–F98) Behavioral and emotional disorders with onset usually occurring in childhood and adolescence
See subcellular case: shattered crystals (attention deficit disorder) page 210.
    (F90) Hyperkinetic disorders
    (F90.0) Disturbance of activity and attention
        ▪ Attention-deficit hyperactivity disorder
        ▪ Attention deficit syndrome with hyperactivity
    (F90.1) Hyperkinetic conduct disorder
    (F90.8) Other hyperkinetic disorders
    (F90.9) Hyperkinetic disorder, unspecified
(F91) Conduct disorders
    (F91.0) Conduct disorder confined to the family context
    (F91.1) Unsocialized conduct disorder

(F91.2) Socialized conduct disorder

(F91.3) Oppositional defiant disorder

(F91.8) Other conduct disorders

(F91.9) Conduct disorder, unspecified

(F92) Mixed disorders of conduct and emotions

(F92.0) Depressive conduct disorder

(F92.8) Other mixed disorders of conduct and emotions

(F92.9) Mixed disorder of conduct and emotions, unspecified

See subcellular case: biographical trauma (abuse, prenatal trauma, etc.) page 105; associational trauma (addiction to a caregiver emotion) page 108; see copies page 119.

(F93) Emotional disorders with onset specific to childhood

(F93.0) Separation anxiety disorder of childhood

(F93.1) Phobic anxiety disorder of childhood

(F93.2) Social anxiety disorder of childhood

(F93.3) Sibling rivalry disorder

(F93.8) Other childhood emotional disorders

- Identity disorder
- Overanxious disorder

(F93.9) Childhood emotional disorder, unspecified

See subcellular case: Asperger's Syndrome page 176; biographical trauma page 105.

(F94) Disorders of social functioning with onset specific to childhood and adolescence

(F94.0) Elective mutism

(F94.1) Reactive attachment disorder of childhood

------- *See subcellular case: s-holes page 131.*

(F94.2) Disinhibited attachment disorder of childhood

(F94.8) Other childhood disorders of social functioning

(F94.9) Childhood disorder of social functioning, unspecified

(F95) Tic disorders

(F95.0) Transient tic disorder

(F95.1) Chronic motor or vocal tic disorder

(F95.2) Combined vocal and multiple motor tic disorder (de la Tourette)

(F95.8) Other tic disorders

(F95.9) Tic disorder, unspecified

(F98) Other behavioral and emotional disorders with onset usually occurring in childhood and adolescence

(F98.0) Nonorganic enuresis

(F98.1) Nonorganic encopresis

(F98.2) Feeding disorder of infancy and childhood

(F98.3) Pica of infancy and childhood

(F98.4) Stereotyped movement disorders

(F98.5) Stuttering (stammering)

(F98.6) Cluttering

(F98.8) Other specified behavioral and emotional disorders with onset usually occurring in childhood and adolescence

- Attention deficit disorder without hyperactivity
- Excessive masturbation
- Nail-biting
- Nose-picking
- Thumb-sucking

(F98.9) Unspecified behavioral and emotional disorders with onset usually occurring in childhood and adolescence

Note: this category could cover a large range of trauma, subcellular cases or parasite issues.

↓   (F99) Mental disorder, not otherwise specified

(G40-G47) Episodic and paroxysmal disorders
See subcellular case: viral net page 216. See application: headaches page 252.

(G43) Migraine (Use additional external cause code (Chapter XX), if desired, to identify drug, if drug-induced. Exclude: headache NOS (R51)

(G43.0) Migraine without aura [common migraine]

(G43.1) Migraine with aura [classical migraine]

Migraine:

- aura without headache
- basilar
- equivalents
- familial hemiplegic
- with:
  - acute-onset aura
  - prolonged aura
  - typical aura

(G43.2) Status migrainosus

(G43.3) Complicated migraine

(G43.8) Other migraine (Ophthalmoplegic migraine, Retinal migraine)

(G43.9) Migraine, unspecified

(G44) Other headache syndromes

Exclude:

- atypical facial pain (G50.1)
- headache NOS (R51)
- trigeminal neuralgia (G50.0)

(G44.0) Cluster headache syndrome (Chronic paroxysmal hemicrania)

Cluster headache:

- chronic

> ▪   episodic
>
> (G44.1) Vascular headache, not elsewhere classified (Vascular headache NOS)
>
> (G44.2) Tension-type headache (Chronic tension-type headache, Episodic tension headache, Tension headache NOS)
>
> (G44.3) Chronic post-traumatic headache
>
> (G44.4) Drug-induced headache, not elsewhere classified (Use additional external cause code (Chapter XX), if desired, to identify drug.)
>
> (G44.8) Other specified headache syndromes

(R20-R23) Symptoms and signs involving the skin and subcutaneous tissue

> (R20) Disturbances of skin sensation
>
> > Exclude:
> >
> > - dissociative anaesthesia and sensory loss (F44.6)
> > - psychogenic disturbances (F45.8)
> >
> > (R20.0) Anaesthesia of skin
> >
> > (R20.1) Hypoaesthesia of skin

--------- *See subcellular case: bug-like parasites page 142.*

↓

> > (R20.2) Paraesthesia of skin (Formication, Pins and needles, Tingling skin)
> >
> > > Exclude: acroparaesthesia (I73.8)
> >
> > (R20.3) Hyperaesthesia
> >
> > (R20.8) Other and unspecified disturbances of skin sensation

(R40-R46) Symptoms and signs involving cognition, perception, emotional state and behavior

> (Exclude those constituting part of a pattern of mental disorder (F00-F99))
>
> (R40) Somnolence, stupor and coma (Exclude: coma)
>
> > (R40.0) Somnolence (Drowsiness)
> >
> > (R40.1) Stupor (Semicoma)
> >
> > > Exclude: stupor
> > >
> > > - catatonic (F20.2)
> > > - depressive (F31-F33)
> > > - dissociative (F44.2)
> > > - manic (F30.2)
> >
> > (R40.2) Coma, unspecified (Unconsciousness NOS)
>
> (R41) Other symptoms and signs involving cognitive functions and awareness
>
> > Exclude: dissociative [conversion] disorders (F44.-)

--------- *See subcellular case: column of self – bubbles page 188.*

↓

> > (R41.0) Disorientation, unspecified (Confusion NOS)

Exclude: psychogenic disorientation (F44.8)

(R41.1) Anterograde amnesia

(R41.2) Retrograde amnesia

(R41.3) Other amnesia, Amnesia NOS

Exclude:

- amnesic syndrome:
- due to psychoactive substance use (F10-F19 with common fourth character .6)
- organic (F04)
- transient global amnesia (G45.4)

(R41.8) Other and unspecified symptoms and signs involving cognitive functions and awareness

See subcellular case: vortex page 168.

(R42) Dizziness and giddiness (include Light-headedness, Vertigo NOS)

Exclude: vertiginous syndromes (H81.-)

(R43) Disturbances of smell and taste

(R43.0) Anosmia

(R43.1) Parosmia

(R43.2) Parageusia

(R43.8) Other and unspecified disturbances of smell and taste (Mixed disturbance of smell and taste)

See subcellular case: ribosomal voices page 125.

(R44) Other symptoms and signs involving general sensations and perceptions

Exclude: disturbances of skin sensation (R20.-)

(R44.0) Auditory hallucinations

(R44.1) Visual hallucinations

(R44.2) Other hallucinations

(R44.3) Hallucinations, unspecified

(R44.8) Other and unspecified symptoms and signs involving general sensations and perceptions

See subcellular case: biographical trauma page 105; generational trauma page 111.

(R45) Symptoms and signs involving emotional state

--------- *See applications: anxiety/fear page 248.*

(R45.0) Nervousness (Nervous tension)

(R45.1) Restlessness and agitation

(R45.2) Unhappiness (Worries NOS)

(R45.3) Demoralization and apathy

(R45.4) Irritability and anger

(R45.5) Hostility

(R45.6) Physical violence

(R45.7) State of emotional shock and stress, unspecified

--------- See subcellular case: suicidal feelings page 258.
↓   (R45.8) Other symptoms and signs involving emotional state
            (Suicidal ideation (tendencies))
            Exclude: suicidal ideation constituting part of a mental
            disorder (F00-F99)
(R46) Symptoms and signs involving appearance and behavior
            (R46.0) Very low level of personal hygiene
            (R46.1) Bizarre personal appearance
            (R46.2) Strange and inexplicable behaviour
            (R46.3) Overactivity
            (R46.4) Slowness and poor responsiveness
                Exclude: stupor (R40.1)
            (R46.5) Suspiciousness and marked evasiveness
            (R46.6) Undue concern and preoccupation with stressful events
            (R46.7) Verbosity and circumstantial detail obscuring reason
            for contact
            (R46.8) Other symptoms and signs involving appearance and
            behavior (Self neglect NOS)
                Exclude insufficient intake of food and water due to
                self neglect (R63.6)

(R50-R69) General symptoms and signs
See subcellular case: viral net page 216. See application: headaches page 252.
            (R51) Headache
                Incl.: Facial pain NOS
                Excl.: atypical facial pain (G50.1); migraine and other headache
↓   syndromes (G43-G44); trigeminal neuralgia (G50.0)
*See subcellular case: bug-like parasites page 142; crown brain structures page
148; chakra problem page 185. See application: pain (chronic) page 253.*
            (R52) Pain, not elsewhere classified
                Incl.: pain not referable to any one organ or body region
                Excl.: chronic pain personality syndrome (F62.8)
                • headache (R51)
                • pain (in): abdomen (R10.-); back (M54.9); breast (N64.4);
                chest (R07.1-R07.4); ear (H92.0); eye (H57.1); joint
                (M25.5); limb (M79.6); lumbar region (M54.5); pelvic and
                perineal (R10.2); psychogenic (F45.4); shoulder (M75.8);
                spine (M54.-); throat (R07.0); tongue (K14.6); tooth
                (K08.8); renal colic (N23)
            (R52.0) Acute pain
            (R52.1) Chronic intractable pain
            (R52.2) Other chronic pain
            (R52.9) Pain, unspecified
                Generalized pain NOS

(Z80-Z99) Persons with potential health hazards related to family and personal history and certain conditions influencing health status

(Z91) Personal history of risk-factors, not elsewhere classified

Excl.: exposure to pollution and other problems related to physical environment (Z58.-); occupational exposure to risk-factors (Z57.-); personal history of psychoactive substance abuse (Z86.4)

(Z91.0) Personal history of allergy, other than to drugs and biological substances

Excl.: personal history of allergy to drugs and biological substances (Z88.-)

(Z91.1) Personal history of noncompliance with medical treatment and regimen

(Z91.2) Personal history of poor personal hygiene

(Z91.3) Personal history of unhealthy sleep-wake schedule

Excl.: sleep disorders (G47.-)

(Z91.4) Personal history of psychological trauma, not elsewhere classified

---------- *See subcellular case: suicidal feelings page 258.*

↓   (Z91.5) Personal history of self-harm

- Parasuicide
- Self-poisoning
- Suicide attempt

(Z91.6) Personal history of other physical trauma

(Z91.8) Personal history of other specified risk-factors, not elsewhere classified

- Abuse NOS
- Maltreatment NOS

Glossary

Apex phenomenon: Coined by Dr. Roger Callahan, it refers to the common occurrence that after an issue is eliminated by a therapy, the client tries to explain the change by something they know, such as being distracted, even though the explanation doesn't fit. The definition has been extended to include the phenomenon of the client forgetting (to the point of disbelief) that the healed issue was ever a problem.

Blastocyst: An embryonic developmental stage that starts about four days after conception and ends at implantation. It is characterized by a cavity that forms in the morula (embryonic cells), with an outer layer that later becomes the placenta, and an inner layer that becomes the fetus.

Body brain: The reptilian brain, at the base of the skull. It thinks in gestalt body sensations (called the 'felt sense' in Gendlin's Focusing), and experiences itself in the lower belly. It is called the *hara* in Japanese. It is the brain that we communicate with when doing dowsing or muscle testing. At the subcellular level, it is the endoplasmic reticulum.

Body associations: The body brain makes non-logical associations during traumas that then direct its actions later in life. For example, this is the basis of the 'Pavlov's dog' connecting a bell sound with food.

Brains: Refers to different portions of the brain that have separate self-awareness: the mind (primate) heart (mammalian), and body (reptilian) of the triune brain model. Their awarenesses are extensions of the organelles' inside the primary cell, which in turn are extensions of the sacred being blocks. Also refers to the extended triune brain model: perineum, body, solar plexus, heart, mind, third eye, crown, navel (placenta) and spine (sperm tail).

BSFF (Be Set Free Fast): A meridian therapy that only uses a few hand points, targets guarding traumas to eliminate psychological reversal, and has a variation that can trigger the healing process by using a key word.

Bubble: A fungal structure that 'looks' like a bubble in the cell that can hold awareness trapped fully or partly inside, causing impairment. Found inside the merkaba in the nuclear core.

Bypass (trauma): A structure inside the nucleus that covers a stuck gene at the base of a trauma string. This blocks the feeling without actually healing the problem. Can result from NLP approaches to trauma healing. Sometimes called a 'trauma bypass'.

Cellular memories: Memories of the sperm, egg, and zygote, usually of a traumatic nature. These include sensations, feelings, and thoughts. Also applied in the literature to memories of the body consciousness alone.

CoA (Center of Awareness): Using a finger, you can find your center of awareness by pointing at where 'you' are in your body. Can be at a particular point, or diffuse, or in more than one location, or both internal to the body and external.

Collective consciousness: A consciousness that is built out of individual units of consciousness, but it has different qualities than its subunits and does not reside in any particular subunit. Some examples are Gaia, sperm, mitochondria, and 'oversouls'. Other terms for this phenomena are 'group mind' or 'composite awareness'.

Collective experiences: The person feels the pain of a subset of all past humanity. For example: the suffering of all prisoners who were tortured; the agony of mothers throughout time who died in labor, etc. This is not generational trauma. Sometimes categorized as a spiritual emergency. It is called 'racial and collective experiences' by Grof. Treated with the Courteau Projection Technique.

Composite awareness: See 'collective consciousness'.

Cords: It describes a dysfunctional connection between two people (actually, between a trauma in each person) that can be seen as a 'tube' or 'cord'. These cause the real-time sensation that others have a 'personality' (emotional tone) when one thinks about them. It is actually tentacles of a fungal organism that penetrates the cell.

Chain: A structure inside the nuclear core that looks like a chain that connects the 'ring' with the 'merkaba'. It is the source of core (spine) trauma; it kinesthetically overlays on the actual spinal column.

Chakras: A fungal organism on the nuclear membrane. Gives rise to experiences of 'energy centers' along the front vertical axis of the body. It contains broken crystalline material that corresponds to trauma.

Coalescence: The precellular organelles combine to form a primordial germ cell at the coalescence stage. This occurs inside the parent who is still a blastocyst inside the grandmother.

Coex (Condensed experience): Coined by Dr. Stanislav Grof, it describes the phenomenon in regressive healing that sensate related traumas are activated together and interrelate.

Column of Self: A column structure in the nuclear core of the primary cell. Different kinds of damage to this column cause different, often serious symptoms. It is fungal in nature.

Copies: A duplicate of someone else's emotions or sensations on one's own body. Copies are caused by a bacterial species that lives in the cytoplasm.

CPL (Calm, peace, lightness): The endpoint to healing a trauma. It occurs when the client enters the present moment, albeit usually temporarily.

Crown brain structures: They 'look' like cables or containers inside the body. They can appear like the movie idea of an alien implant to some clients. The crown brain creates them during certain kinds of trauma. They often cause physical pain.

Destabilization: After healing an issue, symptoms from another issue surface. The presenting problem was actually there so the client could avoid the deeper, more painful issue. Healing their issue 'unstabilized' the client.

Developmental events model: Explains the presence or absence of peak states, experiences, and abilities due to pre-birth trauma. This also applies to mental and physical diseases.

Dominant issue: A trauma-based problem that blocks a client's ability to feel their peak states.

Differential diagnosis: When a symptom can have different causes, the therapist narrows down to the real cause by checking to see if other symptoms match one of the possible choices.

DPR (Distant Personality Release): A PeakStates technique that eliminates transference and counter-transference between people by dissolving 'cords' (and the corresponding traumas) between them.

EFT (Emotional Freedom Technique): A therapy that uses tapping on meridian points to eliminate emotional and physical discomfort. Classified as a power therapy, in the subcategory of 'energy' or 'meridian' therapy.

EMDR (Eye Movement Desensitization and Reprocessing): A regression trauma healing therapy involving the repeated movement of attention from left to right, either with the eyes or by touching the body on alternate sides.

Eukaryotic cell: A cell that contains a nucleus and other organelles. All multicelled organisms are made of eukaryotic cells.

Evil: A sensation that is captured well in horror movies. This is not a type of behavior in the context of our work but rather an experiential quality.

Extended triune brain model: Based on the Papez-MacLean triune brain model, it describes a nine-part structure to the brain. These parts are commonly called the perineum, body, placenta, solar plexus, heart, spine, mind, third eye, and crown brains.

Flattened emotions: A condition where the client has a greatly reduced ability to feel emotions. They can still feel positive and negative feelings, but it is like someone turned down their volume.

Gaia commands: Developmental events can be broken down into biological steps, with each step being described by a short phrase. In regression, these phrases are experienced as commands sent from an external source we call Gaia, the living self-aware biosphere of our planet, which guides our development in real-time.

Gateway structure: These subcellular structures act as gateways to past, shamanic or spiritual events. The best-known are ribosomes on a stuck mRNA string that act as gateways to events in the past.

Generational trauma: Subcellular structural problems passed down through the family line. They cause emotions that feel very 'personal', that something is very wrong with oneself. They can be eliminated with a variety of techniques.

Group mind: See 'collective consciousness.

Guarding trauma: a trauma that causes the client to want to keep a problem. It is the cause of the 'psychological reversal' phenomenon. A person can have several layers of these guarding traumas.

Heart brain: The limbic system, or old mammalian brain. It thinks in sequences of emotions, and experiences itself in the center of the chest.

Hell realm: During regression to certain developmental moments, or in certain locations inside the primary cell, the person has an experience of being in a sort of hell, surrounded by pure evil. This is caused by a bacterial parasite located below their body image.

Holes: Clients can sometimes see what 'looks' like black holes in their body, which feel like infinitely deep deficient emptiness. They are brought to awareness during some therapies. They are caused by physical damage to the body.

Kundalini: Characterized by the sensation of a small area of heat (about and inch in diameter), which moves slowly up the spine. This can go on for months and in some cases years. Kundalini stimulates traumas and other unusual 'spiritual' experiences, creating severe problems for most people, as well as reduced sleep.

Meridians: Energy channels that wind through the body. Used in therapies such as acupuncture and EFT. Caused by tubes in the cytoplasm of the primary cell that connect to the 'chakra' fungal organism on the nucleus.

Merkaba: A fungal organism that looks like a 3D geometrical merkaba, found inside the nuclear core.

Mind: The neocortex, or primate brain. It thinks in thoughts and experiences itself in the head. At a subcellular level it is the nucleus.

Mitochondria: Each cell has hundreds of small organelles that look a bit like hot dog buns in the cytoplasm. These organelles correspond to the solar plexus brain. They create the chemical (ATP) equivalent to oxygen that the cell needs to 'breathe'.

Mother/Father columns: Two additional columns besides the column of self can be 'seen' in most people. These 'feel' like the mother and father respectively, because these are left over awareness material that was supposed to combine to form the new consciousness in conception. These columns, particularly if large with respect to the column of self, can cause problems for some people. They are a fungal structure.

MPD (Multiple personality disorder): Now called 'dissociative identity disorder' in the DSM4. It describes people who have different selves that take over at times without the awareness of the main personality.

Muscle testing: Communicating with the body consciousness by using muscle strength as an indicator. Same mechanism as applied kinesiology, and the terms are used interchangeably.

Nuclear core: A hollow volume inside the nucleolus, containing fundamental structures of consciousness.

Nuclear pores: Openings in the nuclear membrane that have sphincters in them that resemble camera irises. There are 4-5,000 pores in the primary cell nucleus.

OBE (Out of body experience): A person's awareness can move outside their body. This phenomenon is most easily noticed in trauma memories that are 'seen' from an OBE perspective.

Organelle: The different types of structures inside a cell that act like various 'organs'.

Organelle brains: The self-aware organelles in the sperm, egg, or fertilized cell. There are seven self-aware organelles in the sperm or egg, and nine compounded organelles in zygote and adult cells. They share consciousness with their corresponding multi-celled triune brains. This label is usually shortened to just 'organelle' in the context of self-aware cell structures.

Over-identification with the Creator: Some people put their consciousness inside a fungal structure in the cell, causing them to lose their human perspective and no longer want to help other people who are suffering.

Past lives: Encountered in some therapies, the experience of having lived in the past or the future with a different body and personality. This is a different phenomenon than ancestral (generational) memories. These are created by a fungal structure on the inside of the cell membrane.

Peak experience: A short-lived, unusually good feeling that enhances functionality in the world.

Peak state: A stable, long lasting peak experience of one of over a hundred different types. These range from exceptional physical abilities to continuously positive feelings to experiences outside the Western belief system.

Perineum brain: The self-aware consciousness at the perineum.

Perry diagram: A diagram using circles to indicate the degree of connection the triune brain awarenesses.

Personality: This is what others sense about a person when they turn their attention to them. Rather than being a mental construct in the observer, it is a real-time experience of particular traumas in the one being observed. It is caused by the borg fungus. The DPR process is used to dissolve this connection.

Pinecone: A fungal structure that looks similar to a pinecone, containing tiny 'bubbles', and found in the nuclear core.

Placental brain: The self-aware placental consciousness. It corresponds to the Golgi apparatus. Sometimes called the 'navel brain'.

Power therapy: A phrase coined by Dr. Figley who also originated the psychological category called post traumatic stress disorder (PTSD). It applies to extremely effective therapies (originally EMDR, TIR, TFT, and VKD) that remove symptoms from PTSD and other issues.

Precellular organelles: The self-aware organelles before they combine to form a primordial germ cell. The different types are identified either by their biological name in the cell, or by the triune brain they share a continuity of awareness with (e.g., body, heart, etc.).

Precellular trauma: Trauma that occurs to precellular organelles.

Pretend identities: Equivalent to 'triune brain self-identities'. The identities that the different triune brains pretend they are.

Primary cell: The only cell in the body that contains consciousness. It acts as the master pattern for all other cells. Formed at the forth cell division after conception.

Primordial germ cell (PGC): The original cell that eventually matures into a sperm or egg. They are first formed in the parental blastocyst shortly after implantation inside the grandmother.

Prions: Prions are infectious pathogens that cause a group of invariably fatal neurodegenerative diseases. Prions are devoid of nucleic acid and seem to be composed exclusively of a modified protein. We suspect prions are the class 1 bug-like parasites seen in the primary cell.

Projected identities: Each triune brain typically projects identities onto other triune brains. They tend to be very negative. Interestingly, the body brain often feels like a god (or monster) to the other brains.

Prokaryote: A class of simple one-celled organisms that have no organelles (such as a nucleus). Bacteria are in this class.

Psychedelic therapy: It therapy involves the use of very high doses of psychedelic drugs, with the aim of promoting transcendental, ecstatic, religious or mystical peak experiences. Patients spend most of the acute period of the drug's activity laying down with eyeshades listening to non-lyrical music and exploring their inner experience. Dialogue with the therapists is sparse during the drug sessions but essential during psychotherapy sessions before and after the drug experience.

Psychological reversal: When meridian 'tapping' therapies have no effect, the cause is often an unconscious need for the problem. Using a lymph node massage, or eliminating the 'guarding' traumas allows the healing to proceed normally.

Psycholytic therapy: It involves the use of low to medium doses of psychedelic drugs, repeatedly at intervals of 1–2 weeks. The therapist is present during the peak of the experience and at other times as required, to assist the patient in processing material that arises and to offer support when necessary.

Psychosis: The client has lost contact with external reality. Many very different and unrelated problems are labeled this way (for example, see 'shattered crystals').

PTSD (Post Traumatic Stress Disorder): This is the standard name for severe, long-lasting reactions to traumatic events.

Racial and collective experiences: See 'collective experiences'.

Realm of the Sacred: Some clients access a level of consciousness where the environment looks like dark outer space lit by fluorescent black lights. This is how the 'sacred beings' perceive their environment. See Tom Brown Junior's *The Vision* for more descriptions.

Regenerative healing: Physical healing characterized by extreme speed (seconds to minutes) and capability to heal virtually any physical problem (from scars to broken bones). It can be done on oneself or induced remotely into clients. It is an extremely rare. It uses a fundamentally different mechanism than trauma healing.

Ring: A fungal organism that can look like a ring or sphere, found inside the nuclear core. It makes the fungal column-of-self crystalline structure in early development of the grandchild consciousness.

Rule of Three: After a client's issue is fully healed, the therapist plans on doing two more sessions to make sure the healing was stable. The first session is a few days later, and the second session is a week or two later. This catches problems due to subsurface genes and time loops becoming activated later.

Sacred beings: The triune brains awarenesses originate in sacred-feeling cubes that perceive themselves in the 'realm of the sacred'. They are symbolized by totem pole figures or pagodas. These extremely tiny structures are found at the center of the nuclear core.

Scan: Using unusual peak states, the primary cell can be examined for some common structural problems. This is used for clients who are hard to diagnose using only questions and answers.

Self-identity: Each of the biological brains pretends it's someone or something else. This need to pretend is driven by a subtle discomfort in the triune brain's core around not being able to do their particular function properly.

Sensate substitute: During traumatic events, the body consciousness can associate its surroundings with survival. In the present, it drives the person to acquire substitutes that feel similar to the original surroundings to help it feel safe. These substitutes are usually in the subcellular environment and in the person's daily life.

Shattered crystals: Awareness can be 'shattered', so that it is very difficult to focus awareness. This is caused by what look like shattered crystals or broken glass in the primary cell's cytoplasm.

Shutdown (brain): The condition of a triune brain awareness being partially or completely shut off. When this happens, the person loses the ability that the brain gives them. For example, shutting down the mind brain causes the loss of the ability to form judgments, heart shutdown causes others to feel like objects and not people, and so on.

Soul loss: A phrase used in shamanism describing pieces of self-awareness that have left the person. This person will typically feel lonely, sad, and miss the person who triggered this problem.

Sperm tail organelle: This is the lysosome in the cell. In prenatal development it is the self-aware sperm tail consciousness. Its multicellular counterpart is the spine.

Spine brain: A self-aware triune brain whose focus of responsibility is the spine. It corresponds to the sperm tail in the sperm, and the lysosome in adult cells.

Spiritual emergency: An experience from various spiritual, mystical or shamanic traditions that becomes a crisis. This is not the same as a crisis of faith.

Structural problems: Client has emotions or sensations that are not due directly to trauma, but rather the result of structural problems in the primary cell. For example, dizziness due to damaged mitochondria.

Subcellular psychobiology: Many psychological (and physical) symptoms are directly caused by various biological disorders or diseases inside the cell. Subcellular problems are treated with various psychological-like techniques that directly interact with subcellular structures; or with trauma-healing techniques that repair early developmental damage that directly or indirectly caused subsequent subcellular issues.

SUDS (Subjective Units of Distress Scale): A relative measure used to evaluate the degree of pain or emotional discomfort. Originally from a scale of 1 to 10, common usage is now from 0 (no pain) to 10 (as much pain as it's possible to have).

Third eye brain: A self-aware triune brain whose area of major function is located in the center of the forehead. It should be paired with the placenta, but rarely is due to fungal infections.

Time loop: a structure in the primary cell that causes trauma to return after being healed. It is experienced as an egg shaped structure in the body, or in regression as time flowing in a repeating loop. It is found in the pinecone in the nuclear core.

TIR (Traumatic Incident Reduction): An excellent power therapy that uses regression.

Toxicity (cell): The primary cell can have areas in the fluids, or in the membranes that are toxic. This causes symptoms in the client that in the extreme involve nausea, sickness and weakness. Areas of toxicity 'look' grey or black in the primary cell. The primary cell fluids and membranes should look transparent – however, this rarely occurs.

Transpersonal biology model: Triggered developmental events and corresponding structures in the primary cell are the origin of all transpersonal experiences. A dual viewpoint often exists: one based on awareness without biological component; the other based on the corresponding biological structures in the cell.

Trauma: A moment in time, or string of moments when sensations, emotions, and thoughts are stored from painful, difficult or pleasurable experiences. They cause problems because they make fixed beliefs that guide behavior inappropriately. Severe trauma creates post-traumatic stress disorder.

Trauma flooding: The triggering into consciousness many random traumas simultaneously.

Trauma phrase: It is a short phrase, usually 1 to 3 words that translate body sensations during a trauma moment into language. It is used with the Whole-Hearted Healing regression therapy when a trauma healing won't complete.

Tribal block: The influence of culture in people. It also causes cultural conflicts and hostility between members of different cultures. Caused by a fungus.

Trigger phrase: The short phrase that stimulates the client into maximum discomfort (i.e., the highest SUDS rating).

Triune brain: The full name is the "Papez-MacLean triune brain model". The brain is built out of three major, separate biological structures formed in evolution. They are the R-complex (body), the limbic system (heart), and the neocortex (mind). Each is self-aware, built for different functions, and thinks by using either sensations, feelings, or thoughts. They generate the phenomenon of the subconscious. With a certain peak state they can be communicated with directly.

Triune brain shutdown: See 'shutdown (brain)'.

WHH (Whole-Hearted Healing): A regression therapy technique. It uses awareness of the out-of-body experience ("dissociation") associated with trauma to heal.

Zygote: The cell resulting from the union of an ovum (egg) with a spermatozoon (sperm) at conception. The zygote stage ends at first cell division (although it is sometimes defined as including the multicelled organism that develops from the first cell).

Index

C

D

J

K

cerebral aneurysm · 253
Kornfield, Jack · 41
kundalini · 68, 80, 199, 271
    and trauma flooding · 243
kundalini experiences · 6

L

landmine · 85
large signal models · 84
lethargy
    as depression · 250
liability
    readers · vi
liability form · 48
life path trauma · 229
life's purpose · 229
lithium · 221
logos · 36
loneliness · 71
    abyss · 173
    as soul loss · 128
loss
    as soul loss · 128
loss of sexual attraction · 257
lost in the story · 49
lost peak state · 160
lotus birth
    for Wholeness state · 261
    to minimize later suicidal
        feelings · 261
loving feeling
    as s-hole symptom · 131
low functioning clients · 62
    parasite resistance to change · 231
LSD · 251, 252
Lukoff, David · 80, 266

M

MacLean, Paul · 10
male/female archetype state · 256
mammalian brain · *See* heart brain
mania · 80
medical applications
    overview · 9
medical problems
    curse · 150
meditation

and spiritual emergency · 270
    triggering over-identification with
        Creator · 206
mental issues · 67
merging consciousnesses
    dangers · 274
    triggers parasite activity · 159
meridian tapping · *See* EFT
meridian therapies · 60
meridians
    fungal origin · 21
merkaba · 114, 192
migraine headaches · 216
mind (primate brain) · 11
mind chatter · *See* ribosomal voices
mitochondria clumping · 201
mitochondrion
    damage causes vortex · 168
monotone voice · 193
monster in the basement · 174
motion sickness · 168
MPD (multiple personality
    disorder) · 33, 74, 80
    column of self fractures · 203
mRNA · 105
MSG causing headaches · 253
multicultural problems · 134
multiple sclerosis
    and psychological reversal · 222
multiple trauma roots · 106, 233
muscular contraction or tension
    hole · 155
music in my head · 167
mystical experiences · 271

N

NAET · 248
nail, invisible
    curse · 150
naming conventions · 8
Napoleon
    mitochondria clumping · 201
nausea · 183, *See* fungal parasites
    fungus · 138
navel touching
    to localize suicidal feelings · 260
near-death experiences · 265, 271
needs constant attention, to be special
    due to s-holes · 131
negative emotions

Q

R

T

CPSIA information can be obtained at www.ICGtesting.com
Printed in the USA
BVOW06s1209260615

406337BV00028B/437/P